500-1 – The Miracle of Headingley '81

By Rob Steen and Alastair McLellan

Dedication

To Ian and Rupert – that summer feeling's going
to haunt us the rest of our lives.

To Anne, Shirley and Jane, aka Pillars Inc.

Published by
BBC Worldwide Ltd,
80 Wood Lane, London W12 0TT

First published 2001
© Alastair McLellan and Rob Steen 2001
The moral rights of the authors have been asserted.

ISBN 0 563 53820 1

Picture Credits: All photographs © Patrick Eagar except those in picture
section one: page 1 (top) John Frost Newspapers; 1 (bottom) Corbis/Bryn Cotton;
2 (top) and 4 (bottom left) PA News; 2 (bottom) and 4 (bottom right) Rex/Sipa
Press; 3 and 7 (bottom right) Hulton Getty; 4 (top) Corbis/Jeff Albertson; 5 (top)
Allsport/Tony Duffy; and 5 (bottom) Ronald Grant Archive; and those in picture
section three: page 3 (top) Hulton Getty; and 7 Allsport/Adrian Murrell.

Commissioning Editor: Ben Dunn
Project Editor: Rebecca Kincaid
Book Design: Sarah Ponder
Picture Research: David Cottingham

Printed and bound in Great Britain by Butler & Tanner Ltd, Frome, Somerset
Jacket and plate sections printed by Lawrence-Allen Ltd, Weston-super-Mare
Typeset by Keystroke, Jacaranda Lodge, Wolverhampton

Contents

Acknowledgements

A book of this nature is nothing without its voices. Without the memories of the participants, the authors' words would be mere bones. Heartfelt thanks are due, therefore, to (in batting order): Mike Brearley, Graham Gooch, Graeme Wood, John Dyson, David Gower, Graham Yallop, Dirk Wellham, Trevor Chappell, Peter Willey, John Emburey, Bob Taylor, Barrie Meyer, Chris Old, Ray Bright, Graham Dilley, Geoff Lawson and Peter Philpott.

We also owe a substantial debt to those who were intrinsic to the story of Headingley '81 despite never so much as muddying their boots, namely Trevor Bailey, Richie Benaud, Keith Boyce, Ted Corbett, Frank Crook, Bill Frindall, Pat Gibson, Christopher Martin-Jenkins, Brian Mossop, David Ryder, Mike Smith, Tony Smith and Steve Whiting. And to those who helped with nudges, winks, tip-offs and shoves in the general vicinity of the right direction: Rick Allen, Scyld Berry, Matthew Engel, Peter Hayter, Michael Henderson, Tim May, Kevin Mitchell, Brian Murgatroyd, Mark Ray, Martin Searby, David and Keith Summerfield, and Jim Woodward. And above all to Bob Harragan, whose hand-written transcription of the *Test Match Special* commentary made up handsomely for the absence of 'live' television footage. We salute you all.

Merci beaucoup, too, to those who made this project possible: John Pawsey for accepting the pass and running with the ball; Ben Dunn at BBC Publications for having the wisdom and foresight to commission us; Rebecca Kincaid, Michele Savidge and Marian Thornley for their noble editing, and of course Patrick Eagar for his inimitable elegance with zoom lens and shutter.

Muchas gracias, finally, to all those who responded to our letter in *Wisden Cricket Monthly* by supplying their own reminiscences, however peripheral they may have felt. We sincerely hope that the editing process (impelled by the fact that we never suspected for a moment that we would get such marvellous feedback) meets with your approval. If a public event is defined by its witnesses, this is your story above all.

Alastair would like to thank his friends, family and those at 151 who helped in the research and writing of this book. He would particularly like to thank Rob for making the whole endeavour a pleasure and an education.

Rob would like to thank Anne, Laura, Josef, Evie, Woody and Kit for their love, support and patience. And, of course, Alastair, for demonstrating that great minds really can think alike and not come to blows.

Foreword

by Mike Brearley

Being asked to write a foreword to this book gives me, like other people, the chance to look back on the extraordinary series of the summer of 1981, and look also at the constructions I have settled for, the versions I have accepted through the rosy, yet dark, glasses of nostalgia.

One temptation is to view those events as having happened in the best of all possible worlds, as ultimately fitting, as strangely inevitable. It is even tempting to glaze the past in moral tinges – to come to believe that all that happened was planned and deserved. Through these lenses, the Australians only got what they deserved, as did other players on this stage – Ian Botham, Bob Willis, and also me. Such a view is often implied when the question has been asked, during England's years of cricketing travail, 'What has happened to the spirits and triumphs of '81?', as if there were any real doubt that those successes were earned, fated outcomes of sporting right-mindedness and hearts of stout oak.

Yet such were the margins, not only in the Headingley Test but in all three of England's wins in the series, that the minutest chances, infinitessimal differences, could have overturned the outcomes. Then the story would have been of yet another bad-luck story, or of a team that didn't quite cut the mustard. In *War and Peace*, Tolstoy muses on the realities of historical explanation. One of his themes is how cut off from the chaotic, muddled realities of war are the neat battle plans of the generals. 'For want of a nail' an empire is lost. For less than 1000 measly Florida votes a Presidency is lost. And cricket symbolises as acutely as any game the moments of luck, the turning points on which ultimate success hinges – an umpire sees or fails to see the slenderest edge; this umpire, at that moment, decrees that a particular delivery will indeed hit the stumps.

Yet Tolstoy overstates the case, or rather, as befits a man of his depth of thought, he modifies it. For as the book develops, we see as one of its main dramas the conflict between two styles of leadership, between the narcissistic, militaristic great man, as epitomised in Napoleon, and the homely, unglamorous, fat, ugly, peasant-like Russian general, Kutuzov. And Tolstoy makes it clear in his story that the Russian victory over Napoleon in 1812 would, ultimately, not have happened without the approach of Kutuzov, though what he offered was not adequately represented as battle strategy, or as the conscious planning of events. Unlike Napoleon, who cared only about himself and glory, Kutuzov's strengths lay rather in his deep understanding of, and feeling for, his people. His task was often to restrain the glory-seekers among his own officers, and the superficial and ambitious political pundits at home, from ill-conceived glory-trips and adventures. Kutuzov in his person transformed the Russian army. So according to Tolstoy the outcomes of history are not simply down to the unpredictable, momentary, intuitive movements of the massed individuals, but also lie in the leadership and management of morale.

Thoughts like these are alluring, too, when I review that 1981 series. Things are not all down to the vagaries of chance and the particular actions of individuals when they find themselves in the cauldron of conflict. Morale and strategies – even the strategy of being suspicious of strategies – also need fostering, nurturing. I need not necessarily go along with Fred Trueman's judgement at the end of the Headingley Test that Botham's performance came one match too late; that is, that it was simply chance that he happened on success in his first match after being relieved of, or relieving himself of, the captaincy.

I should say now, as I would have then, that it wasn't accidental that it was only then that he did so well. I have no doubt that he needed someone to bounce off, and to encourage him, for such performances to become once again likely. I remember the interchange I had with him about his bowling. When he first bowled, I took him off after three nondescript overs. He was outraged. 'How can I bowl in three-over spells?' he demanded.

'And how can I bowl you if you bowl medium-paced half-volleys?' I retorted. When it came to his batting, by contrast, I gave him his head, encouraging him to feel that he had permission to attack with all guns blazing. My view was that on this pitch, which was irregular in bounce and in movement, he was more likely to do well in his whole-hearted personification of a village blacksmith, than in trying to bat like a respectable and solemn Test batsman. I feel confident that he could not have batted or bowled as he did had he continued as captain. My feeling is that, though I too had supported him as the right person to succeed me as captain, he had been promoted beyond his sphere of excellence, to the detriment of the huge skills he had in such abundance. This, of course, is a view that he countenances with hardly more ease than does Trueman.

Another puzzle about this match lies in the transformation in Willis's bowling between one innings and the next. We did talk on the night before the last day. My memory is that it was Gooch and Gatting, supported by Botham and me, who encouraged Bob to forget about no-balls (with which he had recently been plagued) and simply bowl as fast and straight as he could. It was, in dressing-room parlance, shit or bust. Without the desperate hope of an almost lost cause, and the chance to redeem ourselves rather as had happened at Trent Bridge, in the first Test of the series, when England lost, but by only four wickets, after Australia had been set, on another unreliable pitch, a meagre 132 to win, just two more than their eventual target at Headingley. Willis had been really miserable about the way things had been going. Two winters earlier, on our last tour together, in Australia, he had looked stiff, uncoordinated and not fully fit. Not a natural athlete *à la* Lillee or Holding, he looked more ordinary when lacking rhythm, when the timing was off. From Willis there were no saving graces, no agile fielding or muscular batting to catch the eye. What one saw was a man who looked past his best. So without that last chance for glory, so gloriously taken by Bob, I think it likely that his Test career would have come to an end.

I wish Rob Steen and Alastair McLellan success with this timely book.

Mike Brearley
London June 2001

Authors' Introduction

I don't remember the 1981 Ashes series. Not really. Not with the same Kodachrome vividness with which I can recall what happened in the 17 series stretching from the Indian tour of 1981–82 to the near-blackwash by the West Indies in 1988.

I was 17 in April 1981 and not interested in cricket at all. I wasn't interested in much really, apart from the normal preoccupations of a teenager growing up in the comfortable vacancy of a London overspill town. I certainly wasn't interested in sport. A decade of being the last to get picked in playground football games and countless other humiliations had put a stop to that.

Before one cross-country race I complained to a friend how being the slowest runner in the class was an embarrassment. 'Don't worry,' he said in a genuine attempt to make me feel better, 'somebody has to come last.' When I did trail in five minutes behind the rest, my friend was standing, waiting, not happy.

'What's wrong,' I asked. 'I thought you said that somebody has to come last.'

'I know,' he replied, 'but why does it always have to be you?' No, sport – not my thing.

I was learning to love music. All right, it was the New Wave of British Heavy Metal that I believed was the only thing worth listening to – but you have to start somewhere and the early Eighties seemed an arid time for pop culture. But I needed something more – and it wasn't just the new Angelwitch single.

During that spring I seem to remember hearing or reading about the impending arrival of the Australian cricketers to contest the Ashes. Don't ask how I knew what the Ashes were. Put it down to race memory. Whoever wrote the piece/broadcast made 'The Ashes' – and the Australian team's presence in the country – sound important and historic.

Then I recall nothing until the Headingley Test. Watching the game standing behind my friend Geoff's normally highly reserved father as he became more and more excited or walking along a beach past scores of transistors all tuned into the Test. Suddenly the pleasure of following a game which both folded into the languors of the long summer holiday and also had everybody talking, began to pull me in.

My father took my two younger brothers and me to see Kent at Canterbury and Folkestone. We adopted Chris Tavaré as our hero on the basis of his regular and violent dismantling of county attacks. Our father told us that Kent's glory days had been the Seventies. 'Rubbish,' we thought. Tavaré, Dilley, Benson, Taylor, Aslett and Potter would soon put those achievements in the shade.

By the time England set off for India in the winter of 1981 I was hooked. I was waking in the early hours to listen, through whistling static and the odd burst of Lithuanian folk singing, to the broadcasts from Delhi, Bombay and Calcutta. Did I lose interest when the series turned out to be as tedious as the Ashes rubber had been deliriously exciting? No, I just assumed that it was part of the game's rich tapestry and went even deeper.

My brothers and I started playing cricket too. We would walk to a nearby playing field, knowledgeably debating whether Don Bradman or Jack Hobbs had been England's greatest batsman. Right from the start the game's history entranced and intrigued us. It took us a little while to get up to speed, but within a year even my 13-year-old brother Rupert knew who Victor Trumper was.

The first time we marked out a pitch we couldn't believe how far apart you had to set the two pairs of stumps and doubted that anybody could propel a cricket ball accurately over such a distance. Unfortunately there was no miraculous discovery that I had any cricketing talent. I was terrified of the ball – unfortunate because Rupert turned out to be a decent pace bowler, and being terrorised by a 13-year-old was not cool – and could only bowl incredibly slow semi-lobs. But we played all through the autumn and most of the winter. Those that knew better kept telling us that cricket was a summer sport.

For the next seven years, all through my late teens and into my early twenties, I was besotted with the game. It was not until 1989, when I both fell in love for the first time and started writing about cricket, that I was finally able to get some perspective on my passion.

When I look back on those early years 1981 does not loom large. The defining moment was England regaining the Ashes in 1985. We puffed up with pride when Richard Ellison, like Mark Ealham (whom Rupert once played alongside) from my home town of Ashford, destroyed the Aussies with wicked late swing. Important, too, was the dreadful summer of 1986, which finally convinced me and others like Peter Hardy, the editor of the first cricket fanzine, *Sticky Wicket,* that the game we loved was going to hell in a hand-basket and that we should start doing something about it.

The biggest talking point was not Botham's captaincy or form, but the rebel tours to South Africa. Swanton meant nothing compared to Matthew Engel's brilliant iconoclasm in the *Guardian.* Many of the English players from the '81 series also seem to belong to an earlier age. Boycott, Brearley, Knott, Old and Hendrick, although I saw most play in county cricket, were ghosts. We pinned our hopes on Graeme Fowler, Geoff Cook, Paul Downton, Derek Pringle and Neil Foster.

No, I don't remember much about the 1981 Ashes. But I do know it changed my life. I suspect I'm not alone in that.

Alastair McLellan
London June 2001

I was dreaming of reporting Test matches but working as an estate agent in Hampstead. I detested every minute with the vehemence I reserved for Thatcher, Marmite and that flesh-curdling Gothic look beloved of the prettier denizens of London's trendier clubs.

One of the few advantages – aside from working within a minute's walk of a top-notch Jewish deli, a naughty Belgian chocolatier, England's leading crêperie stall and the Everyman cinema and, of course, seeing how the unnecessarily rich live – lay in appointments that kept me legitimately out of the office for sizeable chunks of the day. This meant being able to pop home – an 8 ft by 4 ft hutch in Belsize Park in a flat shared with four others – during lunch intervals.

Getting caught in a traffic jam in Highgate between appointments on the Monday also had its plus points, allowing me to listen to Botham's innings on *TMS.* I hated the choccie cake'n'pigeons chat and despised Trueman's in-my-dayisms, but this was no time to be picky. That evening I genuinely felt there was a chance of an England victory, however slender, but then I always have been an incurable hopeful romantic. When the West Indies set England 435 at The Oval in 1976, I thought the boys were up for it when Amiss and Woolmer adjourned on the penultimate evening on 43–0. Which is why I never fully appreciated Holding's eight-fer the next day.

As far as I was concerned, Lillee and Marsh were the Kings of the Bogeymen. I'd missed the Ashes-recovering wins of 1977. (Being in Israel at the time I got my fix from the World Service, even traipsing round Haifa on a bus with radio glued to chest – none of that weenie transistor nonsense, mine was a Party Boy, a forerunner of the ghettoblaster; my girlfriend cited it in the divorce petition.) Since I had also missed 'Underwood's Match' at Leeds in 1972, this meant that I had not seen England win an Ashes Test since Old Trafford in 1972. I was 14 then; now I was 23. They owed me. Big.

On the Tuesday I booked myself out of the office for lunch with a house-viewing to follow at 2 p.m. Fortunately, I remembered to take the client's phone number. I got back to the flat just in time to see Hughes and Yallop go, so after much contemplation of conscience and navel, I rang the lady in question to say that I had been unavoidably delayed. Something feeble about a domestic crisis (we were out of loo rolls). Had Bright and Lillee dallied much longer I would have been obliged to miss the climax – phew!

Drove along Hampstead Lane afterwards. Trees and Heath had assumed a deep, revivifying green. Sun puckered up for what seemed like the first time all summer. For the first time in months it felt good to be alive.

It took me a further six months to quit the real estate trade (as opposed to the pretend one), and another five years to report my first Test (Botham, good as gold, took a wicket with his first ball). Still, I'd like to think Beefy and Goose played their part in bucking me up and giving me the push, in persuading me it was worth pursuing lost causes.

Rob Steen
Falmouth June 2001

Part 1

Where we were then

State of play

Think of what our Nation stands for,
Books from Boots and country lanes,
Free speech, free passes, class distinction,
Democracy and proper drains
John Betjeman

Prince Charming, Prince Charming
Ridicule is nothing to be scared of
Adam and the Ants

The gloom that enveloped England's dark and unpleasant land in 1981 was not exclusively metaphorical. Not since 1941, the Met. Office would reveal, had the country endured a cloudier year. In January the Gallup poll annually commissioned by the *Sunday Telegraph* had done little to raise spirits. While 20 per cent of respondents believed an improvement was in the offing, 58 per cent felt that their lives would deteriorate: for the third year running, the pessimists had beaten the optimists.

As if losing John Lennon, Jean-Paul Sartre, Jesse Owens and Peter Sellers the year before had not been sufficiently sobering, Planet Earth was robbed of an uncommon number of good guys in 1981. We bade adieu to Bob Marley, Bill Haley and Joe Louis, allegedly the only man ever to reduce Muhammad Ali to a public display of inferiority. To Jessie Matthews, William Holden, Natalie Wood and Hoagy Carmichael. To Mike Hailwood, rated as one of, if not *the* most formidable of motor cyclists, the fellow who had won the George Medal for rescuing fellow Formula One driver Clay Regazzoni from his blazing Ferrari – killed, somewhat inevitably, in a car crash. To Christy Brown, the doughty Irishman afflicted with cerebral palsy who had transformed himself into an author by learning to grip a piece of chalk with his toes. Unlike Egypt's progressive President Anwar Sadat and his Bangladeshi counterpart Ziaur Rahman, Ronald Reagan, Pope John Paul II and Bernadette McAliskey survived assassination attempts. There are those who will remonstrate quite forcefully that the gods had got things – in the vernacular of the Big Smoke – arse about tit.

Shudders scudded through homes from Land's End to Ponders End following the confession in April by Peter Sutcliffe, 'The Yorkshire Ripper', that he had murdered 13 women. January brought an outrageous case of daylight robbery: Rupert Murdoch, Australian press tycoon and owner of England's two best-selling newspapers, the *Sun* and *News of the World*, was permitted to acquire *The Times* and *Sunday Times* (from, it should be noted, Canada's Thomson Organisation) without so much as a flinched eyebrow from the Monopolies and Mergers Commission, much less the Dirty Digger's chum, Margaret Thatcher. Whereupon, to widespread astonishment, Murdoch hired the brash, oafish, scruple-free Kelvin MacKenzie as editor of the *Sun*. In the Middle East, just for a change, Jews and Muslims were failing to bury hatchets anywhere other than in each other's skulls, ditto Catholics and Protestants in Belfast. Ulster's premier political streetfighter, Bobby Sands, the imprisoned IRA hunger striker, announced his candidacy in the Fermanagh and South Tyrone by-election, and won it shortly before he died.

The Conservative government had begun to flex its icy muscles and exert its vicious, vice-riddled grip, extolling the virtues of a new political cause: Thatcherism. Two years into her term of office, Britain's first female Prime Minister was already the most unpopular political leader the country had elected since the not-strictly necessary invention of the opinion poll. Nor was there much confidence in her cabinet. Angelic as he was by comparison with his opposite number, Labour's Michael Foot was still the most unpopular opposition leader since records began. Politicians had run out of credibility.

Having fleetingly revealed her humane side by promising more funds for the ailing coalmines, the Iron Lady pained even more of her constituents by announcing that British Aerospace would be sold off, the latest step down the road to privatisation that would deprive so many of transport and identity, and lead to the fatal train accidents that would scar the start of the next century. Unemployment was heading for three million, a figure expected to climb for the foreseeable future. Merchant seamen, prison warders, postal workers, fishermen, civil servants, customs officers and even bank staff came out on strike. Ford laid off 15,000 men rather than accede to the wage demands of 400 lorry drivers; British Steel downsized its workforce by 22,000. Ken Livingstone, a shrewd left-winger, was elected leader of the General London

Council, largely on the strength of his promise to cut public transport fares by 25 per cent, this at a time when the Government's decision to slash its grant was adding £1.35 a week to his constituents' rates bill. While the average annual rise in wages had halved to 11 per cent, the increase in the cost of living over the last year had jumped by 15 per cent. A cue, surely, for Government investment? Not according to the new monetarist dogma. Chancellor Howe's Budget saw public spending slashed by £3.5bn, the public reaction a mixture of shock and resignation. The only people pleased, it seemed, were the bosses: the Confederation of British Industry was calling for 400,000 public sector jobs to be cut. The nation's economic future, it appeared, rested on the outcome of an arm-wrestling match between labour and employers with strikes and redundancies their blunt instruments of choice.

Come summertime, the living was anything but easy. A cocktail of boredom, resentment – a million teenagers were seeking jobs – and rising racial tension in the inner cities finally bubbled over, the upshot an eruption of civil unrest that, while tame next to the mayhem of Detroit and Paris in 1968, had not been witnessed in England for a century. As passions soared and a confused generation vented its spleen, the title of Heaven 17's hit grew ever more pertinent, for some if not all: *We Don't Need This Fascist Groove Thang*.

Refuting allegations of harassment and brutality, police officials blamed the looting and vandalism on a 'copycat' element while diminishing the provocative involvement of their reinforcements, the notorious Special Patrol Group, aka SPG. Right-wing Tories blamed everything on the black community, and demanded curbs on immigration. As, rather less subtly, did the avowedly racist members of the National Front and British Movement. In a front-page editorial, *White Power*, the 'paper of National Socialism', declared: 'The integrity of our race and nation is in jeopardy and our anger deepens to a point beyond endurance. If we cannot have our homeland, then nothing is more certain, nor shall the alien horde.'

'Blood on our Streets' screamed the *News of the World* amid the disturbances that ravaged the London borough of Southall in the first week of July. Enoch Powell reiterated the warning he issued after the Brixton riots – 'You have not seen anything yet.' Former Powell aide and Tory MP Harvey Proctor called for the repatriation of immigrants. The following week, Toxteth in Liverpool exploded and the *Sun* claimed that 'Mob rule grips the cities' as it reported on riots in London, Wolverhampton, Birmingham and Hull. Even High Wycombe gained its first taste of 'urban unrest'. According to *The Times*, 'Special Branch detectives are trying to identify the 'Four Horsemen' of the rioting epidemic – four masked men who it has been established were present at major incidents in Southall, Liverpool and Manchester.' The story concluded: 'Special Branch detectives believe the riots are politically motivated, but they do not know from which side.' In the same paper, a 22-year-old black man involved in protests along London's Kingsland Road was quoted saying: 'Our parents took it. They gave everything and they didn't get anything in return. If they had done this a long time ago they would have got something.'

'We cannot take our freedom for granted anymore,' proclaimed PM Thatcher. 'We have to do something to ensure it continues. The veneer of civilisation is very thin. It really does have to be cherished.' In the week before the Headingley Test, Home Secretary Willie Whitelaw announced that army camps would be used to take the pressure off over-crowded prisons and that CS gas and rubber bullets could be deployed against rioters. He added that if armed vehicles were to be used on the streets of Britain, they would have to be painted police blue.

Not that the riots constituted the sole evidence of rebellion. In January, driven from the Labour bosom by what they interpreted as creeping extremism, the so-called Gang of Four, Shirley Williams, David Owen, Bill Rodgers and 'Woy' Jenkins, formed the Liberal Democrats, having considered but ultimately ditched the title 'New Labour'. During the Trooping of the Colour on the Mall in June, a month before the Prince of Wales was due to wed a Sloane Ranger barely half his age, Marcus Sargeant, an unemployed lad from Folkestone, fired six blanks at his Queen. A month earlier, Ronald Zen, a 42-year-old Zen Buddhist from Brooklyn claiming to be an incarnation of Jesus Christ (there were quite a few doing the rounds), sent a package to 'The Queen, London, W1'; within lurked a matchbox containing grains of soap powder, four matches and a piece of wire, plus a picture of a bomb, accompanied by a partially-burned photo of the bride-and-bridegroom-to-be. Further afield, millions of Polish workers risked their jobs as well as the wrath of their Communist bosses, staging a four-hour strike in March that paralysed industry from the Silesian coalfield to the Baltic shipyards. Organised by the Solidarity party, this latest show of defiance presaged a summer of union action that would ultimately overthrow the Soviet yoke. On 29 July, by stark contrast, the Mall would be awash with joy and harmony as Prince Charming wed his fair Diana, the ancient order still firmly intact.

Utterly out of tune with this mass of dismal cumuli, April had afforded a more rewarding glimpse of fantasy-made-flesh. Advised two years earlier that cancer would kill him before the decade was out, jockey Bob Champion had defied all medical forecasts by returning to the saddle in the high summer of 1980. His avowed ambition, the goal that had sustained him through times of despair, was to win the Grand National, but then his chosen mount, Aldaniti, began to display alarming signs of fragility. Word swept round: the horse's legs were no longer strong enough; predictions that he would never race again were repeated and insistent. Eerily enough, the pair began to heal at roughly the same time, and lo and behold, they duly found their way to the starter's gate at Aintree, setting up the most profoundly sentimental celebration of animal exploitation in sporting history. Hearts gatecrashed mouths as Aldaniti struck the first fence with a resounding clatter, and for a few moments during the run-in Spartan Missile threatened to pass, but the Fates were just teasing. Not for the first time, sport had refreshed the parts other drugs cannot detect.

Australia struck the first blow in the pre-Ashes skirmishes. The recently-deceased John Lennon had spent six successive weeks at No.1 in Radio 1's *faabulous* Top 40 – and would spend another couple thanks to Roxy Music's respectful interpretation of *Jealous Guy* – when along bumbled the ridiculous: Joe Dolce's *Shaddap You Face*, a crass piece of cod Italiana from Sydney that did for barbers and trattoria waiters what Harry Belafonte's *Banana Boat Song* and Peter Sellers' *Goodness Gracious Me* had once done for bus conductors and Asian GPs. Andrew Sachs, better known as Manuel the waiter from *Fawlty Towers*, had the presence of mind to adapt the song into Spanish; a court injunction prevented him from releasing it before Joe's version and it eventually peaked at No.138. The year may have opened with those twee choristers of St Winifred's atop the pile with *There's No-One Quite Like Grandma*, but English tolerance of the irretrievably naff runs only so deep. As the miserable failure of Joe's follow-up, a truckers' ditty entitled *Ain't No UFO Gonna Catch My Diesel*, bore out.

Indeed, once one got past the schlock of Neil Diamond and the pre-Army, post-taste Elvis clone that was Shakin' Stevens, the airwaves were as chockful of mavericks as they were of androgynous androids toting serious expressions, excessively daft haircuts and remixed 12-inchers. Eddie 'Tenpole' Tudor, who claimed to be descended from the well-known medieval wife-hopper, evoked his ancestry with *Swords Of A Thousand Men*; Buster Bloodvessel, a 20-stone skinhead with a wickedly winning grin, fronted Bad Manners, a bunch of ska/bluebeat revivalists equally happy to restore the Can-Can to prominence. Fred Wedlock was *The Oldest Swinger In Town*. Landscape, a bunch of serious jazzers, went electro with *Einstein A Go-Go*. Thursday evening at 7.30 was still the bolthole for *Top of the Pops*, now an uneasy mix of bland, blond and cor blimey.

January brought an early warning. The hippest band in England were Visage, a bunch of so-called 'New Romantics', a brand name bestowed on anyone discovered to be in possession of a gothic aura, a ghostly stare, a synthesiser and a ton of Boots No.7. The frontman, a wealthy young Welsh entrepreneur with plans for world domination, went by the soubriquet of Steve Strange. 'We fade to grey,' he intoned ad nauseam. Dissolve, more like.

Thank heavens for Madness, the self-styled 'Nutty Boys' from Camden Town, a band of jolly japesters sporting *March for Jobs* badges and a flagrant social conscience. They could call a song *Grey Day* and still induce smiles. Mercy buckets, too, for Adam and the Ants, the self-styled 'Kings of the Wild Frontier', who merged panto and video in a bodacious marriage of African drumbeats, Apache threads, Dick Turpin chic and Diana Dors. The *Virgin Rock Yearbook* predicted big things for salsa (a tad previous), The Necessaries, Wesley Strick and the Stereotypes, and The Urban Verbs, as well as Paula Yates, The Cure, Spandau Ballet, UB40 and U2. Fired by the likes of Heaven 17 (*Penthouse and Pavement*), Kraftwerk (*Computer World*), Black Uhuru (*Red*), Grace Jones (*Nightclubbing*) and The Beat (*Wha'ppen*), reggae and electronica were alive and kicking; rock 'n' roll, with all due respect to Mr Stevens, had gone to meet its maker. From the States emerged Kid Creole and the Coconuts with their groovy ode to Olive Oyl and the replenishing powers of spinach, *Me No Pop I*. And, lest we forget, the Dead Kennedys, donors of the immortal *Too Drunk To Fuck*. The next big thing? All signs pointed to those trailblazing rappers from the bloody, drug-addled, horribly neglected streets of The Bronx, Grandmaster Flash and his (suitably) Furious Five.

Amid this pre-multiplex era of Odeons, Plazas and ABCs stormed the Britannia-Used-To-Rule-Waves-Shock of *Chariots of Fire* and the windswept canoodling of Jeremy Irons and Meryl Streep in *The French Lieutenant's Woman*. In *Clash of the Titans* Laurence Olivier assumed the role he'd spent his entire career building towards, namely Zeus, only for Sean Connery to trump him with a supreme Agamemnon in *Time Bandits* (both, mind, were outdone by Nicol Williamson's batty Merlin in *Excalibur*). While *An American Werewolf In London* showcased the latest chilling advances in prosthetic makeup (and the best use of a Van Morrison song in celluloid history), Bill Forsyth's *Gregory's Girl* found warmth and poetry in Glasgow and puberty. Julie Andrews got a few things off her chest in *S.O.B*, including – to the chagrin of diehard fans – her bra (well, hubbie Blake Edwards was in the director's chair). Michael Crawford swapped hapless Frank Spencer for the super-dolt antics of *Condorman*. In *Body Heat,* a shameless but engrossing update of Billy Wilder's epic *Double Indemnity*, William Hurt and Kathleen Turner steamed up the dress circle something rotten with their moonlit romps. In *Cutter's Way*, Czech émigré Ivan Passer's empathetic take on the mental plight of the Vietnam veteran, John Heard's Alexander Cutter III outlined how his reaction to watching the war on TV had metamorphosed from 'I hate the United States of America' to 'There is no God' and, finally, to 'I'm hungry'. In *Stardust Memories*, Woody Allen turned away from the chuckle-free angst of *Interiors* with a hilariously scathing depiction of menopausal angst – primarily, one strongly suspected, his own. When Woody/Sandy Bates meets a group of aliens they declare themselves fans of his movies, especially 'the early, funny ones'. He asks them what he can do to help mankind. The advice is unhesitating: 'Tell funnier jokes.' With a fittingly surreal sense of symmetry, the President of the Free World, ex-actor Ronald Reagan – who duly apologised to his wife for forgetting to duck – proved to have been the proposed scalp of an oil tycoon's son bent on impressing 18-year-old Jodie Foster, starlet of *Taxi Driver* and *Bugsy Malone* fame. Only in America ...

As ever, the state of the British film 'industry' was a subject for despair. In April, John Schlesinger, Joseph Losey, Richard Lester, the Boulting Brothers and sundry other filmmakers signed a 'Save Our Industry' open letter: in 1980, only 32.4 per cent of cinema programming, a record low, had been devoted to British or EEC-related productions. By year's end, Lord Grade had closed his ITC international and UK selling arms, both subsidiaries of Associated Communications Corporation, sold half a dozen unreleased films (including *Sophie's Choice*) to EMI, and flogged half of ACC's non-voting shares to Robert Holmes à Court, the Australian tycoon. The Grade empire, giggled *Screen International*, had gone from 'vertical integration to virtual disintegration'. Still, at least Lou still saw plenty of possibilities, chomping that omnipresent cigar with renewed vigour as he waxed lyrical over the 'exciting future [in the] revolution that's sweeping the country' – i.e. pay TV, cable, satellites et al.

As it was, the goggle box proffered a good deal fewer plums than prunes. The heartier laughs were incited by *Not the Nine O'Clock News*, *Shelley*, *To the Manor Born* and *The Kenny Everett Video Show*, with scorn rightly reserved for *OTT*, a purportedly adult version of the marginally more manic, slightly-less-silly children's favourite, *TISWAS*. Dramas included *Bergerac* (trials of a detective in sleepy Jersey), *Tenko* (tribulations of women in Japanese prisoner-of-war camp) and *Triangle* (non-seductive saga of cross-Channel ferry).

For fans of *schadenfreude* there were game shows such as *3,2,1* with Ted Rogers and his able assistant Dusty Bin. Peter Davison (ex-*All Creatures Great And Small*) was crowned the new Doctor Who, yet the most talked-about programme, somewhat inevitably, was a dramatisation of Evelyn Waugh's *Brideshead Revisited*, its longing nod to a statelier past needlessly reaffirming the Englishman's predilection for yesterday. Still, Vivian the Punk from *The*

Young Ones did call his hamster SPG.

On Tuesday 21 July, to take a day entirely at random, London's West End offered *Cats, Evita, The Mousetrap* ('29th Year') and *No Sex Please – We're British,* all trading their cosily familiar licks with Dario Fo's somewhat grittier doubleheader, *Accidental Death Of An Anarchist* and *Can't Pay? Won't Pay!* Dame Anna Neagle had been wheeled out for *My Fair Lady,* Petula Clark to sing Do Re Mi in *The Sound of Music.* Following the genuine *Nine O'Clock News,* BBC1 promised helicopter crews in *Rescue Flight* and Raymond Brooks-Ward commentating on *The Royal International Horse Show;* BBC2 countered with psychiatric drama *Maybury* and a chat with Lord Brockway (nee Keir Hardie) on the seemingly premature *The 20th Century Remembered;* Granada proffered *News at Ten* and an hour-long film about the London Symphony Orchestra's main man, Claudio Abaddo (the options stopped right there). John Peel held down the 10–midnight slot on Radio 1, Mike Read ran the Breakfast Show with anorakish zip. On Radio 4, *News Briefing, Farming Today* and (on Long Wave) the Shipping forecast preceded the *Today Programme.* ITV opened for business at the civilised hour of 9.30 a.m., BBC2 at a positively decadent 11. Nothing was on after 12.30 a.m.

On billboards throughout the land, there was Busby, the cartoon bird employed by British Telecom to promote its wares, urging us to pick up the phone and 'make someone happy'. 'Save our skins – save our lives' pleaded a car window sticker opposing seal culls, reported 'Peterborough' in the *Telegraph.* Having the front seats of the vehicle upholstered in sheepskin, the diary added, rather diluted the message. On the letters page, Mary Whitehouse offered her blueprint for a good night's rioting 'n' looting: 'Take a running kick, jump back as the glass falls, spring smartly forward over the debris, and take your pick. No one will interfere, there's no danger of hurting yourself, there's loot in abundance, and it's fun into the bargain.' Mervyn Jones came at it from another angle in the *Guardian*: 'Doors broken down – furniture smashed – homes made uninhabitable. Clearly this is a case of imitative violence. Can't Mr Whitelaw do something to stop the police watching TV?' Thomas Forshaw, a butcher in his army days, began a life sentence after admitting to Chester Crown Court that he had stabbed his mother to death and severed her head with a carving knife, whereupon he placed it in a holdall, carried it into the woods in Deeside and hid it under a pile of leaves. A psychiatrist said that Mr Forshaw, who had discharged himself from 'a mental hospital' a fortnight earlier, had had his brain cells permanently damaged by years of alcoholism.

The average age for a first-time mother was 24 years six months, the *noms du jour* Thomas and Sarah. Six per cent of homes had video recorders (VHS or the confounded Betamax). The most popular meal out was steak and chips, usually at a Berni Inn and swilled down by a 57p pint of lager. On the foreign exchanges, the pound had closed the previous day at $1.8675. A room in Hampstead could be yours for £30 a week, a secluded Cornish cottage in St Agnes ('slps 12') for barely twice that. Anyone fancying booking a flight to see England's winter Test in Bombay would have to shell out £270. The bare necessities? Consider the following:

Average weekly wage	£158
Average house price	£18,166
High-rate tax (£27,750 up)	60%
Prescription charges (per item)	80p
Colour TV licence	£46
Car tax (per year)	£70
Litre of petrol	34p
Season ticket, Liverpool FC	£20

Richard Brooks and Partners placed an ad in the *Telegraph* seeking a sales manager in Saudi Arabia for 'a major US international company', the carrot £17,000 'tax free'. The National Trust was willing to cough up £5,500 for a qualified secretary; a sales rep for an abrasives firm in East Anglia, Kent or Dorset could pull in £8,000, a lecturer in Political Science at Preston Polytechnic £10,431. Austin Motors was giving the big push to its hatchback Maxi (wider than a Volvo 345 or a Renault 14, '40mpg at 56mph'). Production of the new Mini Metro, Lady Diana Spencer's preferred mode of pre-Royal transport, formed part of the Government's four-year corporate plan for British Leyland; state funding of £620 million making the £10m the Tories were handing over to see the De Lorean sports car emerge from its Belfast factory seem quite reasonable.

Shop wisely and you could snap up the latest *Wisden* (softback edition) and *Sound Affects*, the newest LP from The Jam, and still get change from a tenner. Morrant's spring catalogue proffered the new Duncan Fearnley 'Magnum' Bat (Non-Oil) at £46.85, the Winit 'Bob Willis' Bowling Boot at £28.25, and the Sunil Gavaskar '331' Cricket Shoe at £27.05. Walkmans and CB radios were in with a capital I. Hip, too, were blue eyeliner (à la Lady Di), black lipstick, big hair, combat fatigues, padded shoulders, power-dressing and PVC. The latest passport to heaven was aerobics. The gospel according to Jane Fonda, Oscar-winning actor, political activist, feminist icon and now leotard model, was simple: keep fit and dance a lot.

In Yorkshire, Charlie Brown, the *Telegraph* reported, had been a bit of a cheeky chappie, persuading customers at a pub auction in Worsborough, near

Barnsley, to snap up 'tights at 1p a pair and glass vases, said to have been made in Italy, at £1 a set'. The vases, it transpired, stemmed from Stoke, while the tights adhered to the Trades Descriptions Act in every respect bar the bit about having two legs. Evidently lacking a sense of perspective, the court ruled that Charlie had breached the Mock Auctions Act and fined him £150. After all, reasoned Andrew Crowthers, the defending counsel, nobody had suffered. 'Whether the vases came from Stoke or Italy, they were still a bargain. Customers who complained about the tights got back their 1p.'

Back across the pond, discerning New Yorkers, Texans, Bostonians and Floridians were tuning in and turning on to Steven Bochco's *Hill St Blues*, a radical cops 'n' robbers show that had about as much in common with *Z-Cars* as Kim Hughes had with his distant cousin Ted. Rippling with multi-layered plots, lent verisimilitude by shaky hand-held cameras and endless tracking shots, its impeccable blend of humour and graphic realism served as a backdrop to characters as ragged and rugged as they were rich in diversity and depth. Such as undercover cop Mick Belker, the unkempt, sharp-toothed Jewish mother's boy who eschews guns and bullets but enjoys a nicely-turned ankle ... or nose ... or ear. Then there was Sgt Phil Esterhaus, who ends every dawn roll-call with the heartfelt imprecation, 'Let's be careful out there', while shamelessly juggling the amorous attentions of an interior decorator and a 17-year-old schoolgirl named Cindy. Imagine a song-free update of *Camelot* directed by Luis Bunuel. For King Arthur read Captain Francis Xavier Furillo, Frank to his squad and 'Pizzaman' to his girlfriend, arguably the most put-upon policeman in history, and definitely the most decent.

An episode aired in May, 'The Rites of Spring', finds Detective John 'JD' LaRue, the luckless wide boy, on his uppers. Plans for a chain of 'saloondromats' scuppered, ethics and professionalism in shreds, job and life on the line, he seeks refuge, as ever, in the bottomless bottle. But no bar will serve him. Reluctantly, he drags himself to an Alcoholics Anonymous meeting. As he introduces himself to the gathering, he spots a familiar face: Furillo. Slowly, disbelievingly, JD's helpless hopelessness melts into a relieved smile. Furillo's gaze is knowing, approving, but above all compassionate. In the summer of 1981, we all needed a slice of the Pizzaman.

On the fields of play, 1981 was not so much another country as another solar system. Birmingham supplied the champions of the Football League, Exeter its highest goalscorer, Ipswich the UEFA Cup winners, Merseyside the European Cup winners, Nottingham the county cricket champions, Edinburgh the Olympic 100 metres champion, Brighton the 800m champion, Sheffield the 1500m champion (respectively Aston Villa, Alan Kellow, Ipswich Town,

Liverpool, Nottinghamshire, Allan Wells, Steve Ovett and Sebastian Coe). The best pitcher in baseball was a fellow known as Rollie Fingers, the finest distance runner Mirus 'The Shifter' Yifter. For the first time, the US Open golf champion, David Graham, was an Australian; in John Watson, the British Formula One Grand Prix had its first Irish winner.

Northern Ireland, rather more improbably, won soccer's Home International Championship, and Chesterfield the Anglo-Scottish Cup. In women's tennis, the Wightman Cup was also still going, albeit not exactly going strong: the Americans won for the third time running, a sequence they would extend to 11. Britain and Ireland had yet to request continental reinforcements in the Ryder Cup, though a pair of Argentinians (Ricky Villa and Osvaldo Ardiles) helped Tottenham win the FA Cup and a brace of Dutchmen (Frans Thijssen and Arnold Muhren) fuelled Ipswich's UEFA charge. Not that this stopped English attendances falling by the thick end of three million. 'Suddenly,' wrote David Lacey in the *Guardian*, 'those running the game realised that the declining public interest was not a rumour put about by the media but an actual threat to soccer's position as the leading spectator sport. Moreover, the growing apathy had spread to Europe where even the once thriving West German league was becoming worried about falling gates and rising debts.' Rivalling Brian Clough and Jimmy Hill for the title of Mouth Almighty was John Bond.

Alex Ferguson was managing Aberdeen, Brian Close was coaching Scotland and Tiger Woods was five. Brighton were in Division One, Wimbledon in Division Four. Manchester City played Manchester United twice without bowing the knee. Kevin Keegan was scoring for Southampton, Bryan Robson was tackling for West Bromwich Albion (until a record fee of £1.5m took him to Old Trafford in October). Ron Greenwood's England lost in Basle and Oslo, prevailed in Budapest and only scraped into the World Cup finals when Romania, whom they'd failed to beat, performed a passable impression of Devon Loch.

The Oaks, the 1,000 Guineas, the Ascot Gold Cup and the Jockeys' Championship all fell to Lester Piggott. A gifted if mysterious steed won The Derby and King George & Queen Elizabeth, name of Shergar. Chosen – in a deft piece of PR opportunism – to cox Oxford in the Boat Race, Sue Brown did not react well to the omnipresent media scrum, prompting a protective team-mate to bark, 'Go back to Lady Diana, you vultures.' A last-minute penalty saw England's rugby unionists extend their fallow run in Cardiff to nine visits; they also lost three rugged Lancastrian Lions to the ravages of time and body – Fran Cotton, Tony Neary and Roger Uttley. A try was still worth four points, a Football League victory (until August) two. Queens Park Rangers unveiled their plastic pitch; Sunday football blinked back into the light as Mansfield visited Darlington; red and yellow cards were dispensed with. (And if you're expecting a rose-hued reminisce about Torvill and Dean, forget it: any activity where music, artistic impression and subjective judgments play integral roles cannot be classed as sport.)

The only homegrown player in the top seven of the first-class bowling averages was Arnie Sidebottom, subsequently to become the last man capped by England while spending his winters moonlighting on a professional soccer field. David Lloyd, Mark Nicholas, Peter Roebuck, Vic Marks, Derek Pringle and Mike Selvey were still some way from swapping Ralgex for press pass and commentary booth. Norman Gifford, 41, took 63 wickets for Worcestershire, a move to arch-rivals Warwickshire still to come. Eifion Jones, 39, and Alan Jones, 42, were still stump-minding and new-ball-repulsing for Glamorgan and St David. Gloucestershire's top six numbered four Test players – Chris Broad, Sadiq Mohammad, Zaheer Abbas and Mike Procter – and, in Alistair Hignell, an England rugby union full-back.

Essex's trip to Lord's in May brought a Championship first as Middlesex fielded 11 Test players. Not that this cowed Norbert Phillip, the whippet from Dominica whose return was delayed by 10 days when debris from landslides blocked the airport runway: a Championship-best six for 40 all but consigned the hosts to defeat in a tad over two days' play.

Unfortunately, beyond the boundary, and sometimes within, the sweet was being subsumed by the unsavoury with numbing frequency. Scotland beat England at Wembley without much support from their devoted fans: provoked by past acts of vandalism and hooliganism, the Football Association had resolved not to make tickets available to gentlemen in tartan (not that this deterred thousands). That fitfully august body had also announced a code of conduct: life bans for persistent troublemakers, firmer action on foul play and even identity cards. Englishmen, after all, posed far more grievous headaches. In Turin the previous summer, a European Championship match against Belgium was marred by crowd trouble; police deployed batons and tear gas, the latter spreading to the field and holding up play for five minutes; more than 70 were hospitalised. Action was swift: the next day, Lancaster Gate was fined £8,000. What with bribery allegations against AC Milan and other Serie A clubs being compounded by the national side's unremittingly sterile tactics, neither were the Italians the happiest of bunnies.

From the United States came the latest episode in a bitter struggle for the sporting soul. Accorded the status of chattels for more than a century, professional baseballers had finally struck back in the 1970s under the tireless emancipating influence of Marvin Miller, the first executive director employed by the Players Association. Free agency had finally arrived in 1976, tilting the balance of power. Yet the players still resented their treatment, and rightly so. Other thorns remained, primarily the new labour contract, commonly referred to as the 'basic agreement'. In 1980, the club owners demanded that any team signing a sought-after player (i.e. one of the top 50 per cent of pitchers and batters) be obliged to send in return a member of their own roster. Miller was livid, declaring it a blatant attempt to reverse a legally approved concession; if the compensation clause did not revert to its previous wording, tools would be downed. Compromise saved that particular season – the deadline for settling the basic agreement was extended – but by the time April rolled around again a resolution was conspicuous only by its absence. Irked by Miller's insistence that they were 'unnecessary', the owners quite happily provoked a strike. In a letter to the *New York Times* Bart Giamatti of Yale University damned both parties; fans, asserted *Time*, were being alienated. The end came after 50 days. If the season had not been altogether ruined in practice, it was assuredly bankrupt of credibility, let alone spirit. The Los Angeles Dodgers, who emerged from the mess as World Series champions, claimed to have lost more than $7m, the players had to forego nearly $30m in salaries, and the owners reported losses of around $72m, yet the ultimate fall guys were Lloyd's of London: the insurers sold the owners a policy guaranteeing $50m in compensation over a six-week period at a rate of $100,000 per game lost.

The title of World's Ugliest American, for all that, was won on the cloistered courts of Wimbledon. That John Patrick McEnroe had driven himself to become the finest racketeer of the day was indisputable. Assured of touch, audacious of spirit, his swaggering four-set win in the Wimbledon singles final over Bjorn Borg, winner of the five previous titles and unbeaten in 41 contests, defied all contradiction. His behaviour, however, offended many, and not exclusively the stuffed of shirt and rigid of outlook. 'I worry how I act,' he confessed after his opening engagement within those prissy ivy-clad walls had seen him docked points for racket abuse, calling the umpire 'an incompetent fool' and the referee something even less complimentary.

'It's unnecessary, it's bad. I am just hurting myself. I have no one to blame but myself. Others accept bad decisions and so should I.' It certainly sounded sincere, but credibility was soon lacking as he accused a linesman of bias then, in the semi-finals, threw another wobbly. Insult was duly added to injury when he declined to attend the traditional champions' ball, which at least evinced a measure of consistency. There was greater tolerance among those less enamoured of what Wimbledon represented, who harboured sympathy towards pumped-up professionals being forced to accept judgments from amateurs: it was all good, reasonably clean fun, a snook cocked at establishments everywhere (provided, that is, one discounts the possibility that the tantrums were merely a cunning plan to unsettle opponents). Yet even McEnroe's supporters had cause for dismay. Had it truly come to this?

Melbourne was the scene of sport's most distressing incident. With New Zealand needing six to win off the last ball of a World Series Cup final, Greg Chappell, Australia's highly-respected captain, instructed his younger brother, Trevor, to deliver the ball underarm, along the ground. The ruse worked a treat and embarrassed a nation. Within 24 hours, a shame-faced Australian Cricket Board (ACB) had changed the rules to prohibit any repetition, and Chappell Major had insisted he would never do it again, but the damage had been done. According to a Sydney radio station, several aggrieved callers urged Canberra to recall Australia's ambassador to New Zealand. Sir Donald Bradman 'totally disapproved'; Richie Benaud plumped for 'disgraceful'. Bob Vance, chairman of the New Zealand Cricket Council, dubbed it 'the worst sporting action' in his experience. 'Victory at this cost,' he added, 'was at the sacrifice of Australia's tremendously proud cricket heritage.' Malcolm Fraser, Australia's PM, denounced it as 'a serious mistake, contrary to the spirit of the game'; Robert Muldoon, his New Zealand counterpart, went a good deal further: 'It was an act of cowardice and I consider it appropriate that the Australians were wearing yellow.' Even big brother Ian blanched: 'Fair dinkum, Greg, how much pride do you sacrifice to win 35,000 dollars?'

Seldom, indeed, had sport been in sorer need of reasons to be cheerful rather than fearful. The tone had been set at the outset of the avaricious Eighties, when the normally moderate President Carter, desperate to score points in an ultimately futile American election campaign, demanded that the West boycott the Olympic Games in solidarity over the Soviet Union's invasion of Afghanistan the previous year, and that the event be relocated. Maggie Thatcher, his British counterpart, concurred with the former measure (the latter, Carter had not realised, was an impossibility); in the event, most if not quite all the Iron Lady's subjects ignored her entreaties, though Seb Coe may have felt a tad guilty about his 1500-metre gold as he rose through Tory ranks.

In May 1981, The Troubles persuaded the Football Associations of England and Wales to cancel matches against Northern Ireland scheduled to be staged in Belfast, forcing the Home International championship to be called off. Nevertheless, apartheid, inevitably, was at the root of most of the evil, if only because its proponents were so obsessed by sporting prowess as a cure for wider ills. The New Zealand Rugby Union defied its own government by extending a welcome to South Africa's whitest Springboks: arriving in Gisborne on 20 July the party ran a gauntlet of 100 Maori protestors before learning that four hunger strikers in Christchurch had ended a 12-day fast because one had been smitten with an abdominal complaint. In due course, the West Indies Cricket Board of Control withdrew its invitation to New Zealand to tour in 1982, an unequivocal statement of fraternal dismay at such acquiescence towards an abhorrent regime. At Lord's in late July, fearful of such an eventuality, the International Cricket Conference (as was) emphasised its avowed objections to 'sanctions on cricket as a result of actions by other autonomous sporting bodies' while slamming the door firmly shut on rumours that South Africa would be re-admitted. 'What more can we do?' lamented Rashid Varachia, the president of the South African Cricket Union, having assured the gathering that Mr Botha's government intended to exclude sport from the three pillars of apartheid policy that hindered the development of a multi-racial game. That nobody was able to provide him with a suitable answer spoke eloquently of the delegates' leanings.

In February, England's provocative/naïve (take your pick) decision to summon 35-year-old Robin Jackman to Guyana in place of the broken-down Bob Willis had almost caused a tour to be abandoned. One of a cadre of hard-nosed professionals who had decided they had a right to earn their corn in the Republic regardless of how those meddlesome politicos might frown, Jackman had married a South African, yet he was not the only transgressor. Reporting in *Wisden*, Michael Melford pointed out that David Bairstow, one of two wicketkeepers in the party, had captained Griqualand West in the Currie Cup the same 1977–78 winter that saw the signing of the Gleneagles Declaration. This was a well-intentioned if confusing concord urging governments to deploy their 'best endeavours' to dissuade and prevent teams from competing with, or in, the home of the accursed Bothas and Vorsters. Bairstow's faux pas, though, had more innocent roots, being largely a question of timing. Besides, Jackman had continued to flaunt his apparently tacit approval (upon retirement he became a prominent TV commentator in South Africa). This, moreover, was Guyana, the most politically-charged region in the Caribbean.

Two days before the second Test was due to start, once it had become plain that the Guyanan government objected to Jackman, Hector Munro, the British Sports Minister, described the Gleneagles agreement as wholly irrelevant to this particular case: it did not, after all, extend to individual contacts. Later that day, nonetheless, Jackman was obliged to surrender his visa and told to leave the country. AC Smith, the England manager, and the Test and County Cricket Board (TCCB) released simultaneous statements: the tourists would not go ahead with the Test 'as it is no longer possible for the Test team to be chosen without restrictions being imposed'. Attracting sympathy and support from other Caribbean countries, Smith and team, accompanied by the ever-thickening media entourage, left for Barbados the next morning. Within days, a heart attack had killed Ken Barrington, the avuncular coach-cum-assistant manager dearly loved by the players. An intense patriot once characterised by Wally Grout – who endured his determination from the rear in all too many Ashes conflabs – as walking to the crease trailing a Union Jack. It would be misguided to describe England's distraught display in losing the Bridgetown Test as strictly coincidental.

Many surmised that the Guyana affair had all been a ruse by Forbes Burnham's government to deflect attention from Lord Avebury's unfavourable report into election-rigging. Others, such as the former Jamaican premier, Michael Manley, espied the bigger picture: 'The action of the Guyanese government, however painful for the cricketing public, was completely within their competence to take as a sovereign entity. Forbes Burnham was throughout his life a passionate and consistent advocate for and supporter of anti-apartheid causes. He and his government concluded that they could not, consistent with their own principles, accept Jackman. They risked unpopularity, even opprobrium, in acting on conscience rather than in accordance with the actual terms of the Agreement. This they were entitled to do because Gleneagles called for a minimum programme by consensus, but did not prevent any government going further if they felt justified in so doing.'

In a letter to *Wisden Cricket Monthly*, R Hale from Liverpool drew on history and fine print: 'Guyana should be congratulated on the principled and firm stand it has taken ... when, some years ago, the Guyanese people had the audacity to elect democratically this party as their government, Britain responded by sending in an invasion force to overthrow it. It ill-behoves, therefore, certain elements in this country to lecture Guyana on malpractices and undemocratic behaviour! The claim by EM Wellings that apartheid is practised against Europeans in West Indies is ludicrous and just mischievous nonsense. Eligibility to participate in political life and to vote does not depend on the colour of one's skin, as is the case in South Africa. Neither is enforced racial segregation in all spheres of human activity enshrined in West Indian constitutions. Nor is it a crime to have sexual relations with a person of a different skin colour!'

As late as September, England's selection of the two Geoffs, Boycott and Cook, would keep the winter tour of India in doubt until Prime Minister Gandhi stepped in: both openers were on a UN blacklist of sportsmen with South African links, along with candidates such as Bob Woolmer and Paul Parker. Intriguingly, when Graeme Pollock, arguably the finest batsman to play less than 25 Tests nor grace the county circuit, came to The Oval the following May for Jackman's benefit match, only 1,400 turned up to pay homage; Pollock, symbolically perhaps, was out for 13.

How sobering now to re-read Editor's Notes in the 1982 *Wisden*, composed by the admirable, likeable John Woodcock: 'When two countries wish to meet each other, it is no longer a simple matter of their respective boards of control arranging a tour and knowing that it will go ahead. Given half a chance the politicians will use it as a means of applying pressure on South Africa to renounce the system of apartheid.' The inference was clear: pressure of that ilk was wrong, unfair. In other words, even in the view of decent coves such as Woodcock, politicians had no right to poke their noses into sporting affairs. The logical extension of this is that sport, in short, should be free of social responsibility. When apartheid finally closed for business, it bears recalling, Nelson Mandela was quick to thank the boycotters for their part in its liquidation. Woodcock was unquestionably right on another score. 'In the autumn of 1981, while England's tour [of India] was in doubt, the world of cricket came close to being split into two halves, the dividing line being one of colour. The white and non-white countries are, in fact, so inter-dependent in a cricketing sense that for this to happen would be a setback from which the game might take generations to recover.' Was it really that different in the autumn of 2000?

The build-up to the 50th official Ashes series brought its usual delights and posers. The weather gods, mind, could scarcely have been less encouraging. On 24 April, the players fled Fenners during the match between Cambridge University and Essex due to the intense cold; the only precedent anyone could muster had occurred during the 1903 Gents v Players match at Hastings – in September. So foul were the elements, Zaheer Abbas did not manage so much as a single first-class run in May (though he would still be the first to 1,000). On 28 April, more than 600 friends attended a memorial service at Southwark Cathedral for dear old Kenny – the address was by David Sheppard, Bishop of Liverpool and a confrere of Barrington's on the 1962–63 Ashes expedition; Peter May and Botham rendered the lessons; Harry Secombe sang *Amazing Grace*. Two days later, according to a *Daily Telegraph* correspondent, 'Somerset soon introduced a spanner at the pavilion end'. Kenny, the maestro of malaprop, would have appreciated that one.

The civil war had been over for two years but cricket's head was still dizzy. The Packer Revolution – peeved at the loss of TV rights to old pals' act between board and senior channel, Australian media tycoon tempts the most illustrious performers with sums worthy of their talents and puts on own show – had fractured friendships, polarised normally sensible folk and shaken the game to its core. True, Kerry Packer's World Series Cricket and the Australian Cricket Board had both lost a fortune, but the cold shower had been a long time a'coming. The upshot was a more vibrant game, a more aware game (if prone to excess on the japes-in-jammies front), happier and better-rewarded players. Those who liked to be thought of as purists prided themselves in deploring the influence of the new commercialism in Australia, yet it was Packer's offshoot, PBL Sports Ltd, now the board's official marketing arm, who egged the ACB into proposing that the country stage a quadrennial World Cup Test series.

The most visible outward change, a direct result of broadcasters having a firm if not always judicious hand on the tiller, was the glint of the golden goose, the one-day, limited-overs game – conceived in Blighty, baptised in Oz. Not so much the fielding circles – or ovals, as Mike Brearley corrected – but night matches, white balls, triangular tournaments and all that jazz. In the winter of 1979–80, the Test and County Cricket Board initially rejected certain aspects of the Packer package adopted by the ACB – coloured togs, pads and gloves – only for Brearley's England tourists to decide, rather admirably, that sticking with white under floodlights would disadvantage their *opponents*. All the same, while consenting to day-glo pads and gloves, they drew the line at the technicolour trims and piping favoured by Australia (yellow) and the West Indies (maroon). Not that that did much to placate Disgusted of Tunbridge Wells after he'd watched the highlights. For those of a delicate or squeamish disposition, seeing Yorkshire's Graham Stevenson and David Bairstow scamper off the field in dark blue pads flushed victory of every dram of pleasure.

If Richie Benaud had been happy to take Packer's shilling and serve as WSC's most esteemed consultant, this did not blind him to the overkill in his homeland. Cheapening the game was never his aim. That said, he resolutely defended the variant from attack on other grounds. '[Twenty-five years ago] traditionalists decried the concept of the one-day game played by first-class cricketers. Now, in the 1980s, they are still at it with all the supercilious snobbishness they can muster, defending what they regard as being *their* game. Cricket is not their game at all ... cricket is a game for everyone.' Including 'the new spectators, many of whom have been brought to the game by the one-day fixtures of the past 20 years. They are the ones who would never in a million years have been guilty of being found at a boring five-day match or an equally boring three- or four-day county or Sheffield Shield match which may produce no result.' In the soggy summer of 1980, England's six Tests – five against the West Indies plus the Centenary bash against Australia – had attracted 351,523 paying customers, a daily average of nearly 12, 000 (*Wisden* had excised the figures for the four Tests against India the previous season, in the interests, presumably, of discretion). The four 55-over Prudential Trophy one-dayers – an apparently necessary antidote to the indulgences of the previous summer's World Cup — drew 70,000, the mean 17,500 (compared with 20,000 for the 13 matches staged at larger venues in the 1979–80 World Series Cup). The times and tastes they were a-changin'. What price the 30-hour match come 1991?

Back, though, to the shires. *The Cricketers' Who's Who*, now in its second edition (complete with Foreword by IT Botham), revealed that Kent's David Nicholls had once been a store detective and Derbyshire's John Walters a nightclub bouncer; Pringle, the Cambridge captain, cited his leisure pursuits as conchology and phenomenology. South Africa named a purely theoretical Test XI and included Allan Lamb, the Lasher of Langebaanweg, now in the final year of a shamefully brief four-season residential qualification period with Northants and about to become Anglicised. Within the space of a few months Michael Holding, Andy Roberts and Clive Lloyd all sired sons in England, for all the good it did their birthplace; even more regrettably, the search for a Scottish grandmother for Zaheer, who against Somerset improved on his own world record by making a century and a double-century in the same match for the fourth time, proved fruitless. A compatriot of Zaheer's was invited to umpire 17 first-class fixtures, the name Rana, Shakoor Rana. Gloucestershire's Sunday League match at Bath produced record Somerset receipts of £11,500. British Telecom's Cricket Information Service — 32m calls in 1980 — celebrated its 25th anniversary.

Some notables announced their arrivals. Alec Stewart, 18, debuted for Surrey — as timber-minder. Robert 'Jack' Russell, 17, postponed his A levels to answer an SOS from Gloucestershire, and claimed seven catches plus a stumping. On second XI duty were Hugh Morris, John Morris, Robin Smith, Neil Fairbrother, James Whitaker, Rob Bailey, Alan Wells, Richard Illingworth and Steve Rhodes, each a future Test player. Matthew Fleming made two and two for Eton against Harrow; Peter Moores, the 2001 England A coach, kept wicket for MCC Schools against the National Association of Young Cricketers. The Sri Lankan tourists, Test status pending, brought two de Silvas (neither, as yet, an Aravinda), an 'old-fashioned approach', a refreshing reliance on strokeplay and spin, and an over rate of 20 per hour. 'How will such methods serve them in Test cricket?' asked a plainly sceptical *Wisden*.

From India came a major blow for the discerning cricketaste: Bishen Singh Bedi, the Little Richard of left-arm spin, had retired. A bit much to swallow on top of a winter in which Jack Fingleton, Eric Hollies, Dudley Nourse, George Geary, Brian Sellars, Arthur Wellard and Jack Crapp had shuffled off their seemingly immortal coils. *Wisden Cricket Monthly* announced that Alec Bedser, twin brother of Eric, had perished following a Johannesburg car accident; happily for most, this Alec Bedser turned out to have been a 33-year-

We Don't Need This Fascist Groove Thang – The summer of 1981 found Thatcher's England in the grip of record unemployment, strikes, racial strife, right-wing terrorism and civil unrest unseen since the nineteenth century. The media were not short of copy.

THE Sun

SPORT STARTS ON PAGE 26

Saturday, July 11, 1981   10p

MOB RULE GRIPS THE CITIES

- **Southall: 1,500 go on rampage**
- **Brixton: Looting gangs run wild**
- **Dalston: Petrol bombers swoop**
- **Wolverhampton: Shops wrecked**
- **Birmingham: 400 in riot**
- **Hull: Centre under siege**

BATTERED . . . A wounded PC during last night's riot in Brixton

FULL STORY: Pages 2, 3, 4, 5, 6 and 7

LUKE'S KITCHEN
GOOD FOOD

Can't Happen Here – Southall burns, early July: 'If we cannot have our homeland,' declared the so-called National Socialists, 'then nothing is more certain, nor shall the alien horde.' The following week Toxteth was engulfed in similar riots, prompting Rupert Murdoch's latest acquisition, the *Sun*, to ram home the message: 'Mob rule grips the cities'.

Above: **She's a Bad Mama Jama** – The rise to power of Margaret Thatcher, Britain's first woman PM, did rather less for feminism than envisaged. In 1981 she began to batter the unions into submission while embarking on the privatisation drive that would prove so divisive.

Right: **Funeral Pyre** – Bobby Sands symbolised the defiance of the Irish Republican movement. The hunger striker became an MP shortly before his death.

Opposite: **Prince Charming** – Street parties were *de rigeur* the week after the Headingley Test as the nation forgot its woes, let down its hair, grabbed its Ronald McDonald hat and celebrated the union of Prince Charles and Lady Diana Spencer.

Fade To Grey – Mourning for Bob Marley (top), reggae emperor and stoker of black pride, was hardly alleviated by the arrival of Bucks Fizz (left), first UK winners of the ever-fluffy Eurovision Song Contest for five long years, and the New Romantics (above), 'Blitz Kids' responsible for Duran Duran and Spandau Ballet but also Classix Nouveaux and Flock of Seagulls.

Right: **Stand and Deliver** –
John McEnroe became the
latest standard-bearer for
sport's declining manners,
winning the Wimbledon
singles title while alienating
as many as he entranced.

Below: **All Those Years Ago** –
'The British are coming,'
asserted scriptwriter Colin
Welland after *Chariots of
Fire*, the saga of unlikely
British triumphs at the 1924
Olympics, had won the Oscar
for Best Film. On
contemporary fields of play,
few were quaking.

Chosen for The Royal Film Performance 1981
CHARIOTS OF FIRE A

You Might Need Somebody – The England 12 at Lord's, where stalemate left the hosts 1-0 down in the Ashes series, an advantage no Australian side had wasted since 1888.
Back row, l-r: Gatting, Woolmer, Willey, Dilley, Emburey, Gooch, Gower. Front row, l-r: Taylor, Willis, Botham (capt), Boycott, Hendrick. Chris Old returned at Headingley, as did captain Mike Brearley.

Musclebound – Patronised on arrival, Greg Chappell led the list of absentees. The largely inexperienced Australian tourists initially made light of internal ructions as captain Kim Hughes (front row, fourth from right) and senior pros Dennis Lillee (back row, fourth from right) and Rod Marsh (front row, fourth from left) struggled bitterly for power.

Body Talk – A pensive Ian Botham
(bottom, inset) prepares to lead England's
1980-81 tour of the Caribbean, where,
despite Geoff Boycott's optimism, defeat
in the Test series was overshadowed by the
'Jackman Affair' and the death of much-
loved coach Ken Barrington (right). In the
Lord's Test, Botham was dismissed for a
pair and returned to the pavilion (below)
in stony silence, captaincy and credibility
in tatters. 'Right,' he thought, 'Bugger ya!'

Walk Right Now – As the series got underway at Trent Bridge, the hitherto anonymous Terry Alderman made an immediate and decisive impact on his Test debut, taking 4 for 68 and 5 for 62 as Australia won by four wickets. Here he traps Paul Downton.

Can Can – Emerging from his sick bed, the ailing Lillee proved his menace remained undimmed. Here he takes the first wicket of the rubber as Graham Gooch edges to Graeme Wood.

old South African (of fervent cricketing stock, one presumes). But what's in a name, eh? The Nottinghamshire squad numbered an Illingworth and a Dexter, not to mention a Fraser-Darling, a Bore and a Hacker. Somerset Seconds moistened a few eyes by featuring one D Compton. Yorkshire hopefuls included a Brearley as well as a Heritage. Cornwall fielded a Cock and a Willcock, Norfolk a Pilch. The Samuel Whitbread Village final would tickle aficionados of the dreaded 'other' game, pitting St Fagans' Toshack against Broad Oak's Greaves and McCreadie. In the John Haig Trophy final, Blackheath's top order would be wrecked by a Moor from Scarborough.

The names that caused the most fervent discussion, however, were those of the overseas players on county books, whose continued presence left the scapegoat-mongerers, the pragmatic and the cognoscenti at loggerheads. Dividing the best into two teams should give an idea of the lustrous riches on show. Not a genuine spinner in sight, nor even a specialist keeper, but a lineup eminently worthy of the Elysian Fields:

Rest of the World: *Glenn Turner, John Wright, Sadiq Mohammad, Ken McEwan, Zaheer Abbas, Javed Miandad, Geoff Howarth, Imran Khan, Clive Rice, Kapil Dev, Richard Hadlee.*

Caribbean Crusaders: *Gordon Greenidge, Viv Richards, Alvin Kallicharran, Clive Lloyd, Eldine Baptiste, Andy Roberts, Joel Garner, Malcolm Marshall, Michael Holding, Sylvester Clarke, Wayne Daniel* (when one has that many quality quicks, what side would require more than four batsmen?).

From 1982, it had already been decreed, teams would be permitted to field only one player ineligible for selection by the acolytes of St George. Tart and provocative as ever, that trenchant little Englander E.M. Wellings was still not satisfied: 'If the money lavished on foreigners had been devoted to our own products, an Englishman rather than West Indian Richards might now be regarded as the most exciting batsman in our English cricket – as invariably used to be the case.'

Historians and statisticians were left spluttering at the depletion of WG Grace's career return in *Wisden* by 685 runs (54,896 to 54,211) and two centuries (126 to 124), causing the new editor so much grief that he reversed the ruling in time for the next edition. John Woodcock, who had succeeded to the throne vacated after 29 years by the death of Norman Preston, had much to contend with in his inaugural address: tardy over-rates, neutral umpires, helmets, MCC members jostling with umpires during Centenary Tests (no thanks), night cricket (not here), county imports (better off over there). He began it by reflecting with customary perceptiveness on the fact that the most pressing matters advanced by his five most recent predecessors in *their* maiden notes – a fairer lbw law (1934), consecutive losses to Australia and West Indies (1936), a lack of 'great' English leg-spinners (1939), an absence of fast, level pitches (1944) and a dearth of culture and enterprise (1952) – all remained relevant. While the counties' decision to scrap the 100-overs restriction on first innings in Championship fixtures was applauded, the introduction of full covering of pitches prompted a few boos. Pointing out that the last time this was attempted, in 1959, 'the experiment was soon discontinued', he lamented the loss of the 'sticky dog' as a theft of heritage. More pertinently, he communicated the concerns of groundsmen who feared that constant protection from the elements would increase the danger of disease à la the 'fuserium' that helped Derek Underwood spin out Australia in the contentious Headingley Test of 1972 and hence ensure England retained the Ashes.

Over the previous 12 months, the counties had indeed been busy. Pricked after blocking Barry Wood's proposed move from Lancashire to Derbyshire within 48 hours of banking a benefit cheque of £62,429 – the threat of legal action clarified minds, bringing a swift reduction in his suspension – they had agreed to ease movement between clubs, albeit while rejecting a football-style 'compensation' fee. They had given the thumbs-up to Sunday play in Tests, fielding circles, the National Westminster Bank as heirs to Gillette as sponsors of the major one-day competition and Mike Procter's rebirth as an Englishman (the latter, it should be added, was far from unconnected to the import restrictions). After three months and £50,000, Warwickshire finally installed what came to be known as the 'Brumbrella', a revolutionary pitch-covering device weighing in at 11 tons. Not to be outdone on the innovation front, neighbours Worcestershire bowed to the wishes of their membership and agreed that the playing hours for nine of their home Championship fixtures should be 11.30am to 7pm. Points for a Championship win rose from 12 points to 16 and prize money went up to £38,000 – £12,000 for landing the three-day title, £7,500 for the 40-over John Player League, £8,500 for the 55-over Benson and Hedges Cup and £10,000 for the new 60-over NatWest Trophy. 'A cacophonous name,' grumbled Alan Gibson, adding that, in contrast to the competition's previous soubriquet, 'there is nothing smooth and soothing about it. [It] suggests the irritant midges that cop you when you are walking the dog on a summer evening in Somerset.'

The counties even proposed that the ICC adopt their system of fines for slow over-rates, one that would see a dozen counties docked up to £2000 apiece amid a season in which Nottinghamshire (19.59 overs per hour) pipped Sussex

(16.61) to the championship. The offer, sadly, was spurned, as was the TCCB's suggested daily minimum of 100 in the Tests. Amusingly, Perrier were roped in as sponsors for a Fast Over Rate Award, offering £3,000 to be shared among any counties averaging 20 per hour, only for Schweppes, sponsors of the County Championship, to raise vaguely understandable objections about supporting competitors; the venture, placing unreasonable store by quantity, died a mercifully quick death.

The counties had also given notice (as from the end of August) to Alec Bedser, chairman of selectors since 1969, in order 'to revert to the previously established practice of looking at the chairmanship to span the period between Australian tours'. Interestingly, Peter May, his successor, would endure until 1988 despite presiding over an era in which Australia were the only side England bettered with any regularity and as such no longer (however fleetingly) a barometer.

Having declared a 1980 surplus (the p-word was never mentioned) of £1.439m (up from £1.425m), the TCCB distributed the pickings among the first-class and minor counties, MCC, the Irish and Scottish Cricket Unions and − wait for it − the Combined Services. Players' and umpires' Test fees, nevertheless, were pegged at £1400 and £1050 respectively. For the common or garden shirehorse, life was appreciably tougher. In 1980 the minimum wage for a capped player was £4,850, for a 21-year-old aspirant £2,850 (one of the authors was earning £3,000 as a standing orders clerk). Even so, the total wage bill of £1.25m represented a rise of £500,000 in two seasons. The Cricketers Association responded by stating, according to *Wisden*, that 'the counties might be discouraged from re-engaging "marginal" or older players'.

By common consent, the pitches were the source of gravest concern. The board's executive committee had reminded the counties of their obligation to at least try and prepare 'dry, hard, and fast pitches at all times', the latest in a succession of futile attempts to dissuade them from malfeasance. Not that there was much anybody could have done to thwart the members of the United Liberation Front for Socialist Thamleelam who damaged the surface at The Parks in June while the Sri Lankans were tackling the Combined Universities. Dear old Norman Morris, in his final week before retiring after 50 years' service as assistant and head groundsman, might have wished for a less dramatic farewell.

Soil was also uppermost in Woodcock's mind, albeit only in terms of the effect he felt certain players were having on the game's purportedly good name. Beyond the Chappells − by way of compounding the crimes of his siblings, Ian had twice been suspended for dissent − the prime cause lay on page 67, at the very start of a 12-page photo section that did its best to put flesh on the bones of those endless statistics (55 pages of schools' averages no less). While New Zealand's John Parker casually adjusts his gloves as if nothing in the slightest bit untoward had occurred, there was Michael Holding, owner of the planet's second most aesthetically-pleasing bowling action (after Bedi), frozen in a follow-through that would scarcely have disgraced Liverpool's centre-forward or the Leicester fly-half, two stumps removed from their moorings, two fingers thrust at the umpire's word. If the words overhead – 'Unbridled Dissent' – were characteristically genteel, Woodcock, untypically, was drawn into a definitive statement: 'In all the years that *Wisden* has been published, there can have been no more shocking photograph.' If he neglected to mention that, during the same fractious tour, one of Holding's West Indies colleagues, Colin Croft, had shoulder-barged an umpire, one can only assume this to have been, unusually, a case of either ignorance or forgetfulness. The New Zealand public, according to RT Brittenden's report, were 'glad to see the back of them'.

And so to the nation's flannelled representatives. At Sabina Park on 15 April, David Gower played the innings of his life, enduring for nigh-on eight hours against Holding, Croft and Garner to make 154 not out, guiding England past 300 for the first time in eight attempts and securing the most honourable of draws. A few weeks earlier, as the tourists lined up before the Barbados Test, tears slid from every blinking eye, and defeat duly followed, putting the seemingly unstoppable West Indies two up with two to play; yet such was the hardy resilience of Graham Gooch, Geoff Boycott, Peter Willey, Paul Downton and Gower in Antigua and Jamaica, the margin remained the same, honour regained.

Behind the noble revival, though, lay rising tides of unease. Bob Willis's early departure appeared to have spelled the end of the road for the country's finest fast bowler since John Snow. Ian Botham's captaincy, moreover, was felt to be sorely lacking. 'I thought I'd performed reasonably well in the first Test,' recalls Chris Old, 'but I'd criticised Ian for getting out to Viv [Richards] with a hopeless shot towards the end of a day, with only Emburey, Downton, Dilley and myself to come. The new ball was taken, Geoffrey got one that ballooned off a length after playing brilliantly, and the wickets tumbled. I was sitting on the balcony alone, putting my helmet on, when Ian rushes out and says, "Two hours to go – it could rain". I said: "Look, you've just slogged one up against the spinner and we've got to face Holding, Roberts, Garner and Croft with a new ball – I've got a wife and three kids at home and I'd like to see them again." When I got out there to face Garner there were eight men stationed 30 yards behind me. Got a brute of a ball: Dill [Graham Dilley] and I had a laugh about it as we were coming off – "how could you play that?" – that sort of thing. Ian saw it and wasn't happy. He requested a private meeting, where I took the opportunity to suggest he should utilise the experience around him, and that no one would think any less of him. He liked to do things his own way, I appreciated that, but when people asked him how the meeting went, he told them that so long as he was captain I'd never play for England again.'

With the benefit of hindsight, Botham would confess his shortcomings. 'I freely admit that understanding what motivates players has always been a difficult area for me. Chris was one who tended to be overawed rather than inspired by playing for his country. We were in Bridgetown preparing to play Barbados on a wicket that could have been tailor-made for Chris, and Kenny said we should have him in the side. I said he did not seem that keen on playing, but Kenny insisted. Ten minutes before we were due to toss up, Chris came up to me and said he couldn't play. "What do you mean you can't play?" I asked him. "I've been stung." "Where?" "Somewhere," he said, and walked off [Old claims it was a migraine]. I could think of no other reason for his actions [other] than he had simply bottled out. I was so incensed that instead of trying to talk him round I bawled him out, leaving him in no doubt as to my assessment of his character. Now if I had been Mike Brearley, I would have walked up to Chris and told him that the wicket was ideal for him, that he was the best man for the job and I really needed him. Instead, I was getting myself psyched up for the game, I was winding up the other players and just didn't have the time or inclination to get involved with this kind of nonsense. I should have bitten my tongue, counted to ten, and tried to coax Chilly back on board because we all knew what great qualities he had as a bowler.'

Most perturbing, however, was the detrimental effect that responsibility was having on Botham's wand. Prior to the first Test of the 1980 series against the West Indies – having been appointed to succeed Brearley, who had bowed out to spend his winters concentrating on his second career as a psychotherapist – Somerset's young Achilles had played in 25 Tests with imperious results: 140 scalps at 19.33 (at a strike rate of 45.83 balls per wicket), 1336 runs at 40.48, six centuries, 14 five-fers and three match hauls of 10 or more. It had taken him only 21 outings to complete the 1000 runs-100 wickets double: unheard-of urgency. Pete Townshend had him down to a T: 'What is it? I'll take it/Got a bet there/I'll meet it/Getting high? You can't beat it.' Alas, in 10 outings as captain – save the Centenary Test against Australia, all against the West Indies, who were shaping up as the game's most irresistible combo since the 1948 Australians – the opposition made the Lord of the Lads look all too vincible: 242 runs at 14.24 with one fifty; 29 wickets at 34.79, strike rate a smidge under 64, with a best return of 4–77. In losing three and winning none of those games, England had escaped lightly: accommodating weather and pitches designed to draw the sting of Roberts et al had conspired to keep the 1980 scoreline at 0–1, while only Boycott's diligence held Lillee and Co at bay after the follow-on had been enforced. There was one patently obvious alibi, but then acknowledging enemy superiority has never been an Englishman's most glaring weakness.

'I didn't think he was a very good captain, to be honest,' says Willey of Botham, echoing one and all. 'He was just one of those people who was a natural cricketer. And that sort of cricketer doesn't have to think too deeply about the game. He just went out and did things. He was good enough to do that. [But] he was really down. The press had been after him for off-the-field things in the West Indies and he was sick to the back teeth with it.' Willis felt his friend lacked the mindset for the job. 'Ian was not an able enough captain to divorce himself from his own failings yet instil the sense of purpose that any team needs. To a significant degree, our results were inextricably tied to his form. If Botham was playing well England would win, and if he failed they would fail. It was a needless agony to see the captaincy destroying such an important component.'

Criticism of Botham, though, merely masked a sea-change in the game's pecking order. Under the endlessly shrewd stewardship of Ray Illingworth, England strung together a record run of 26 unbeaten Tests starting at Lord's in 1968 and ending at The Oval four Augusts later. Indeed, since losing to the West Indies at Headingley in 1966, they had lost just once in 37. In the six years before Kerry Packer assembled his Flying Circus in the winter of 1976–77, however, they had laboured heavily: successive Ashes series were lost (the first, in 1974–75, by the length of Oxford Street), twice they were walloped at home by the West Indies, and two rubbers were dropped to India – one, unprecedentedly, on terra familiar. In 1971, but for Edgbaston's rain and an hour's reckless batting at Headingley, Pakistan would have secured their first series success in the northern hemisphere. Had Ken Wadsworth not spilled Geoff Arnold's third-ball snick at Lord's in 1973, New Zealand would have gleaned their first five-day victory over England. Packer's emissaries still alighted on quite a few Poms – Tony Greig, Dennis Amiss, Bob Woolmer, Derek Underwood, John Snow and Alan Knott came aboard, Boycott, Willis and Old declined – but the gulf between the amount of talent emerging from overseas and that being sired by the counties was becoming ever plainer. Under the sagacious command of Mike Brearley, promoted upon the defection of Greig, Botham's South African-bred doppelganger, England won 11 Tests and lost just two during the lifespan of World Series Cricket (which just happened to coincide with Botham's entrance) – against Australia, New Zealand and Pakistan XIs deprived of most of their essential components. Packer did English cricket a good deal fewer favours than he did the pockets of the game's underpaid practitioners.

By the time they returned to the fold in the winter of 1979–80, hardened, not unnaturally, by having pitted their skills and wits against each other on an unnervingly regular basis, the 'rebels' had grown ever more formidable. When, in the interests of Commonwealth harmony, England consented to tour Australia that winter, Brearley cannot have been entirely devoid of selfish motives when he argued, successfully, that the Ashes should not be up for grabs. Retained so ruthlessly against Graham Yallop's second-stringers 12 months earlier, the urn would indeed have been at grave risk. The composition of the sides could hardly have contrasted more vividly. While Underwood returned for England, Australia welcomed back Rick McCosker, Bruce Laird, Greg and Ian Chappell, Rod Marsh, Ashley Mallett, Ray Bright, Dennis Lillee, Jeff Thomson and Lenny Pascoe, the upshot three defeats out of three, by 138 runs, six and eight wickets.

Only in the final 'dead' encounter at Melbourne's MCG did Botham batter the bowlers in the manner to which we had grown accustomed. Seemingly over-eager to impose himself on the equally macho, if cannier, Lillee (Achilles did have a dodgy heel, did he not?), he had scrabbled together 68 in five knocks when, with the score 88 for five and his side requiring a further 83 to make the hosts bat again, he assembled a relatively composed 119 not out, trebling the total. From there he proceeded to Bombay for the Golden Jubilee Test, took 6–58, dragged his team from 58 for five to 296 with a vibrant 114, then sealed the spoils with 7–48. Then they made him captain.

All that said, the coming summer's opponents were Australia, not the West Indies. An inexperienced platoon of baggy green caps shorn of its captain and best batsman, not to mention all but four of the XI that had prevailed at the MCG. There was no immediate prospect of the captaincy changing hands. Two members of the proudly proletarian selection committee – Charlie Elliott and, more tellingly, Close, his svengali at Taunton – had always been firmly 'agin' elevating Botham; in common with Bedser, though, John Edrich, Barrington's replacement on the panel, felt he warranted a chance against 'manageable opposition'. Even with His Beefiness still distracted, respite was in the offing. That sobering run of 10 successive Tests without victory was surely about to end.

Yet Packer's intervention, Brearley's brain and Botham's self-belief had disguised a fact so unpalatable it was ritually denied. Namely, that the rest of the world was either catching, had caught or had overtaken the cradle of the game. Hence the preference for over-rate penalties over punitive action for pitch-rigging. Hence the insistence on three ever-so-subtly varied varieties of limited-overs rave-ups ahead of a rigorous examination of the possibilities offered by a four-day Championship, let alone a proper streamlining of the first-class game to sort wheat from chaff, ambitious athletes from time-servers and never-could-bes. Hence the diffidence that greeted three-day 'matches' in which one side gifted runs in the third innings for an agreed number of silver-plattered overs to compensate for rain and expedite a declaration. Hence the hoopla over imports – what else could one conclude but that the counties sincerely believed they possessed scores of simply ripping tenderfoots whose potential could not possibly be realised until the mercenaries left town – while renationalised Southern Africans were encouraged to take their places anyway. That Botham, Gower, Gooch and Willis had all served apprenticeships against the galaxy's finest never occurred. The cradle had begun to rock; the bough was bending.

'If I were a betting man,' pronounced Lillee on his arrival at Heathrow in mid-May, tongue buried in cheek, 'I wouldn't know who to put my money on.' To many, given that the words emanated from a mouth renowned for neither modesty nor understatement, this sounded suspiciously like a grudging acknowledgement of frailty. Which bore out the popular view. In Kim Hughes, Australia were led by the youngest captain to conduct a tour of England since Billy Murdoch in 1880. A second-choice captain whose crew included no fewer than nine men with no experience whatsoever of English conditions. Even with Lillee, Marsh, Rodney Hogg and the up-and-coming Allan Border in tow, how cocky could they afford to be? 'The press said that we were the weakest Australian side ever to arrive in England,' recollects Trevor Chappell, 'but then they said that about all the Australian sides back then.'

Two of Australia's more ferocious spear-chuckers were missing: Pascoe, who had totted up 20 wickets in the WSC 'Supertests' of 1978–79 and hounded England the next winter, withdrew with a knee ailment; the fitness of Thomson, irresistible and occasionally petrifying in the Ashes debates of 1974–75, was regarded as too great a risk. Nose and elbow operations, moreover, had compelled Lillee to miss the preliminaries in Sri Lanka (as did Marsh, with knee trouble); now he was said to be suffering from bronchial congestion. So prolific everywhere but England, Doug Walters was omitted too, prompting a vengeful backlash. That rousing all-rounder Alan Davidson, now a selector and president of the New South Wales state association, received a death threat from one aggrieved fan; other selectors sustained their share of abusive calls, as did Davidson's wife. Barry Cohen, a Labour MP, demanded the selectors' heads, and there were street protests around the state. That Walters hadn't managed a century in four Ashes tours was conveniently forgotten.

The most alarming absentee, nonetheless, was undoubtedly Greg Chappell. Although hinted at for several weeks before the end of the Australian season, one that had culminated in a series-squaring mugging by India on an MCG slagheap, his unavailability was confirmed just 48 hours before the party was announced, catching the selectors totally unawares. Family and business reasons were cited. Since he and his partners were planning a major expansion in real estate and insurance, he would be better off staying at home in Brisbane.

Adrian McGregor, Chappell's biographer, ignored this element, concentrating instead on the objections of his wife Judy, an avid consumer of books with a feminist slant such as Gail Sheehy's *Passages* and Colette Dowling's *The Cinderella Complex*. Brother Ian's recent divorce, McGregor stressed, had also had an impact. 'I was being paid for the stress of it,' said Chappell of the captaincy. 'It wasn't part of [my family's] job. They just had to cop it.' But for Packer, he would have retired already. 'I think I made the assumption that [Judy] was happy in her role as a mother with the children, and that she fully understood what cricket meant to me.' They reached a compromise: no more long tours. The 'Underarm Incident' was another unstated factor, having left him 'pained and disillusioned'. Was this an opportune moment to pause for breath, to let the dust settle, to invigorate the appetite, to leave the board to imagine life without him? Besides, he had stated his willingness to return to the helm for the subsequent visits by Pakistan and the West Indies.

Chappell's withdrawal caused the selectors – Davidson, Phil Ridings, Sam Loxton and Ray Lindwall – to change tack. They decided that this was the moment to implement a rebuilding programme, hence the exclusion of Walters, despite topping the winter lists with 397 runs at 56.71 in six Tests, and the reluctance to take a punt on Thomson's body. That said, for all that was made of the callowness of the squad, perspective and a keen grasp of history dictated caution. Of the four preceding parties to England, collectively speaking, only Ian Chappell's 1975 model boasted more caps; Greg's 1977 side numbered half a dozen men with but one between them. Hughes could also call on more batsmen with at least 20 caps than any predecessor since Bob Simpson in 1964. 'I would have liked [opener] Bruce Laird and [off-spinner] Bruce Yardley,' admitted the skipper, 'but I had no say.'

For Peter Philpott, an occasional Test leg-spinner in the Sixties, now named as coach-cum-cricket manager, Chappell's exit made life exceedingly tricky. 'Greg asked me to be the first-ever coach of NSW. It was very successful and so Greg asked me to come to England with the team. I was a boarding house master at King's House School in Sydney and getting the time off was very difficult. But I did it because Greg was a good friend and we worked so well together. When he said he wasn't going I was surprised and disappointed. I was put into a very unwelcome position; if I'd known he wasn't going to tour I'd never have gone.'

In saying he felt 'unwelcome', Philpott alights gingerly on a touchy area. Exacerbated by the preponderance of New South Welshmen and 'Westies', the antagonism between Sydney and Perth, old world and new, was not to be sniffed at. As Wagga Wagga's Geoff Lawson, one of the maiden voyagers, underlines: 'I didn't feel any resentment towards me personally. The problem lay with individual personalities and the Western Australia resentment at Peter Philpott. This I found very hard to believe but WA had the best domestic team, and they'd built it with ferocious parochialism: they believed their man, Daryl Foster, should have been the coach – which many of us didn't believe at all, given Foster's lack of experience and Philpott's high standing in the game. The conflict *within* the WA group was far more significant, the Lillee and Marsh v Hughes conflict worse than anything. It was the veterans and the World Series players versus the young Establishment player. Lillee was adamant that Marsh should have been captain once Chappell had decided not to come. The tension between those three, all from the same state, was on a precipice waiting to tumble into catastrophe at the merest slip of self control.'

Frank Crook, a reporter embarking on his maiden UK tour for the Sydney *Sun*, was less than chuffed with the chosen batsmen. 'Some of them, you look back and think, "Jeez, how did he get in?" Hughes was an awfully nice bloke but he could be very impetuous. He could be like a 14-year-old. When he'd had a few drinks he might get stuck into somebody and we'd have to remind him that's not the way an Australian captain should act. Most of the press boys thought that Rod [Marsh] should have been captain. But we were pretty confident.'

Philpott's reservations centred on the bowling, not that he dared express as much publicly. 'Fred Bennett, the manager, said it was the best-prepared side he'd worked with but there was a great question mark over Kim Hughes's leadership and we were worried about Lillee's fitness. Hogg wasn't the bowler he was in 1978–79, Lawson and Alderman were inexperienced and we were very thin in spin – so Lillee's fitness was very important to us. We were sent to Sri Lanka to prepare: it wasn't a very successful trip because it rained all the time. It was the monsoon season – our board knows nothing about geography.'

Raw as he was, Lawson experienced few tremors. 'I always rated our chances as very good. There was no apprehension about the quality of the opposition as you might get with the West Indies. England were beatable if we played to anywhere near our potential. Greg Chappell was a big loss but we had some very talented players. And English conditions were always going to favour our bowling.'

For the Australian Cricket Board, the South African spectre had caused a few sleepless nights, persuading it to enlist Government support in scuppering plans for a private tour in April. Geoff Dymock, the left-armer who had played such merry hell with English outside edges in 1979–80 and was still contracted to the board, was said to have agreed to lead a party including Gary Gilmour, another contender passed over for Ashes duty. Dr Ali Bacher and his one-eyed varmints had been thwarted – for now.

In his Journal for *The Cricketer*, Alan Gibson observed less than enthusiastically that this was 'the fifth time in seven years that Australia had dispatched a party to these shores' (counting the 1979 World Cup). 'The magic of my youth – when Australia came once every four years, and as soon as a tour was over we began discussing prospects for the next – has gone.'

Part 2

So far, so bad

Botham eclipsed (or The Alderman and the Old Tart)

There was FOT, FOT, giving 'em the V a lot
On the tour, on the tour
There was Rowd, Rowd, reading porno books aloud,
On the tour, on the tour

Each member of the 1972 Australian tourists had his own personal verse adapted to the ribald strains of 'The Quartermaster's Store'. 'Rowd', short for 'Rowdy', was Rod Marsh; the acronym 'FOT' denoted 'Fuckin' Old Tart', an Ian Chappell-inspired soubriquet for Dennis Lillee. Even if their 1981 successors had not had a seam attack so unversed in English conditions – Hogg, Alderman and Lawson were all on their maiden Ashes tours – the well-being of the FOT would have been the single greatest concern for colleagues, captain and management alike, so critical to the cause had he been for a decade. Having him laid up in hospital during the opening weeks was not seen as a helpful way of raising chins left downcast by the abysmal weather.

It was while ghosting his 'column' for the *Daily Star* that Ted Corbett glimpsed the FOT at his most vulnerable. 'He was out late in London and got caught in a storm and soaked to the skin. He contracted viral pneumonia and was sent to an isolation ward in North London. I took him some paperbacks; because of his infectious condition I had to wear a face mask. Thirty minutes after I turned up, Allan Border and Rod Marsh arrived – and they both had masks on as well. It was a surreal sight.'

Pluvius, ever the patriot, saw to it that Hughes and crew took time getting cranked up. They were whisked out for 106 by the olden goldies of the Duchess of Norfolk's XI in the Arundel curtain-raiser, then sat and moped for the most part. The four first-class fixtures in Wales and the south-west scheduled as a lead-in to the Prudential Trophy series were reduced to barely a day apiece. Not once did the tourists bat a second time, nor take five opposition wickets, nor forge a century stand. Among the specialists, only John Dyson, Trevor Chappell and Graeme Wood scaled the heights of 50, much less 100. Holt Lloyd's offer of £150,000 for winning all 11 county engagements was as safe as a Page Three model stepping out on the town with Danny La Rue.

Botham, meanwhile, was in no shape to gloat. Appearing before Scunthorpe magistrates on 29 April, he elected for trial by jury having been charged in connection with an assault the previous December on an apprentice seaman. Also hanging over him was the claim by Henry Blofeld, the journalist and commentator, that Botham had physically accosted him at Bermuda Airport. He had been reappointed as England captain but strictly on a Test-by-Test, suck-it-and-see basis. Worse yet, form remained distant. In the Championship he scored five and took 1–71 against Hampshire, whereupon six Lancashire scalps at Old Trafford were offset by a Holding-inflicted duck. In the group stages of the Benson & Hedges (B&H) Cup against Essex, Gooch took him apart, 11 overs for 74 being followed by an innings of eight. When the Australians came to Taunton he disposed of Wood and Chappell but the elements denied him a bat. All told, his only score of any note in advance of the one-dayers was an unbeaten 57 in another zonal clash with Kent.

Other English pillars were looking equally wobbly. Subtract that thunderous 138 against Somerset in the B&H and, in all competitions, Gooch had mustered 96 in nine crease visitations. Boycott, too, was floundering, seven Championship knocks producing a peak of 51 against Warwickshire, though Willis did race out of the blocks in that match with a deceptively encouraging 5–61. The openers proved more obdurate in the opening one-dayer at Lord's on 4 June. Gooch made 53 and Boycott an unbeaten 75 as England overcame the loss of the former as well as Mike Gatting in the penultimate over of Lillee's rugged stint, some meaty clumps from the skipper speeding them home with six wickets and 20 balls in hand.

The next instalment, at Edgbaston, was tinglingly nip-and-tuck. Wood (55) and Yallop (63) were the mainsprings of Australia's 55-over score of 249–8, Gatting (96) drove England to 224–5, 26 needed off six, only for Hughes to cling onto Botham's attempt to locate Mars. Making his second appearance behind the stumps, Geoff Humpage was too nervy to impose himself with the bat as he did for Warwickshire. When Geoff Lawson capped his three wickets with an impressive leap in the final over to intercept Gatting's boundary-bound biff, the task of scoring three off the last two balls was always going to be too arduous for Willis and Mike Hendrick. The latter duly succumbed to the Lillee–Marsh double act. Marsh also apprehended Eric McManus, a far from glamorous streaker who was subsequently fined £25 for his foolhardy if inoffensive intrusion.

One-sided as the opener had been, the decider was what the Americans call 'a laugher'. On a Headingley pitch of unusual pace and bounce (i.e. there was a modicum of both), Wood (108) and Yallop (48) added 130 for the second wicket, only 20 fewer than England aggregated off the bat; Hogg's 4–29 sealed a 71-run victory. All told, Botham picked up five wickets at 29 while yielding a shade more than four runs per over, ejecting Marsh three times, yet this was largely nullified by scores of 24, 5 and 13 not out, the wand still riddled with rust. Not so the turnstiles: total attendance for the three games was 48,894, takings £230,325. Better still, after Edgbaston had been saturated by a midday storm of 40 days' and nights' intensity, the 'Brumbrella' was estimated to have saved at least two hours' play. On arrival, Hughes had talked of taking advantage of the opposition's internal difficulties, of giving them 'a bit of a shake'. Mission speedily accomplished.

Defeat in the series, on the other hand, had left Botham on his uppers. '[My wife] Kath begged me to resign there and then; it was clear to her that the selectors were holding a gun to my head. When I got back home after dealing with the press she said, "It's not worth it. Why don't you just give it up?"'

Australia's batting woes resumed in the last two sodden first-class matches before the first Test, Yallop and Dyson alone getting to 50. As a consequence, Martin Kent lost the No. 3 berth for which he had been earmarked, and although Dirk Wellham, the bespectacled, studious-looking New South Wales youngster with only five Shield outings behind him, played impressively on a turgid pitch at Derby, Chappell won the nod as first-drop. Before the off, says Graeme Wood, it felt too close to call: 'Botham looked to be on his last legs as captain, and Willis was struggling. But, that said, Alderman was an unknown and Lillee had spent a week in hospital.' Not that you would ever have guessed as much. Notwithstanding his ill-health, Lillee was certainly productive when he trod grass, taking 5–59 in the first two Pru games and 5–41 against Middlesex's all-Test XI. Ray Bright, who had won a tour berth despite not having featured in either of the winter's victorious home series against New Zealand and India, did little to merit selection for the first Test at Trent Bridge. But then, spin was never going to be in either side's plans on a pitch that turned out to be every bit as conducive to the seamers as the purists feared, if not more so.

The death of Ken Barrington continued to cast a pall over the home XI chosen for the first Test, eight of whom had resisted the West Indies in Jamaica with Bill Athey, Roland Butcher and Jackman making way for Bob Woolmer, Gatting and Willis. The last-named felt the loss more acutely than most: 'When I heard of [Barrington's] death, my mind flashed back to the time when he visited my flat in Streatham Hill to try to persuade me that I still had a future with Surrey, the county where he had played all his cricket. He was an eternal worrier, and it was this, I suppose, which killed him. If it is possible, he cared too much about the game and about his players, becoming so involved in the problems of each one of the lads that, in a sense, he was suffering the traumas with them.' The funeral drew a rare outburst of emotion from one of the country's sturdier stoics. 'Tears,' he confessed, 'ran uncontrollably.'

With only marginally less urgency, proceedings by the Trent ran away from England as soon as Hughes won the toss. Lillee (3–34), Alderman (4–68 on debut) and Hogg (3–47) polished off their first effort inside 57 overs, Dilley's haymakers bringing him 34 to drag the hosts from 116–7 to 185 all out. England's pace quartet of Willis, Dilley, Botham and Hendrick left Australia in even direr straits but Border's tenacity and some shoddy work in the cordon – notably when Downton fluffed the southpaw's attempted cut off Hendrick at 51–4 – kept the deficit down to six. Alderman (5–62) and Lillee (5–46) soon had the home order at sixes and sevens, 13–3 begetting 125 all out and a target of 132. The first Sunday's Test play on English soil ended at 5.49, the tourists completing a four-wicket victory, 7500 spectators groaning in unison as chance after chance went down. The whole shebang lasted 236.2 overs, less than three days' worth. But for the rains there would have been no need to despoil the Sabbath, as some saw it. Which may, in turn, say something about the Almighty's view of such purported sacrilege.

'There were complaints of a shortfall in quality, but it was a contest from which one dared not avert one's eyes,' wrote David Frith, who accepted that England had been hoist by their own petard. Others were less amused. To John Dyson, the pitch smacked of panic: 'The wicket was a horror. I thought, "This could be typical". When a side's under pressure they tend to prepare result wickets.' This may or may not explain the combativeness of Chappell, who whacked a ball to deep mid-on after it had fallen in his crease and also hurled at the stumps while Boycott was 'gardening'. Fortunately, and uncharacteristically, he missed, averting a diplomatic incident.

Ted Dexter vented his spleen in *Wisden Cricket Monthly*. 'As a spectacle in its own right it was absorbing enough, but as a milestone in the degradation of

Test cricket towards an unvaried stereotype it was as significant as the go-slow 80-over day at The Oval last year perpetrated by the West Indies. The over-rate was again painfully slow after the Australians had perversely rejected the plan to ensure 100 overs per day.' The contest's saving grace, in Lord Ted's estimation, was the Australian catching, the worst aspect 'the reduction of batting skill to something near a lottery'. If 'this style of cricket is acceptable at the highest level,' he concluded, 'then I despair for the enjoyment of future generations — although, having known nothing better, they may never realise what they've missed.' He also quoted the assertion in the *Book of Common Prayer* about there being nothing more certain than that any human invention, sooner or later, will be corrupted.

Botham had looked in reasonable fettle in the second innings at Trent Bridge, top-scoring with 33 before being undone by a terrific slip catch from Border, one of those predatory, instinctive takes that had contrasted so alarmingly with England's butterfingered escapades. In the B&H quarter-finals, though, he was dispatched for a duck by Peter Hartley, an untried Yorkshire seamer. After the Lord's Test, no earthly amount of Setlers was going to supply express relief.

'We were pleasantly surprised when we won the first Test,' reflects Brian Mossop of the *Sydney Morning Herald*. 'We realised we'd underestimated our blokes a bit. The spirit was sky-high and it could only get better.' And so it did, if not quite in the manner envisaged. Hogg's fitness problems before the second Test resulted in a call for Bright (for a few days, indeed, speculation was rife that, with Thomson having undergone a hernia operation, the tourists would send home for reinforcements, Greg Chappell the favoured candidate if not the logical substitute). Bedser and Co. made two alterations, handing Downton's gloves to Bob Taylor and recalling off-breaker John Emburey in Hendrick's stead. After Hughes had inserted once again, a lifeless surface saw both batting orders recover a measure of respectability, Australia answering England's 311 (Willey 82 despite an injured right index finger) with 345 (Border, Hughes, Wood, Marsh and even Lillee all making at least 40). On the second evening, the compensatory extra hour came into operation but, after going off for bad light, the umpires assumed, wrongly, that there could be no further play. Shortly after 7 p.m. the light improved markedly, but by then the players had been instructed to pack up and go. Aggrieved punters threw cushions on to the field and up into the Tavern hospitality boxes, prompting the TCCB to apologise with due humility the following day.

It was an indication of Botham's tentative mental state that so bold an adventurer should eventually set a target of 232 in 170 minutes, although Willis's hamstring was acting up and he was also fighting off a virus. Shortly before he declared, the captain was bowled behind his legs sweeping at Bright – his second duck of the match. As he wended his morose way up the pavilion steps, MCC members greeted him – if their behaviour can be so dignified – with silent disinterest. 'It was,' remembered Christopher Martin-Jenkins, 'one of the most embarrassing moments for a cricketer I've ever experienced.' Botham had now extended his run as England's most unsuccessful captain to 12 win-free Tests. Something had to give. Within an hour of Australia shutting up shop at 90–4, he had tendered his resignation.

Willis 'rued the day' his friend was appointed. 'The job was plainly not only having a detrimental effect on Ian's cricket but on his whole life. The myth that he, or anyone else for that matter, has an indestructible temperament was quickly crumbling, the sparkle fading.' By reappointing Botham in such piecemeal fashion, Willis argued, the selectors were 'forcing him to walk the plank, a sword poised above his shoulder blades'.

From an Australian perspective, Lawson remembers being both baffled and encouraged. 'Any team that has its leader's credentials endorsed in such a short-term way can have doubts about their collective future, particularly when the captain is clearly the best player. Even Ian Botham needed security, or the outward appearance of it. I was surprised at his temporary appointment and we saw it as a weakness of the whole England set-up. On the other hand, we couldn't give a rat's arse about what the opposition were doing.'

On the Monday morning at Lord's, Botham had padded across the dressing room to Willis and informed him of his intention to stand down (he told the rest of the side later). 'I don't for a moment suppose that Ian wanted me to try and talk him out of it, because once he makes a decision he normally abides by it. I certainly had no intention of trying to dissuade him. Frankly, I thought it was the only option open to him if he was to rescue his own career; I also thought it the best thing that could happen to the team ... we had undoubtedly lost our way.'

'It wasn't a happy time,' affirms Dilley. 'I don't think we were ever going on to the field thinking that we were going to win a game. Both found it very difficult to get his points across without there being that air of defeatism about him.'

Taylor was of a similar mind: 'Some of the criticism [of Botham] was fair. He was too much one of the boys. Making him captain was doing England a disservice – it would have been better to leave him to look after his own game.'

What dismayed Botham – and many others besides – was the behaviour of the Chairman of Selectors. Shortly after the plainly hot and extremely bothered-looking ex-captain, head bowed, had advised Peter West and the BBC viewers that he had stepped down, Bedser admitted that yes, Botham had jumped before he could be pushed. Declining to oblige when Botham sought assurances that he would be in charge for the remainder of the series, they had resolved to sack him anyway, though Bedser did concede, a mite sheepishly, that this was not supposed to be the way it was portrayed. Was this revelation absolutely necessary? Pat Gibson, then cricket correspondent of the *Daily Express*, places Bedser's words in a more innocent light. 'A few of the journalists asked Alec, who's as honest as the day is long, and he told us straight. That was him. Ask a straight question, get a straight answer.' And dear old Alec, of course, never was one for schmoozing. It still suggested a teacher wanting the final word with an errant 11-year-old.

'[Botham] was not taking the easy way out,' stressed Willis, 'which would have been to bury his head in the sand and blunder on. He was being quite brutally honest with himself, making what amounted to a public confession that the job was getting him down. What a pity the selectors had to spoil it all.'

Dilley concurred: 'You had to feel sorry for the bloke. Nobody wants to go through that public humiliation. It would have been a lot more dignified to let him fall on his sword.'

'Without doubt, and whatever Botham's view may be,' warranted Brearley, 'it was a relief to him to be captain no longer.'

Botham himself has said little to dispel the conviction that a stone had been removed from his shoe. 'Because I had only been given the captaincy on a match-by-match basis, I was never sure where I stood. That caused me to be withdrawn and moody and, as usual, Kath had to bear the brunt of it. It was the same old story: I didn't need anyone's help to sort out my problems, not even Kath's. I snapped at her and the kids; even Tigger, our boxer dog, started moping. [Kath] also became quite depressed, so much so that she lost about a stone in weight.

'So when we walked through the Grace gates on the first morning [at] Lord's to be confronted by a newspaper hoarding shouting "BOTHAM MUST GO", that was more than enough as far as I was concerned.'

He mewed to Lillee about his tribulations over a pint of beer. The recommendation, as ever, was plainly put: 'Why don't you just give it away?'

So effervescent were the suds in this particular soap opera, even BBC2's high-minded *Newsnight*, which barely pays lip service to sport at the best of times, had been airing a daily item entitled 'The Botham Trial'. The presenter was hard-pressed to suppress a smirk as he recounted the latest developments, complete with 'Case for the Prosecution', a litany of the skipper's on-field sins. *Weekending* on Radio 4 chipped in with a running joke: 'Botham's been made captain until the end of the next over.'

Then came the 'reception' from the bacon-and-egg tie brigade after completing that Lord's pair. 'Not a soul among the members mumbled "bad luck" [nor] looked me in the eye,' Botham would recollect. 'They all just sat there dumbstruck. Some picked up their papers and hid behind them, others rummaged in bags and a few just turned their backs on me. Needless to say, I was fuming.' Nor would the grudge be forgotten; for the remainder of his career he treated MCC members with 'contempt'; whenever he played at Lord's, he would never so much as raise his bat to acknowledge them. 'Right,' he thought, 'Bugger ya!'

The pity of it all, he would insist, was that he felt he was getting to grips with it all. 'I had been forced into a position where all I could do was resign, but the irritating thing was it came at the point when I felt that at last I was getting the hang of the job; I was coming to terms with all aspects of it and I was ready to bloom. Not for one minute would I agree that the captaincy affected my form. Everyone has ups and downs and for a while I was in a slight cricketing trough. Given time, though, I'm certain I would have come good as a captain.' Unanimity on that score is scarce. Seldom do the instinctive and phenomenally successful make good leaders: how can they truly empathise with those less blessed, those to whom it does not come naturally?

Nonetheless, some, such as Robin Marlar, then cricket correspondent of the *Sunday Times,* believed it may well have been a case of right man, wrong time. 'Botham was given the job too early. Looking back, the decision seems more monstrous than it did at the time, like lobbing a hand grenade, with the pin long out, into the hands of the most promising recruit. Botham was given the job in circumstances that demanded that he also be given a chance. As a chance, two consecutive series against the West Indies is that of a snowball in hell.'

Cultural differences, the contrast between new world and old, exerted an influence here. While Australian sides in this position would have expected backing from their own media, England's tabloid circulation wars, together with the growing predilection for 'nanny goats' (quotes), had exacerbated an already prickly stand-off in the opposing camp. The ever-mounting number of ex-players sitting in judgement, particularly in the commentary boxes, widened the chasm. In July 1981, Botham, Brearley and Willis were all in varying states of high dudgeon, refusing to speak to various newspapers (even though Botham had a column in the *Sun*).

Not that this was anything unusual for Willis who, as the son of a journalist, at least had a better insight into the beast than most. 'I always believed I had a good relationship with the press until the day in 1977 when it was revealed that I had decided not to join WSC. I deliberately avoided talking about the issue, not wishing to become embroiled in any controversy.

'A Birmingham evening [newspaper's cricket correspondent] wrote a piece of some length in which I was widely quoted. The only thing was, I had never spoken about the matter. He was duly sacked, but the incident set me more on my guard than I had ever thought necessary. Before long I stopped reading most of the papers to avoid getting angry.

'Perhaps my criticism is too intolerant [but] I do have a rudimentary knowledge of the job and its requirements [and am] aware that whatever licence may sometimes be permissible, it can never include sheer invention. My anger [in July 1981] was directed at the clutch of writers who seemed intent on making utterly untenable the position of England captain ... the very writers who had been boldly campaigning for [Ian] to be given the job were now cruelly consigning him to the rubbish patch.'

'It was the time when cricket was starting to make the transfer from back page to front,' recalls Pat Gibson. 'I'd done front-page leads from Guyana, and when Tony Greig was made captain, and when the England players threatened to strike in Pakistan. Our relationship with the players was the same but they resented the new corps of news reporters. In the Caribbean, things went badly for Botham on and off the field. There was the Jackman affair, Barrington's death, losing Tests. I remember Kathy Botham arriving somewhere – Barbados – and when her husband went to meet her at the airport the TV crews were there. I objected, saying they ought to give them a bit of peace. I was told by one member of the crew, very forcibly, to mind my own business.'

'The relationship between the English press and the English team was very tense,' notes Frank Crook of the Sydney *Sun*. 'Most of the English players wouldn't talk to their press boys, but they were happy to talk to me. Bobby Willis told me, ''Cricket writing in this country has gone down the gurgler.'' We used to sit in press conferences and chuckle at the way the English press and players would have a go at each other. The English press didn't get on with Brearley; he was on a different intellectual level. But they liked Hughes. He was the sort of bloke they could have a man-to-man chat with.'

Handed back his pips for three Tests with an option for a fourth, Brearley believed his main rivals were a pair of public schoolies, John Barclay of Sussex and Roger Knight of Surrey, both uncapped. The only viable option considered, however, was Essex's Keith Fletcher, 'The Gnome', whose own acuity (favoured, incidentally, by Willis), was counterbalanced both by the four years that had passed since his last cap and by concern for his batting. The visiting hacks were cock-a-hoop. 'We really thought that losing the captaincy would take the wind out of Botham's sails,' says Crook. 'It was a victory for the Australians. [We] had a bit of a chuckle over the appointment of Brearley. We didn't think he was a Test cricketer.'

Adds Mossop: 'Although we respected the bloke, Brearley had retired from international cricket. "The Poms are in panic mode," we thought.'

The Australian players, too, welcomed the decision to reinstate Brearley. 'He was always seen as an astute leader but a very moderate opening batsman,' reflects Lawson. 'I simply thought that the team was weakened by not picking the best opener.'

There was 'great glee', says Philpott of Botham's exit as captain. 'The English side was semi-shattered. The English press were giving them a hard time, which could only be good for us.'

That said, the tourists, as Lawson reiterates, were riven by their own leadership headaches. 'Kim [Hughes] certainly had the majority's respect, but it is damned difficult to maintain respect when two of the greatest – and most respected – players of contemporary Australian cricket were intent on undermining that respect in nearly every waking hour. The lesser WA players preferred to follow the lead of the elder statesmen rather than defend their skipper, which also didn't help. Some of us were just playing our first few Tests and did not have the status to be questioning Rod and Dennis's actions to their faces, although in private their actions were not considered very "Australian" or "true blue". There was no doubting the team's endeavours on the field, but in almost every other sense we were a divided group.'

Still, it seems safe to assume that one statistic united them in delight. Not since 1888 had Australia lost an Ashes rubber after going one up.

Part 3

Headingley, July '81

The stage

Headingley, headquarters of Yorkshire CCC and Leeds RLFC, is not alone in doubling as Test venue and international rugby ground. It is safe to say, however, that it outdoes its Antipodean and South African counterparts in its unabashed flair for controversy. To Australians born since the Second World War, for all that the urn was won or retained there in 1964, 1968 and – courtesy of the 'Free George Davis' campaigners – 1975, this homely area of suburban Leeds has long held all the allure of a week in Hades. Indeed, those of a suspicious bent might suggest that the protestors who poured oil on the wicket were acting, not at the behest of Mr Davis, but at the urging of some vengeful Cobber.

Management of the site has long been vested in the Leeds Cricket, Football and Athletic Club, but Yorkshire's lease is similarly long. The only covered accommodation is in the members' stand and the main stand that curls around the southern section of the arena. The infamous Western Terrace, den of throaty support and gratuitous insults ('the pit of hate' as some have dubbed it), is the most popular place to sit. A winter practice shed was recently demolished in favour of offices and dressing rooms, behind which lurks a bowling green.

'The deep embankments and the concentration of roofed buildings to the south leaves Headingley with a pleasantly open atmosphere, and the old paved cycling track encircling the turf increases the sense of spaciousness,' wrote J.M. Kilburn in the second edition of *Barclays World of Cricket* published in 1980. 'But players find sighting the ball as difficult as they would against a darker background.' There are no sightscreens, leading to incidents such as that which befell Peter May on his Test debut there in 1951, although admittedly en route to a century; failing to pick up his very first delivery, he groped forward and edged the ball down the legside. Fielders sometimes complain not only of losing the ball against spectators or foliage, but of a north–south slope that inhibits accurate judgement of the pace of shots. 'Yet all Headingley's remarkable cricket and adventurous by-products,' warranted Kilburn, 'have left the ground still without any marked quality and character.' It has 'the commercial rather than the domestic appeal' giving, in short, 'no obvious cause for either affection or dislike'.

Of late, it has been England's lucky ground. They retained the Ashes here in 1972 and regained them in 1977. Of the eight tussles for the urn since 1948 they have lost only one. Not that such good fortune lacks precedent; in 1934 they were heading for defeat when a thunderstorm flooded the premises. Two of Ray Illingworth's finest wins as England captain came here – against the West Indies in 1969 (by 30 runs after Sobers' men, seeking 303, had reached 219–3) and against Pakistan two Julys later (by 25 runs after Intikhab Alam's combo, requiring 231, had been looking equally pregnant with expectation at 160–4). Another gripping contest was the 1976 Test against the West Indies. By stumps on day one, Lloyd and his fleet-batted forces had scorched to 437–9, yet so spirited was the home recovery (centuries from Greig and Knott, 5–43 by Willis in his comeback) that, chasing 260, they were 140–4 and, later, 204–8 before Ward and Willis fell to Holding in consecutive balls, leaving Greig high and dry on 76. That Willey (36 and 45) made his debut in this contest cannot have been entirely coincidental. After winning three of their seven Tests here immediately after the war, England won six on the reel from 1956 to 1962. Sobers, Kanhai, Griffith, Hall and Gibbs combined to give the West Indies victory by 221 runs in 1963, and a year later Peter Burge's saucy sally against Trueman saw Australia regain the Ashes, but since then the hosts had lost only twice to all-comers in 15 Tests. A bastion by any other name.

Two of the more unstoppable assaults in Test history occurred here in successive Ashes rubbers: Charlie Macartney's century before lunch on the opening day in 1926, and Don Bradman's triple century on the first day four years later. Bradman enjoyed himself hugely here, racking up 963 runs in six Test innings at a heady 192.60, his rewards – honorary life membership of Yorkshire CCC and, in Kilburn's words, 'The most stirring public acclaim, by his own reckoning, of his whole career.' It was here in 1948, moreover, that Bradman led the first 400-run chase in five-day annals, on a pitch that often turned right angles. His compatriots have been paying for his nerve ever since.

It was here in 1953, with Australia needing 66 in 45 minutes with seven wickets intact, that Trevor Bailey, under the approving eye of Len Hutton, stifled the charge by shamelessly firing the ball well wide of leg stump for six overs. Neil Harvey found it 'absolutely disgusting – Godfrey Evans was standing eight feet wide of leg stump taking the ball. If one-day rules had been in force they would have been wides. I made 34 in about even time and, if they'd've bowled properly, we'd have got them. But they got away with it.'

Lindsay Hassett and Hutton's teams duly shared pints and diplomacies, but the former, observed Evans, 'were absolutely livid and I think rightly so. They had been cheated of victory by the worst kind of negative cricket. They were right.'

Jim Laker's legendary n-n-n-nineteen on that dusty, decidedly iffy pitch at Old Trafford in 1956 was preceded by a Headingley surface for the third Test that brought the Surrey off-spinner a matchwinning return of 11–113, prompting the declaration (some years later) by Ian Johnson, Australia's captain, that it was the worst track he'd ever clapped eyes on. 'It played all right until tea on the first day, then it started to go. Richie [Benaud] bowled a ball late on the first day that gripped and spun over Peter May's right shoulder. And I thought, "My God! This will be a shocker." Then it rained and got wet, so I don't think anyone really appreciated how bad it was.'

On the next tour, five years later, Aussies past and present fumed anew. 'A disgrace,' was Ray Lindwall's pithy summary in his syndicated column.

'A tennis net seemed more appropriate equipment here than two sets of stumps,' noted Ken 'Slasher' Mackay. 'The wicket was the colour and texture of a crumbling ant-bed tennis court.'

Before the off, Mackay was idling on the putting green at the Hotel Majestic in Harrogate when Laker walked past. 'Have you seen the wicket?' asked Laker. 'Think I'll make a comeback.' Even so, it was Fred Trueman who did the damage, albeit with off-cutters at a considerably reduced pace. A spell of 5–16 in five overs in the first innings was followed by 6–5 in eight overs in the second, including one 24-ball burst of 5–0 as Australia slumped from 99–2, 37 in profit, to 120 all out, ultimately losing by eight wickets in under three days.

In 1972, a fungus by the name of fuserium (or, to give it its full, lesser-spotted moniker, *Fuserium oxysporum*) entered the lexicon. Fuserium, it was asserted, was the cause of the grassless 'dust bowl' that saw Derek Underwood and Ray Illingworth take 14–146 in 92.1 overs, enabling England to win by nine wickets shortly after tea on day three and hence keep their hands on the Ashes. Flooded by a freak storm the previous weekend, continued poor weather had prevented the use of the heavy roller, which led to the pitch being dried by artificial means.

Yet, for all that, Ian Chappell's tourists, in E.W. Swanton's words, took defeat 'philosophically and sportingly', the fuserium line rankled, particularly with that honourable Australian opener-turned-scribe, Jack Fingleton. In order to do its worst, fuserium requires soil temperatures in excess of 75 degrees Fahrenheit – not exactly common in Leeds. The official explanation was that it was the flat covering that had created conditions favourable for fuserium to flourish – an explanation that Fingleton, among others, refused to accept. In *Wisden*, editor Norman Preston was adamant: 'Not for a moment would one suggest that conditions had been deliberately engineered.'

The losers were less convinced. 'The dressing room at the end was like a morgue,' recalled Greg Chappell. 'We felt we'd been cheated.' Even E.W. conceded it was 'an embarrassment'.

Context is all. Having taken the first Test, Illingworth's ageing team had staggered through the next two, were walloped at Lord's and comfortably behind the eight-ball for four out of five days at Trent Bridge as Lillee, Marsh, Massie and the Chappells potted pretty much everything in sight. In 1961, Australia were one up when the sides convened at Leeds, as in 1956. In 1953, as in 1972, the sides were level. Put two and two together, and, if you come from Bondi or Wagga Wagga, Adelaide or Hobart, there is ample fuel for a decent conspiracy theory.

The cast

Statistics by Paul E. Dyson

Includes all 24 players available for selection on the morning of the match

Figures correct up to and including the end of the 2nd Test at Lord's.

SR = Strike rate (balls per wicket)

ENGLAND

John Michael BREARLEY

b. Harrow, Middlesex, 28/4/1942

Cambridge University 1961–64

Middlesex 1961–

Test debut 1976

36th Test (28th as captain)

Test record to date:

Innings	Not out	Runs	Highest score	50	100	Average	Catches
58	3	1301	91	8	–	23.65	48

The reincarnation of the Messiah – or a despairing roll of the dice by panic-stricken selectors? The next five days should supply the answer. At least he has had the good sense to shave off the beard that so antagonised the Australians when last their paths crossed on a Test field, earning him that less-than-fond (if grudgingly respectful) moniker, 'The Ayatollah'.

As his advocates seldom tire of reiterating, his form for Middlesex has been excellent – 570 Championship runs thus far at over 50, including centuries against Essex, Hampshire and Nottinghamshire. A duck against the Sri Lankans, moreover, was followed by an unbeaten hundred against his old sparring partner Lillee. And yes, he really did once score 312 in a day (legend has it that the England Under-25 skipper may have caned North Zone for even more that day in Peshawar; he and Alan Ormond rattled off 234 between them in an hour and three-quarters, leaving one of the local scorers so overwhelmed he gave up with 20 minutes left and fled the premises). For all England's batting frailties, though, such figures, as ever, are encouraging yet irrelevant. You don't get to play in 35 Tests as a specialist batsman – mostly as an opener – while lugging around an average of 23 and a top score of 91 unless you have something else to commend you. 'Brears', happily, has two more harmonious strings to his bow: a capacity to belie an absence of obviously athletic qualities by catching flies at slip, and, in the famous words of Rodney Hogg, 'A degree in people'.

That Brearley possesses the game's shrewdest brain (in addition to a first-class Classics degree) is not in doubt, nor that his leadership acumen has helped transform club and country. He can also be quite charming and, if the mood strikes, something of a card. Interviewed by Tim Rice on a TV chat show, that chunky head of hair swathed in professorial grey, he held up a fluffy grey toy creature (to distract from his own eminence gris-ing?). An odd-looking thing, two-thirds wallaby to one-third Tasmanian devil, he introduced it as 'an Australian friend of mine – called Dennis'. Cue knowing giggles in the stalls. It was a gift, he elaborated, from a nun: 'She told me it was a typical Australian. There's a very small space for the brain – and a very large mouth.' The smirk almost outdazzled the studio lights.

Whether Brearley has also been extraordinarily fortunate is another matter. At Middlesex, where he has presided since 1971, decades of wonky focus and extensive underachievement came to an end with the Championship-winning campaign of 1976, to be capped by not one but two Championship–Gillette Cup 'doubles', a feat no other county had achieved in the singular. He will be the first to confess, however, that he has been blessed with one of the finest crops of talent to represent any county for any significant passage of time. For the opening Championship fixture against Essex at Lord's in May, the home XI, uniquely, read: Brearley, Downton, Radley, Gatting, Butcher, Barlow, Emburey, Edmonds, Selvey, Thomson and Daniel – Test players all. Since Brearley assumed the captaincy for the 1977 Ashes series, England, meanwhile, have been in a position to call on up to seven world-class performers, in Tony Greig, Alan Knott, Boycott, Gower, Botham, Taylor and Willis.

By the same token, Brearley tapped their potential more fully, by demanding more and assisting more, by listening and counselling, inspiring both sets of players to greater deeds than they perpetrated under the less accomplished likes of Peter Parfitt and Mike Denness. Although the fuse is shorter than it was, he remains a communicator par excellence. The rapport he builds up with his charges – even those who do not instantly take to that vaguely superior veneer – is all any leader can ask for.

'He's very good at giving people credit for things if they suggested them and they worked, even though he might have done the same anyway,' says John Emburey, who joined Middlesex soon after Brearley took over as captain. 'He changed the culture at the club. He has a lot of time for young players.' Botham, whose earthward descent over the past two series can surely be blamed at least in part on Brearley's absence, will surely be relieved at his return. At net practice, as if to prove the point, he grabbed his new skipper and threatened to kiss him, for the benefit of the press.

To the solitary of eye, the Ayatollah's record as captain appears as deeply impressive as any in English Test history. Fifteen successes in 27 attempts, balanced by just four reverses, are indubitably the stuff of deification. Closer inspection, however, removes much if not all of the gloss. Only five of those wins – two against India, three against New Zealand – have been achieved against full-strength opposition. Packer saw to that. Seven of the victories came against Australia and Pakistan, whose missing personnel could make up an XI capable of beating all-comers and still have enough spare quality to lend England some eminently worthwhile ringers. Two winters ago, with peace restored and Australia duly reinforced, England were routed. Nor has he led the line against the marauding West Indians. Was his withdrawal before the 1980 tour a tacit admission that his bat would be a luxury the team could no longer afford against a genuinely troublesome foe? Quite possibly.

For all that apparent self-assurance and bookish air, it may console some to learn that fear of failure afflicts him as much as the next man. On the advice of Bob Willis, he went for hypnotherapy with Dr Jackson during the 1978–79 Ashes tour ('I thought there was nothing to lose'), but declined to go beyond a deep trance by entering the full hypnotic state. 'I was just very relaxed. If someone had opened the door I'd have noticed. I found it very helpful. He diagnosed my problems – fear of failure – before the hypnosis then invited me to imagine confronting the bowler – Hogg or Hurst in this case – and visualise my body moving in anticipation as they came in to bowl.'

'The statistics suggest that he is one of the great England captains,' mused Ray Illingworth after Brearley stepped down, recommending Botham as his heir. 'The luckiest would be nearer the truth.' Envy or reality?

Graham Alan GOOCH

b. Leytonstone, Essex, 23/7/1953

Essex 1973–

Test debut 1975

33rd Test

Test record to date:

Innings	Not out	Runs	Highest score	50	100	Average	Catches
57	3	1941	123	11	3	35.94	30

Balls	Runs	Wkts	Av	Best	5w/1	10w/m	SR
738	271	6	45.17	2–16	–	–	123.00

With that drooping moustache and hangdog countenance, Gooch rarely gives the impression of enjoying his trade overmuch. Those muscular, uncomplicated drives belie this to a degree, but since the start of the summer the whimpers have outnumbered the booms. Hesitant and all too often subjugated, he appears to be in urgent need of, if not a furlough, then certainly a lengthy siesta.

What a pale contrast to the bulwark who, having finally secured his first Test century against the West Indies at Lord's last June, five fitful years and 21 appearances after that pair on debut against Australia, proceeded to reel off another couple in the very lair of the most relentless attack the game has ever seen. Bridgetown yielded 142 runs in a match where England's six other specialist bats raised 146 between them. In Antigua he was Horatio once again, making 153 in the first dig while 10 colleagues scraped together 116. Make that Trevor Bailey stuck in fast-forward mode.

That John Bullishness resurfaced on the opening morning at Lord's as he cuffed Lillee and Alderman at will, only for a mistimed hook off Lawson to lob meekly, apologetically, to midwicket. Off he sloped, shoulders sagging. Addressing the bowler with bat held aloft might be just the ticket against Roberts and Holding, but it could be that it works against him in subtler company. There is also a nagging suspicion that, after spending the best part of a year repulsing a far greater threat to life and limb, the tank could well be empty.

The pity is that 'Goochie' has at last nailed down a regular berth, supplying Boycott with his most reliable and trustworthy opening partner since Dennis Amiss's mid-Seventies pomp. So long a prolific runmaker for Essex, transferring that dominance to the next rung with any consistency has proved troublesome. Even when three figures did appear to be within compass, at Melbourne two winters ago, he ran himself out for 99 trying to finish the job – off the last ball before tea. Then came Lord's and affirmation. His present slump may indeed be a natural reaction, an extended 'whew'. Compassion, however, is unlikely to lift that chin off the floor quite so efficiently as a few meaty clumps off Lillee.

A specialist slip and adept seamer renowned for wobbling even the most venerable balls, his Test victims number Ian Chappell, Rod Marsh and Collis King. Should the coming contest look destined to end in stalemate, expect to be consoled by his hilarious impressions of other bowlers; suffice to say our wannabe Mike Yarwood pulls up clutching his back before his 'Chris Old' reaches the stumps. Seeing even a wisp of a grin enliven that apparently frozen scowl would be reward in itself.

Geoffrey BOYCOTT

b. Fitzwilliam, Yorkshire, 21/10/1940
Yorkshire 1962–
Test debut 1964
101st Test (3 as captain)
Test record to date:

I	NO	Runs	HS	50	100	Av	Ct
177	22	7518	246*	40	20	48.50	31

Balls	Runs	Wkts	Av	Best	5w/I	10w/m	SR*
926	380	7	54.29	3–47	–	–	132.29

The stage was not so much set as pre-ordained. Fifth day at Lord's, the great man's 100th Test, a record 60th half-century in the bag, the prospects of a conclusive outcome dim. His timing had certainly been impeccable against the same opponents four years earlier when he collected his 100th century on his home patch at Headingley. Given that peerless knack of stapling himself to the crease, another historic effort, it was assumed, was his for the taking. Whereupon, playing at a widish ball from Lillee he would have ignored 99 times out of 100, he edged to Marsh. Silence descended on the crowd, disbelief profound.

Now he is approaching 41 and showing an increasing desire to give the slip cordon as much practice as possible, the question must be asked once more. Does England's foremost accumulator still have the appetite, the greed, to leave bowlers in a state of listless enervation? We asked it after his unhappy Ashes tour in 1978–79 when he was reduced to mediocrity as well as strokelessness, but between then and the outset of the current rubber he garnered 1474 runs at 52.64 with four hundreds, the force evidently with him as never before. There was that unbeaten 99 in Perth (the first such score in

Test history), a match-saving 128 not out in the Centenary Test and an equally invaluable unbowed ton in Antigua. It says a lot for his resilience and recuperative powers that the latter followed that matchless over from Holding in Barbados, wherein he moved mountains to keep the first five balls out only to be bowled neck-and-crop by the sixth. Technically, none can compare for exactitude. But fancy letting a Warwickshire debutant dismiss you with his maiden first-class delivery, as the far-from-blatantly-gifted Chris Lethbridge recently did. Is it simply that, like Gooch, metal fatigue has set in?

The buccaneering freedom, nay, effusiveness, of Boycott's strokes in the one-dayers on the last trek Down Under startled those who tuned into this particular soap late in the day. The fact is, he has always had it in him, as that sparkling matchwinning 146 in the 1965 Gillette Cup final so eloquently demonstrated; it's just that what almost invariably prevails is the cautious, pragmatic and – come on, let's be honest – selfish Boycott. Mostly, this suits the team just fine, sometimes not. Runs and averages are his bread and water, his very lifeblood, the sole criterion by which he wishes to be judged. Which is why, for all his experience and expertise, he made such an inept leader of men.

That he will persist in dividing opinion is indisputable. Those who sing hosannas in his name do so every bit as lustily as those aiming the brickbats. Bar that self-imposed exile from 1974–77 when a rare bad trot convinced him to withdraw his services, he has served his country admirably.

David Ivon GOWER

b. Tunbridge Wells, Kent, 1/4/1957
Leicestershire 1975–
Test debut 1978
29th Test
Test record to date:

I	NO	Runs	HS	50	100	Av	Ct
47	4	1962	200*	8	4	45.63	14

Surprising as it may seem, if any home batsman has risen above foe and conditions in the series thus far, it has been Gower. Surprising, because that minimalist footwork and legendarily iffy concentration probably ought to have made him a sitting duck. Instead, he has been alone on either side in exceeding 25 in each innings, and, at Lord's, achieved the highest score to date, 89. He also endured longer than anyone during that dismal second innings at Trent Bridge. Luck had something to do with it, sure, but are we witnessing the flowering of a new, less carefree 'Goldilocks'? More importantly, do we want to?

That steadfast stint in Jamaica three months ago hinted at change. Prior to that, the capacity to grit it out appeared to elude him, as if he were above such piffling, mortal concerns. Betrayed by those infuriating firm-footed wafts, had he not been dropped against the same opponents the previous season? Ah, but would watching cricket be remotely as satisfying if the cares of adulthood swamped the positivism of youth?

To cite Gower as the game's most watchable, aesthetically pleasing batsman verges on cliché. A trifle dilettante-ish for the average Yorkshireman, admittedly, and being left-handed definitely gives him a head start; to most of us common or garden right-handers, awe comes all too easy. Get beyond the mechanics, though, and you still have the timing. Cover drives flow and glow, pulls executed with a pirouette of which Baryshnikov would be proud. From the moment he gathered his first runs for England, caressing Liaqat Ali through midwicket at Edgbaston in 1978, expectations have surged as soon as he takes guard. That they have been met as often as they have is a minor miracle, that he averages nearly 46 no less so. A deceptively languid presence in the covers, he intercepts shots as if on castors, throwing in a single movement. He brings beauty, however fragile, to a sport long on unsightly warts.

Grace Road regulars will witter on about his inability to lift himself for the off-Broadway stuff, even if he did recently help set a new high for a Leicestershire second-wicket stand, adding 289 with Chris Balderstone against Essex. Such, sadly, is the way of things as the international game eats up ever greater wodges of time traditionally devoted to county business. For all concerned, tolerance is as obligatory as the glass of vino Gower craves at stumps.

The application has improved but major flaws remain. He doesn't possess a fraction of Boycott's single-mindedness, let alone Gooch's enthusiasm for practice. He will probably never pile up the stacks of runs he should, but let's be realistic. Precious commodities like Gower will always frustrate as frequently as they delight, probably more so amid an era in which the counties' devotion to the instant game plays merry hell with batting techniques. In a shortlived B&H tie against Northamptonshire restricted by rain to a mere 11.2 overs, he still found time to be trapped lbw for 0, for the third time in successive meetings between the sides at Northampton, by Tim Lamb. The Right Hon – but hardly terrifying – Timothy Lamb.

Like the little girl with the curl, the big boy with the curls wavers between the very good and the horrid. Then again, when the good is *this* good, *this* intoxicating – such as that feline 200 against India two summers ago – why fret? A more discernible determination to make the most of his gifts would be nice. As would a drastic reduction in those flirtations outside off stump. But look at that average – 45; not that far behind Boycott, who is himself on the verge of becoming the country's highest runscorer in Tests. Is it too much to ask that Gower should one day displace him, cavalier usurping roundhead? Let's hope not.

As for the selectors, one can only pray they don't do anything silly, such as take too much notice of those pukka public school roots and make him captain.

Michael William ('Mike') GATTING

b. Kingsbury, Middlesex, 6/6/1957
Middlesex 1975–
Test debut 1977
11th Test
Test record to date:

I	NO	Runs	HS	50	100	Av	Ct
18	1	390	59	4	–	22.94	8

Balls	Runs	Wkts	Av	Best	5w/I	10w/m	SR
8	1	0	–	–	–	–	–

The most astonishing thing about this energetic, fit but inarguably dumpy young Londoner is that he once won a medal for ballroom dancing. The second most astonishing thing, for someone who can appear so brassy and bold, is that his highest Test score is only 59. Delve a little, however, and you notice that, of his 17 dismissals, seven have been lbw, and three in this series already. Judgement of line and anticipation of movement demand as much attention as that passion for Branston pickle.

That said, there is no doubt that Gatting, who made a career-best 158 against Yorkshire on a tricky Headingley pitch in May, has taken substantial strides this summer. In and out of the Test side since that painful, arguably premature debut at 20 against the Pakistani spinners (and umpires), he and Border are the only batsmen in this series to glean two half-centuries. In the first innings at Trent Bridge he was in full command, cutting and glancing to resounding effect when, five minutes after tea, he requested a fresh glove. Concentration broken, he pulled lavishly at the next delivery from Hogg only for the ball to jag back and bounce indifferently. Another leg-before. At Lord's he achieved a new Test best, then misread Bright's arm ball. Lbw again. The heart bled.

A bustling seamer and normally dependable close fielder, there is a theory that, for batsmen spotting him perched under their noses at short leg or silly mid-off, that ample frame presents too big a target to resist, hence the frequency with which he finds himself posted there. Affable after hours and a fervent team man, meat and two veg to Gower's chateaubriand, reports suggest he may well have saved John Emburey's life in the Caribbean. Having joined his Middlesex buddy on a catamaran neither had the expertise to control on high seas, Gatting had returned to shore when the off-spinner was swept away by a fierce wind. Gatting alerted the occupants of a nearby boathouse and a motor launch was duly dispatched. The selectors who have shown such faith in his potential will be keenly hoping he has a few more rescue missions in him.

Peter WILLEY

b. Sedgefield, Co Durham, 6/12/1949
Northamptonshire 1966–
Test debut 1976
19th Test
Test record to date:

I	NO	Runs	HS	50	100	Av	Ct
34	5	861	102*	4	2	29.69	3

Balls	Runs	Wkts	Av	Best	5w/I	10w/m	SR
971	406	5	81.20	2–73	–	–	194.20

At the height of England's Caribbean travails last winter, Charlie Griffith, the planet's most feared and controversial bowler two decades ago, accused the batsmen of being 'bloody scared'. Dear old Charlie obviously hadn't been watching Peter Willey very carefully.

To find this stern, indomitable, unfashionably puritanical Geordie featuring in a Test series not involving the West Indies is strange. Of his 18 caps, 11 have been won when the Wisden Trophy has been at stake. Of his six scores of 50-plus, all but the lowest have come when the going has been roughest. No Englishman has batted for longer in this rubber than the 246 minutes he dug in for in the first innings at Lord's. That predicament, though, was a piece of the proverbial cake by comparison with the ditches he retrieved his side from in the space of a fortnight last July.

At Old Trafford, England were 180 on with four wickets intact and nearly four hours to go, but Willey manned the trenches until the coast was clear. At The Oval, he went one better. Entering at 67–6 in the second innings with the runs-time equation almost identical, he looked on in tight-lipped fury as the total slid to 92–9, then found a wholly unexpected ally in Willis. The pair may have won few prizes for artistic impression (Willey's stance, two-eyed and addressing mid-on, is especially hard on the eye), yet they added 117 without being parted, Willey completing his maiden Test century. He was at it again in Antigua in April, coming in at 138–5, wincing as another man went without addition, then carving and uppercutting his way to the newest Test venue's inaugural hundred – undefeated, naturally. 'He could only say that it was "nice on the day ... perhaps the next two or three days", ' recalls Gower, 'but that it was "what you are supposed to do".' According to Gower, he 'doesn't suffer fools at all', and is probably happiest walking his dogs, Topsy and Toffee. 'In cricket things just happen,' says the taciturn Willey of that innings in Antigua. 'I've batted and got a hundred and I've looked back and thought, "That wasn't me out there." Something had taken over; the mind had taken over. You can't say I was going to play that shot off Roberts or Croft. It just happened.'

A callow 16 when he made his debut for Northants, Sedgefield's current claim to universal fame toiled without recognition for a decade before being granted two Tests against the West Indies in 1976. He acquitted himself well, only to be omitted from the ensuing tour to India – where those niggardly off-breaks would have come in decidedly handy – because his technique against spin was considered suspect. Recalled three seasons later, he made his point with 52 and 31 against India, and has since played 15 Tests on the trot, strapping up that bane of a right knee before the start of each day's play. If Tom Wolfe ever decided to bottle the Right Stuff, he could do worse than call it Willey's.

Not that everybody is satisfied, even in his home county. 'More than one critic asked how a man with dodgy knees, whose Championship bowling average topped that of his batting, could be chosen to face one of the greatest Test sides since the war. Perhaps he kindly cuts the crusts off the selectors' sandwiches during the interval or his wife Charmaine occasionally ironed Ian Botham's flannels?' Thus wrote David Hickey in an article for the Northants–Australians match brochure. Brown-nose? Peter Willey? The Man With No Middle Name? Most people would have consulted their briefs in less time than it takes to say Alvin Kallicharran. Fortunately, internal complaints forced the magazine to be withdrawn. Even if it had been published, knowing 'Will', he would have shrugged and moved on, smiling the inner smile of a man too secure in himself to need to tell the world. He'd make a top-notch umpire.

Acclaimed as the only county player ever to make Botham think twice about one of his pranks, the power in those trunk-like forearms has attained mythical proportions. *Et naturellement*, we've had the classic one-liners. Who can forget Brian Johnston on *Test Match Special*, barely able to contain those first-form sniggers as he made the indelible observation, 'The bowler's Holding, the batsman's Willey' (bet it took a couple of choccie cakes to cook that one up)?

He also happens to be the middle man in the ultimate assonant scoreline –
Lillee c Willey b Dilley. It is, therefore, eminently conceivable that his name will
linger longer than that unflinching spirit. He deserves far, far better. Being part
of a Test-winning team, a pleasure he has yet to sample, would be a start.

Ian Terrence BOTHAM

b. Heswall, Cheshire, 24/11/1955
Test debut 1977
38th Test (12 as captain)
Test record to date:

I	NO	Runs	HS	50	100	Av	Ct
56	2	1612	137	4	6	29.85	45

Balls	Runs	Wkts	Av	Best	5w/I	10w/m	SR
8439	3733	174	21.45	8–34	14	3	48.50

When he polished off Australia's first innings at Nottingham with a return
catch off Border, a narrow lead secured, the indifference screamed. John Lee
Hooker's paean to misery rang loud and clear: 'Been down so long, it looks like
up from here.' He looked, at that moment, as if he would rather follow a career
in undertaking. On the night he renounced the captaincy it took a bottle of gin
and the fellowship of Viv Richards, his county confrère and soulmate, to part
the clouds that have spent the past year dulling the most thrilling cricketer of
the era. It remains to be seen whether England's persecuted Perseus – and the
team that so palpably depends on him – can discern blue skies on yonder
Yorkshire moors.

Rumours abound. Did Brearley really suggest that Botham sit this match
out? More important, if only because of what it would say about his state of
mind, did he really warn Brearley that he would wreak ungodly vengeance on
him if he did have the nerve to drop him? 'They were trying to psyche him up,'
stresses Dilley. 'Brearley asked him if he wanted to play and Both said, "You've
got to be joking ..."' Nowt wrong with the desire, then.

The sadness of Botham's decline since he succeeded Brearley is rendered all
the more profound when one considers what the side missed through having
him as captain. A comparison with the incomparable, namely Sobers, is
instructive. By the time the Fabulous Bajan Boy (initially picked, like Botham,
for his bowling) had acquired his first Test century he was winning his 17th
cap; his sixth came in his 22nd Test, when he was 22 (having started at 17);
by that juncture he had taken 23 wickets, expensively. Botham was
24 when he notched his sixth ton in his 25th Test, by the end of which – by

comparison with Sobers – he had harvested more than six times as many wickets.

Then came the armband. Calculated onslaughts subsided into despairing efforts at macho one-upmanship, incisive spells into elongated labours – after all, there was nobody there to stop him bowling as long as he wished. Then, at Trent Bridge, he went to the opposite extreme, holding himself back until the 54th over, then firing a horrendous wide to the third-man boundary (stirring even mild old Tom Graveney to take a leaf out of Fred Trueman's book and pronounce: 'I don't know what's going on out there.'). His back, to be fair, has been giving him gyp, the stress scarcely alleviated by those off-season sallies for Scunthorpe United. That, though, is not the only reason for the recession of that once-irresistible outswinger, or the deadening of that irrepressible bounce. 'Frustrated by his inability to defy single-handedly the fierce West Indies pace attack, his cricket became self-conscious,' observed his Somerset colleague, Peter Roebuck. 'His cricket was inhibited and his personality too tense to relax.'

On the morning after he had decided that he had had his fill of the captaincy – notwithstanding throbbing head, parched mouth et al, having insisted that his wife remain in Humberside because he 'wanted to be alone' – Botham walked into the County Ground at Taunton. 'It was already filling up. I came out of the pavilion to walk across the pitch to the nets and the reception I received from the locals was sensational. They were up on their feet, clapping me all the way across the pitch. It was one of the most exhilarating moments of my career. I thought of those people at Lord's giving me the cold shoulder and I looked at the Taunton supporters and thought, "Hang on a minute, these are the real people, these are the people who count. To hell with Lord's and to hell with the selectors."'

Ever get the feeling that, sooner or later, someone is going to pay a hefty price for all this? Given that longstanding antipathy for Australia's equally combative and patriotic ex-captain, maybe Botham should try imagining there are 11 Ian Chappells out there.

John Ernest EMBUREY

b. Peckham, London, 20/8/1952
Middlesex 1973–
Test debut 1978
Caps 15
Test Record to date:

Balls	Runs	Wkts	Av	Best	5w/I	10w/m	SR
3236	1046	34	30.76	5–124	1	–	95.18

Had Arthur McIntyre not dashed off a consolatory letter of recommendation to Don Bennett, his opposite number across the Thames, it is eminently feasible that the nation's pre-eminent off-spinner might still be slogging away for the Amalgamated Union of Engineering Workers, bound to a desk, chained for life. As it was, the magnanimity of the Surrey coach, who had rejected him and all but broken that loyal south London heart, triggered a career change, even though accepting Middlesex's offer of £600 per week meant taking a wage cut. Less than a decade later, ironically enough, 'Embers' has cemented the regular Test place denied – for reasons not wholly related to talent – Pat Pocock, the fellow whose enduring if unappreciated gifts rendered Emburey surplus to requirements at The Oval.

Pocock and Emburey are technical and spiritual opposites. The former, who took 6 for 79 in his maiden Ashes Test 13 years ago and was promptly ditched, the first in a series of facial slaps, is an enterprising, jocular card who thinks nothing of bowling six different balls in an over; the latter is serious-minded, captivated by the disciplines of his trade and loath to deviate from the curmudgeonly, as a five-day economy rate of barely two runs per over testifies. That is not to say he lacks subtlety, anything but. Indeed, there were times in the Caribbean when he constituted England's sole hope of containing Viv Richards and Co. The only time the West Indies found themselves on the back foot was in Port of Spain, Emburey sending them slithering from 168 for 0 to 257 for 5 on the second day, taking 5 for 81 in 40 overs of crafty Cockney nous.

Tall, straight-backed, shrewd of thought and as committed as they come, Emburey, who tormented Australia in 1978–79, relies on variations in pace and flight, abetted by a wicked arm ball, rather than expansive turn. Had his art been more fashionable, the pitches barer and his left-arm foil Phil Edmonds less averse to tugging forelock, the prolific ice-and-fire double act at the heart of so many Middlesex triumphs would surely have forged a national alliance rather more frequently than the solitary occasion they have been permitted to date. That Emburey has been consistently preferred to Pocock and Edmonds says much for the Peckham man's dependability and that cussed, strictly non-textbookish bat, rather less for English cricket's tolerance of mavericks.

Robert William ('Bob') TAYLOR

b. Stoke-on-Trent, Staffordshire, 17/7/1941
Derbyshire 1960–
Test debut 1971
28th Test
Test record to date:

I	NO	Runs	HS	50	100	Av	Ct/St
35	3	629	97	2	–	19.66	83/6

If you walk on to a cricket field and can remember playing against both umpires, somebody somewhere is probably trying to tell you something. If that is indeed the case with 'Chat', who turns 40 on the second day of the third Test, he is certainly making a terrific fist of ignoring those hints and nudges. Dorian Gray? Pah.

England's wicketkeeper, the fifth the selectors have named in little more than a year, pulled off a stunning catch to get shot of Wood in the second innings at Lord's, flinging that slight, unprepossessing frame with breathtaking dexterity to clasp an inside edge. That ought to have convinced the sceptics. If it didn't, a rundown of the remarkable events in his life over the past hectic month should do the trick.

On 13 June he was awarded the MBE in the Queen's Birthday Honours List. Against Yorkshire on 19 June he thrust two decades of frustration behind him by forging his maiden first-class century. Forty-eight hours later he became the first stumper to tot up 200 John Player League victims. The day after that, he passed Harry Elliott's Derbyshire record bag of 1183 dismissals; then came the news that his testimonial had raised £56,000. Finally, on 28 June, when Paul Downton paid the predictable price for dropping Border at Trent Bridge, came the summons to return to the England XI at Lord's.

The fates certainly owed this sweet, sociable, even-tempered soul a favour or two. Until the twilight of his career, for all that he is arguably his equal behind the stumps, he had been kept waiting in the wings by Alan Knott's fiddle-fitness, sustained excellence and superior bat. At virtually any other time over the past century, Taylor would have been an automatic choice. He had made but one Test appearance before Packer lured away the Kent sprite, and was 36 by the time of his second Test, in Lahore on the 1977–78 tour of Pakistan.

Making up for lost time with aplomb, he conceded a solitary bye in 215 overs.

In Adelaide the following winter came evidence of stickability. England were 137 ahead with only four wickets standing before he and county colleague Geoff Miller formed a seventh-wicket alliance of 135, a ground record for their country, Taylor dominating the stand with a (then) career-best 97. Neat and unshowy, a gent to those adhesive fingertips, he became a fixture with that omnipresent smile and sunhat.

Dame Fortune, though, had not finished her devious little tricks. The Bombay Test of 1980 saw him add 171 with Botham and collect 10 catches, a new Test record, whereupon Knott, who had announced his unwillingness to undertake any further tours, was brought back for the first Test of the next summer against the West Indies. 'I learned of the decision [from] the radio. For the first time in my career I had been confident of keeping my place. I couldn't understand the logic. Surely age wasn't a factor ... Boycott was still in the side and, a year younger, I was just as dedicated towards maintaining form and fitness.'

Alec Bedser's letter of confirmation arrived the next day. 'He said many nice things but it didn't ease the pain. Was this my reward for siding with the Establishment over Packer?' The selectors' vote, Taylor understands, went against him 3–2; the transfer of the captaincy from Brearley to Botham, he believes, was the decisive factor. 'Botham,' he reasons, 'rated Knotty's batting ability.' In the event, Knott failed to sparkle, averaging a meek five, but this did little to console Taylor, who 'slackened off mentally' and contemplated retiring. Had it not been his testimonial season, had J.T. Murray's world record for dismissals not been looming tantalisingly in the near distance, he may well have quit. Instead, 'self-pity and frustration mellowed into a more philosophical state of mind'. Packer, he realised, 'had been my Santa Claus'.

That keen sense of perspective also embraces sympathy for the man he in turn deposed: 'I felt sorry for Downton. During the TV highlights I noticed that he was getting down about two yards before the bowler delivered, leaving himself unbalanced, and therefore in no position to catch Border. I almost rang him but I didn't want him to misconstrue my motives.'

And so to Lord's. 'When I went through the gates on the first day I was *so* nervous. Finally, my first home Test against Australia. Fortunately, I soon caught a reasonable catch off the inside edge against Graeme Wood.' Ah, the humility of the reasonable man.

Graham Roy DILLEY

b. Dartford, Kent, 18/5/1959
Kent 1977–
Test debut 1979
12th Test
Test record to date:

I	NO	Runs	HS	50	100	Av	Ct
18	7	174	38*	–		15.82	2

Balls	Runs	Wkts	Av	Best	5w/I	10w/m	SR
1954	962	36	26.72	4–24	–	–	54.28

Before 'Picca', then 20, was plucked from relative obscurity to tour Australia two winters ago, he worked as a diamond setter in London's Hatton Garden (the sack beckoned after he skipped off to play a match for Kent Seconds). The feeling that England may well have unearthed a jewel of their own is growing. Any bowler who can consistently take wickets with length and radar AWOL, as Dilley did in the first two Tests, must be treasured.

Rapid and rangy, this 6ft 3in blond bomber employs one of the more peculiar, not to say exhilarating, methods in the business. Striding sedately but purposefully to the stumps, the deliberation bordering on vanity, he rocks back, unfurls, arms shooting out at all manner of odd angles, takes one final immense stride then fires the ball in as if it were a javelin. His chief problem appears to be an unhelpful body. He missed the Centenary Test with glandular fever, and that action, for all its splendours, augurs ill for consistent good health.

Kent insiders say his erratic form may be attributable to depression. Could the passing of Ken Barrington be a factor? Even though the assistant manager was twice his age, the pair got on famously. 'He was the ideal guy to help a player through a tough tour,' explained Dilley. 'At the end of a particularly bad session in the field he would be there in the dressing room ready to find the right words that would make me want to go and bowl again 40 minutes later full of fire in the gut. I really did love the old guy.'

Does the loss explain Dilley's intemperate, atypical outburst at Trent Bridge? Fielding at long leg beneath the press box amid one particularly errant spell, he was abused by Nottinghamshire members and, being somewhat unused to such voluble and disrespectful criticism, took it to heart. The riposte came when he had Lillee caught behind by Downton: a swift turn towards his persecutors followed by a raised middle finger (I am told, by those who watch *Happy Days*, that someone called 'The Fonz' is responsible for this craven dereliction of the noble standards set by Winston Churchill and Harvey Smith). Fortunately for him, few reporters noticed and even when the *faux pas* was mentioned it barely rated a paragraph. Not that this dissuaded Donald Carr, the TCCB's stickler of a secretary, from upbraiding him with a stiff missive, warning him that behaviour of that ilk would henceforth not be tolerated. The apology to the selectors was prompt and heartfelt.

Not shy of giving the ball a crack, he is developing into a useful No. 9, swinging freely from an open left-handed stance. He kept Gatting company for an hour at Nottingham, sensibly pushing for singles early in the over to give his partner the strike, although the forward defensive, as yet, seems to have bypassed his repertoire.

Christopher Middleton ('Chris') OLD

b. Middlesbrough, Yorkshire, 22/12/1948
Yorkshire 1966–
Test debut 1972
45th Test
Test record to date:

I	NO	Runs	HS	50	100	Av	Ct
62	8	782	65	2	–	14.48	22

Balls	Runs	Wkts	Av	Best	5w/I	10w/m	SR
8354	3845	138	27.86	7–50	4	–	60.54

As one of the most formidable English seamers of the past decade and one of only two men in Test history to take four wickets in five balls, 'Chilly' has every cause, one might imagine, to anticipate a secure place in English hearts. Alas, he may not even be the best-loved sportsman in his own family. Around the time Chris was hustling India out for 42 at Lord's in 1974, big brother Alan, that fine fly-half, was trumping him in South Africa, booting a record 37 points in a game for the British Lions.

The trouble is, for all the new Yorkshire captain's dutiful and telling service for White Rose and St George, he is often regarded as an underachiever, in this country at least, his contributions either demeaned or taken for granted, which is a pity. Then again, when you step into Fred Trueman's six-league clodhoppers, invidious and unflattering comparisons are, sadly, par for the course.

If anything, he is more highly rated abroad. Had he not just been awarded a benefit by Yorkshire, one of the counties most resentful of Kerry Packer, he would have accepted that offer to join WSC (he stresses, mind, that he 'didn't agree with the whole exercise'). A pelvic strain suffered in Australia kept him out of Test contention in 1979, persuading him to cut his pace and run-up 'to avoid extra strain'. Yet he was much the most impressive home bowler of the Centenary Test, gleaning six wickets with swing and seam, only to fall foul of Botham in the Caribbean.

What, then, of those perennial jibes about Chilly the Hypochondriac? While he accepts that his reputation may on occasion have affected his credibility with selectors and even the odd captain, he rejects the idea that those seemingly endless sick notes might be related to some deep-rooted fear of failure. 'A fast bowler should never play with the slightest injury – you only let yourself and your colleagues down. Surely it's better to have someone giving you 100% than 85%. There's pain and there's pain. A certain amount you can live with [but] if I had a slight problem I'd tell the management, saying I'd play if they want, making it their responsibility if I can't do it. What bugged me was coming round to a Test and Christopher Martin-Jenkins always saying, "Chris Old has turned up with his usual injury problem." That's totally uncalled-for.'

Arriving at Yorkshire as a belligerent left-handed strokeplayer who could turn his arm over at a pinch, the order of priority soon altered. Bustling in rhythmically, the release an explosive flurry that promises greater speed than actually materialises, he won his first cap against the Rest of the World at Leeds in 1970, becoming the middle man in Eddie Barlow's hat-trick, only for the authorities to strip the game of its 'Test' status. Recalled for the subcontinental trek of 1972–73, he took 15 wickets at 24.73 against India, his favourite opponents, with 43 scalps at 19 all told. Asia also supplied the opposition for his proudest hour – four successive wickets against Pakistan at Headingley in 1978. How typical, he must have pondered, that the no-ball in the middle should have denied him a hat-trick.

While two five-day 50s do his talent scant credit, that bat still swings boisterously (in 1977 he thrashed a century in 37 minutes, the third fastest in first-class annals to date, albeit against Warwickshire's generous declaration bowlers). Fulfilment as a Test all-rounder has been blighted, he fears, by a mystifying inability to judge the ball's pace. Hence, perhaps, those cat-on-a-hot-tin-roof antics whenever he is confronted by the genuinely hostile.

His recall for Headingley was made partly on a horses-for-courses basis. The selectors will also have been mindful that Old's frugal line and length ought to compensate should Dilley's philanthropy persist. The key, however, was probably Botham's resignation. In light of the pair's squabbles in the West Indies, it is a toss-up as to who will feel more gratified by the return of Brearley.

Robert George Dylan ('Bob') WILLIS

b. Sunderland, Co Durham, 30/5/1949
Surrey 1969–71
Warwickshire 1972–
Test debut 1970
60th Test
Test record to date:

I	NO	Runs	HS	50	100	Av	Ct
83	38	518	24*	–	–	11.51	23

Balls	Runs	Wkts	Av	Best	5w/I	10w/m	SR
11367	5203	206	25.26	7–78	12	–	55.18

He really has no right being here. Willis returned prematurely from the Caribbean in February, knee wrecked, confidence at its lowest ebb, too depressed to believe, as vice-captain, that he could possibly be of any benefit to his mate Botham. Every man and his dog was sure 'Goose' had bowled his final ball in Test cricket. So, he confided to Gooch and others, was he. Lillee was in his early twenties when he broke down; 31-year-old fast bowlers with awkward actions and twisted limbs don't come back.

Thanks to a Birmingham surgeon and the wonders of arthroscopy, however, Willis defied even his own pessimism, just as he did when both knees collapsed in 1975. And on the opening day of the series he reaped his 200th Test wicket, a figure attained by only Snow, Statham and Trueman among English purveyors of limb-threatening pace, in fewer balls than any Pom of any persuasion bar Trueman.

Comments about the captaincy affecting Botham's form, aired in a radio interview, went down less well – the TCCB demanded an explanation but declined to take action. Willis has never been afraid to speak his mind (he left Surrey over the club's tardiness, as he saw it, in awarding him his county cap), or to express unpopular views. As if being an opera buff and Bob Dylan aficionado (hence the middle name) were not enough to set him apart from the in-crowd, in his newly published tome, *The Cricket Revolution – Test Cricket in the 1970s*, he attacks the benefit system. Propounding the virtues of a four-day County Championship, he also suggests that, instead of the present flat fee of £1400, an England player should earn £1000 per Test with a further £400 going to his county. Not a bad idea at all.

He also admits that, in 1978, he made a serious error (PR rather than ethical) in failing to show concern for Iqbal Qasim, the Pakistan tailender whose face he had just rearranged with an unscrupulous bouncer. The reason for Willis's apparent heartlessness was his concern that the sight of blood would have disrupted his concentration. These days he goes in for self-hypnosis. Small wonder, when bowling for England, that he sometimes gives the impression of participating in a match played exclusively between himself and his demons.

But never mind the quirks, feel the quality. Called to Australia as an untried, unproven replacement for the unfortunate Alan Ward, Willis, then a 6ft 5in stringbean with a high-stepping, straight-ahead action, captured his first Australian wickets in 1970–71. Aggravated by the way his right leg landed, boot pointing straight down the pitch, those knee afflictions set him back; not until the 1976–77 tour to India did he cement a place in the side. Time and again, on even the most placid surfaces, he would generate pace and spiteful lift, that huge mop of Afro curls bobbing in the breeze like some frantically nodding dog on the back shelf of a souped-up Cortina. His best return, 7–78 in the Jubilee Test against Australia at Lord's, came in June 1977. For three years, the new cherry was his by divine right, likewise – despite last summer's heroic stand with Willey – the No. 11 berth.

Age and body, however, are catching up. Against the West Indies at Old Trafford last year he thought he 'bowled as badly as I have ever done', and felt 'utterly helpless and depressed'. Botham's loyalty saved him from being discarded for the next Test, where he twice took wickets with no-balls and was duly dropped for the first time in five years. So far this series, the selectors' touching faith in pedigree has not been entirely vindicated; nevertheless, after seeing him labour productively at Lord's while carrying a chest infection, they were relieved to learn that he would recover in time for this Test having missed last week's Championship game.

AUSTRALIA

Kimberley John ('Kim') HUGHES

b. Margaret River, Western Australia, 26/1/1954

Western Australia 1975–

Test debut 1977

36th Test (10th as captain)

Test record to date:

M	I	NO	Runs	HS	50	100	Av	Ct
35	64	4	2448	213	13	5	40.80	29

Balls	Runs	Wkts	Av	Best	5w/I	10w/m	SR
66	20	0	–	–	–	–	–

Viv Richards apart, does any contemporary batsman show such callous disregard for the done thing? Patrick Eagar's photo in *Wisden* captures the confidence, the elan and the sheer unadulterated audacity – down on one knee, cap rather than helmet atop those buoyant blond ringlets, the follow-through as clean and complete as the shot he has just sent hurtling through the covers. Few men have been named as one of the Good Book's Five Cricketers of the Year on the strength of two innings, but then nobody in the seamy summer of 1980 so entranced an audience. That he chose the otherwise benighted Centenary Test as the stage demanded gratitude as much as admiration.

In regaling us with 117 and 84 not out, he played as if oblivious to the nerves that depleted others while acutely aware that such a grand occasion deserved something fitting. In the second innings, seeking quick runs to offset the rain that had peppered the Lord's parade, and hence set up a declaration, he struck a six off Chris Old, assuredly no slouch, into the top deck of the pavilion – from three yards down the track. Another sally against a fellow quickie saw the ball zip across the ropes at deep point in a crimson blur, ahead of a fielder stationed barely a couple of yards distant.

If expositions of that ilk have been rare this summer – he failed to reach 50 at Trent Bridge and Lord's – the pitches have been largely responsible, and the promise of the havoc he might wreak on even a semi-fast surface remains a source of guilty anticipation for all but the most myopic Pom. What we have glimpsed is a chap trying to do the right thing, to occupy and grind, but unable to restrain himself as fully as he or his side would like – witness the 141 minutes he expended reaching 42 at Lord's until, champing at the bit, he lofted Emburey and failed to clear a backpedalling Willis at deep mid-off. During that fraught second innings at Nottingham, meanwhile, he fell leg-before driving across the line at Dilley. Then again, he has always held fast to a determination to live and die 'by the sword'.

Enjoying a prodigious schoolboy career, Hughes entered senior club cricket at 15; several respected judges considered him ripe for first-class status even at that tender age. Impatience – he was 12th man for Western Australia three times running – prompted him to try his luck in Adelaide only to return with tail firmly between legs. Amends came via scores of 119 and 60 on debut against a New South Wales attack brimming with five Test bowlers; he was donning the baggy green cap himself inside two years, albeit mustering just a single at The Oval in 1977.

Headstrong, brash and often impulsive, it did not take him long to earn the soubriquet 'Howie', the 'millionaire' batsman, after Howard Hughes ('Clag', another, even less reputable *nom de guerre*, stems from a prolific appetite for nocturnal activity). Again, he would atone, compiling an eight-hour 129 on his next Ashes appearance. Later that winter, when Graham Yallop was sidelined by injury, Hughes stepped up and immediately led the side to an unexpected win over Pakistan, giving the board a perfect excuse to make Yallop pay for permitting the Poms to run up their biggest series victory since Charlie Bannerman won the freedom of Melbourne.

In India, Hughes was a model of consistency with the bat and, by comparison with his predecessor, fostered noticeably greater urgency and zest. Demoted to the vice-captaincy when the WSC contingent came back and Greg Chappell was restored, he doubtless looked upon reinstatement for this tour as no less than his due.

The Australian board cherish Hughes all the more because, having rejected Packer's overtures, he is seen as an 'Establishment' man, for which the captaincy, when initially granted, was widely regarded as his reward. At the same time, somewhat inevitably, the WSC exiles resented him, fellow 'Westies' Lillee and Marsh in particular. In his first season as captain of Western Australia, whom Hughes would lead to two Sheffield Shield titles, Lillee and Marsh, the WA 'mafia' dons, refused to serve as his vice-captain. That two sets of selectors deemed Marsh too rambunctious, not to say rebellious, to entrust with either the state or national captaincy, handing both to Hughes, did little to allay the tension. On the field, thus far at least, this has not been obviously apparent, although it could become so should England level the series.

Not for nothing is Hughes also known as 'Jekyll and Hyde'. Unsettled by his antics when under the influence of the dreaded alcohol, team-mates have been even further galled to see him turn to the nearest person in the shower and relieve himself over them. One of the younger members of the party attests that, after being on the receiving end of this unesteemed party trick, any respect he may have held for Hughes the captain dissolved. Yet colleagues and opponents alike find him generous and considerate, the intentions perceived as honourable. The word common to many critiques is 'naïve'.

All that said, let the final word go to Des Hoare, once a bit of a maverick himself, latterly Hughes's first captain in the Perth grades. 'I have most admired him,' enthused the former Australian Test paceman, 'because he has had the courage and ability not to become ordinary.'

John DYSON

b. Kogarah, Sydney, 11/6/1954
New South Wales 1975–
Test debut 1977
12th Test
Test record to date:

I	NO	Runs	HS	50	100	Av	Ct
21	2	365	53	1	–	19.21	1

With seeming disdain for aggression and that penchant for reducing crowds to drowsiness, this unobtrusive, angular-looking PE teacher is precisely what Australia ordered for a summer such as this. The short ball and the outswinger spared spectators in three of his four innings to date but the 38 that underpinned the run chase at Nottingham was invaluable. For nearly two-and-a-half hours he stood upright in that sentry box, content with a solitary boundary, playing and missing with alacrity but never at the cost of composure.

Slender, studious and alert, it was his sound, predominantly front-foot play – and agile close fielding – for the state colts XI that attracted the NSW selectors, who correctly perceived an aptitude for careful, Boycottish acquisition and capacious reserves of phlegm. WSC defections fast-tracked him towards his Test debut, against India in 1977–78, the challenge answered with 53 in more than four hours, yet that remains his zenith at this level, and he did not tarry long. Indeed, while his domestic contributions this past winter – 1028 Shield runs at 57, including 152 in a record opening stand with Rick McCosker of 319 against WA's vaunted attack of Lillee, Alderman, Yardley and Wayne Clark – demonstrated an unsuspected capacity to dominate, 11 knocks against India and New Zealand brought just 213 runs, with a peak of 30.

In sticking with him for this tour ahead of Bruce Laird, an exemplary player of pace who scored four 50s against the West Indies in 1979–80 but whose dive in form had been exacerbated by a ruptured achilles tendon, the selectors clearly felt Dyson could prosper against the laterally shifting ball in conditions where patience is the prime virtue. As much as any single factor, that Australia are ahead in the rubber serves as testimony to that faith.

Graeme Malcolm WOOD

b. East Fremantle, Perth, 6/11/1956
Western Australia 1977–
Test debut 1978
25th Test
Test record to date:

I	NO	Runs	HS	50	100	Av	Ct
47	3	1508	126	6	5	34.27	25

Amid the praise rightly lavished on Hughes for his exploits at Lord's last August, Wood's sturdy century tended to be forgotten, yet without that fusion of determination and sweet on-side drives the scope for frolics would have been slim. The lean, left-handed opener was the soul of sobriety until deftly stumped by David Bairstow, but then advancing down the pitch has seldom been a forte of the man they call the 'Kamikaze Kid'.

Wood was fortunate in his early team-mates; while studying physical education at the University of New South Wales, he played alongside that devout, scholarly opener John Inverarity as well as Ric Charlesworth, the last Australian to be named in international squads for cricket and hockey. Making 37 on his first-class debut for WA against the MCC in 1976–77, he displaced Laird at the top of the order when Packer intervened, whereupon centuries against Queensland and South Australia in his maiden season produced a call-up to face India at Adelaide after just eight first-class outings. A fine hundred against the Packerised West Indies later that winter was capped the following December by a resolute, six-and-a-half-hour, oh so rounded 100 against England on an awkwardly-bouncing track at Melbourne, scene of Australia's only victory of the series. Nobody else in the match managed 50. That was also the series in which his reckless running and calling saw his ennoblement as the Kamikaze Kid. Not since Compton, say some, has a professional crease beheld a bloke so utterly unable to discern between the eminently feasible and the downright dotty.

A tricky period ensued. A painful tour of India coincided with the end of WSC, although many felt he owed his subsequent dropping to a delay in signing his ACB contract. Even WA dumped him for a spell, when he took longer than expected to recover from injury and illness, but the influence of Lillee – his captain at grade club Melville – did its bit and he won selection for the Centenary Test tour, if not for the centrepiece itself. Further hundreds followed against New Zealand and India last winter, and June's Prudential Trophy found him in prime fettle. He made 55 at Edgbaston then 108 at Headingley, more than sufficient for the Man of the Match award in a contest where, once again, no one else got even halfway to three figures, even if he was run out.

How he gets on with Jeff Thomson may be a delicate matter. It was Thommo, after all, who, playing for Middlesex on the eve of the first Test, and nursing a severely bruised ego at his de-selection, pranged the willowy Wood with a short one that dented the temple guard of his helmet, ushering him to hospital for X-rays. Twin failures at Trent Bridge duly incited concern for his well-being yet only Gower scored more runs at Lord's. First time round he made 44 off just 59 balls before Taylor made his staggering interception; after the speedy loss of three wickets, an unconquered 62 in the second innings proved a much-needed steadier of nerves. Has the Kamikaze Kid lost his taste for flames?

Trevor Martin CHAPPELL

b. Glenelg, Adelaide, 21/10/1952
South Australia 1972–76
Western Australia 1976–79
New South Wales 1979–
Test debut 1981
3rd Test
Test record to date:

I	NO	Runs	HS	50	100	Av	Ct
4	1	44	20*	–	–	14.66	2

Whatever marvels Chappell Minor may or may not have before him during his career as a cricketer, he is doubly cursed. As the most junior of Australia's best-known siblings – nine years younger than Ian, four years younger than Greg, his debut at Trent Bridge helped the clan creep ever nearer Pakistan's Mohammad quartet – he is, surely, at enough of a disadvantage. Having one of those brothers insist that he be the perpetrator of the most roundly rubbished, defiantly non-cricketing act of the era was scarcely likely to enhance any thoughts that he might ever be appreciated for being entirely his own man.

How absolutely bloody typical – as Basil Fawlty would surely put it – that that infamous underarm to Brian McKechnie should come just as Trevor was warming to his role. A star turn at Prince Alfred College, he toured the

Caribbean with Australia Schoolboys, making his debut for South Australia in 1972–73. Although he won a WSC contract after relocating to WA, it was not until he joined NSW last year that the shadow began to recede, selection for his maiden tour coming largely on the back of a career-best 150 against mighty WA. Helpfully, he has sampled life in the Lancashire Leagues.

Armed with more of Ian's tenacity than Greg's precision, Trevor is a superb, adaptable fielder and useful seamer who has been seen to optimum effect in the abbreviated game, dispatching Botham during a stint of 3–31 in the decisive Prudential one-dayer. However, one half-century (91 v Proctershire) in 13 innings to date, plus a sniff of unease against the short stuff, render his middle-order berth vulnerable to the elegant Martin Kent. The decision to move him up the order to first-drop may be the answer. Luck, predictably, has not been terribly forthcoming; shortly before lunch on the Saturday at Lord's, he tried to leave a rare brute of a ball from Dilley that somehow still contrived to locate an edge. Nothing, one nonetheless suspects, can ever besmirch the memory of striking the winning runs at Trent Bridge.

Graham Neil YALLOP

b. Balwyn, Melbourne, 7/10/1952
Victoria 1972–
Test debut 1976
28th Test (7 as captain)
Test record to date:

I	NO	Runs	HS	50	100	Av	Ct
51	3	1750	172	6	5	36.46	13

Balls	Runs	Wkts	Av	Best	5w/I	10w/m	SR
144	99	1	99.00	1–21	–	–	144.00

If the sight of Englishmen were to bring this introverted left-hander out in blotches, who could possibly blame him? Leading a team to the wrong end of a 5–1 Ashes drubbing, on home soil to boot, might have been cause for permanent banishment to the Blue Mountain salt mines had he not wielded such a persuasive and silky bat.

As it is, this lofty, moustachioed Victorian remains an integral part of the middle-order trio to whom Australia look for the bulk of their runs. Neither as effervescent as Hughes nor as single-minded as Border, he preceded both onto the international stage with that stooping, almost apologetic stance, not to mention the trademark trailing helmet strap, disguising the panache within.

As England will readily acknowledge. They were subjected, after all, to a brace of centuries during that same 1978–79 rubber, the second, in the final Test, a quite remarkable effort. At 61.11%, his contribution of 121 to a total of 198 was the sixth greediest in five-day history. Few captains have been so beleaguered; even fewer have mounted such a gung-ho riposte.

Educated at Carey Grammar under the wise eye of Frank Tyson, he toured Sri Lanka with Australia Schoolboys in 1971–72, consistent displays for Richmond winning him his state spurs 12 months later. A match double of 108 not out and 95 against NSW led to selection against the West Indies, yet the experience was marred. Yallop would claim that he was all but ignored by senior players irate at McCosker's omission. A dip in form cost him a trip to England in 1977, after which things looked up.

Appointed Victoria captain in 1977–78, he was recalled for the fifth Test against India, making 121, and, apart from having his jaw shattered by a ball from Colin Croft in Guyana, he had a highly satisfactory time in the Caribbean. With Bobby Simpson's second coming drawing to a close and WSC cranked up, he inherited the captaincy, but inexperience combined with a degree of reticence to make it a poor choice in hindsight. Hogg's attempts to show him up by taking the mickey in the field can have done little for self-respect, let alone team morale. Being obliged to compare their man with Brearley, furthermore, could not be said to have improved the perspective of the compatriots who criticised him so viciously.

A torn calf muscle in the second Test against Pakistan presented a perfect opportunity to pass the baton on to Hughes. Indeed, it was a measure of how far his stock had plummeted when, even though he had just steered his state to successive Shield triumphs, Victoria stripped him of the captaincy. Bumped up and down the order in India – he made 167, the best for Australia there, in his first stab at opening – he was pushed out by the WSC returnees until the 1980 tour of Pakistan, where, reintroduced to middle-order duties at Faisalabad, he marched to 172 and shared a record alliance of 217 for the fourth wicket with Greg Chappell. Home appearances, though, remained fleeting, and Doug Walters displaced him last winter.

On the current expedition, with the exception of the second and third one-day internationals, he has been unable to engage even second gear, averaging 5.75 in the Tests. Mike Hendrick's impeccable inswinger and Gatting's astounding slip take proved his undoing at Nottingham, while a sharp one from Dilley induced him to play on in the first innings at Lord's. If a pattern has been set, the summer will be much the poorer.

Allan Robert BORDER

b. Cremorne, Sydney, 27/7/1955
New South Wales 1977–79
Queensland 1979–
Test debut 1979
30th Test
Test record to date:

I	NO	Runs	HS	50	00	Av	Ct
53	9	2219	162	13	6	50.43	33

Balls	Runs	Wkts	Av	Best	5w/I	10w/m	SR
938	298	8	37.25	2–35	–	–	117.25

Had it not been for Barry Knight it is doubtful whether cricket would have won the hand of Australia's most reliable batsman. Ever the gambler, the former Essex and Leicestershire all-rounder emigrated to Sydney in 1969, shortly after taking the concluding wicket in England's series-clinching victory over the West Indies, wed a sheila and set up the first of a string of indoor schools in the old Japan Trade Centre with a little help from his chum Richie Benaud. In 1975, now a fairly advanced larrikin of 20, Border was working as a clerk in a film library when he enrolled for a spot of one-on-one tuition every Thursday; from then on he took things seriously.

'Barry didn't try to change my style,' remembers Border. 'He just tried to strengthen it.' He didn't do a bad job. WSC hastened his climb, but unlike such as Paul Hibbert, Jeff Moss and David Ogilvie, he answered opportunity's knock. After 10 Tests, Knight's stocky left-handed protégé was averaging 60.29, had become the first man to score 150 in each innings of a five-dayer (Lahore 1979–80), and was already seen by opponents as one of the most difficult objects to prise from a crease. Methodical, frill-free and possessed of staggering concentration, let alone a keen thirst for the scrap, he is quite capable of savaging attacks with those pulls and cuts he developed on the baseball diamond, but mostly elects to play the percentages.

Courage is another decided asset, as Dilley will recall. At Perth in 1979 Border had reached 109 against England, completing 1000 Test runs quicker than any Australian (354 days), when he missed a hook off the Kent man and sustained a gash above the left eye. Grabbing a helmet, he was back in the fray seven runs later, five stitches in place, ticker as hardy as Thomas or Oliver.

At North Sydney Boys' High School, alma mater to Graeme Hole, Ian Craig and Peter Philpott, Border was touted as an all-rounder, the accent on his left-arm spin. While that string remains far from negligible, if rarely explored, the bow hums to a different tune now. So quickly has he made his name, it is hard to believe this is his maiden Ashes tour, though he does not lack knowledge of the locale, having served as pro for East Lancashire as well as playing for the villagers of Downend. At Trent Bridge, his first-innings 63 in four-and-a-half hours was the highest, longest and most vital of the contest; at Lord's, a punchier 64 secured a narrow lead after five had fallen for 167. Ostensibly Australia's first full-time professional cricketer, the honour could scarcely have gone to a worthier recipient.

Rodney William ('Rod') MARSH

b. Armadale, Western Australia, 4/11/1947
Western Australia 1968–
Test debut 1970
71st Test
Test record to date:

I	NO	Runs	HS	50	100	Av	Ct/St
110	11	2894	132	14	3	29.23	249/11

Balls	Runs	Wkts	Av	Best	5w/I	10w/m	SR
60	51	0	–	–	–	–	–

And to think they once called him 'Iron Gloves'. When Rod Marsh first surfaced in an Ashes conflab at the dawn of the 1970s, he had a paunch, a follicly-challenged upper lip, an endearing slobbishness and a knack of making even the simplest wicketkeeping procedures seem a task of Herculean proportions. Australian journos, protective towards the popular Brian Taber, were eager to see him return as swiftly as possible from whence he came. Reborn as 'Bacchus', lover of tinnies, life, snarling 'taches and the competitive arts (even though the nickname celebrated a Victorian township), he shed most if not quite all the excess girth and duly forced his detractors to retract, transforming himself into an Alan Knott with attitude.

For all its repetitiveness, nothing more vividly personifies the Australian menace than the death sentence, 'c Marsh b Lillee'. The first half of the equation is far more, however, than an assured poucher of nicks. A poacher unlikely ever to turn gamekeeper – hence those largely unfulfilled leadership aspirations – he continues to defy gathering years, gravity and dumpy physique by clutching catches he has no earthly right to reach. Fleet of hand and foot, uncanny of anticipation and reflex, the one flaw on the CV is that the paucity of quality Australian spinners in his era has confined him to one stumping for every 22 Test catches, though Old, Greig and John Snow will assuredly all vouch for his stealth. As for celebrating his own handiwork, nobody does it better. Keep your eyes peeled – barely has the ball been enveloped in those massive mitts than it will head for the stars as if launched from Cape Kennedy.

Initially a batsman pure and simple – his debut for WA against Gary Sobers' 1968–69 West Indies tourists brought a century – Marsh became the first Australian timber-minder to compile a Test century, at Adelaide in 1972, repeating the feat against New Zealand on the same ground the following winter and, most famously of all, in the 1977 Centenary Test. He might have achieved the breakthrough even earlier had Bill Lawry not declared when he was on 92 at Melbourne in 1971, the first of four scores in the nineties. That he took the skipper's decision in such good heart did much to win over his critics. If those lusty left-handed heaves now tend to take precedence over more pragmatic virtues, his value has declined only marginally. In a one-dayer against New Zealand last winter, he thwacked the first five balls of Australia's final over for three sixes and a couple of fours. Big brother Graham, that maestro on fairway and green, would have appreciated the loft and distance of those drives.

The lack of support for those captaincy ambitions may seem odd. After all, he did once lead WA to a Shield–Gillette Cup double. He is also the focal point of the team in the field, endlessly picking up plummeting crests. The traditional resistance towards keeper-skippers, though, is only part of it. Far more significantly, having been one of Packer's prime targets and a known agitator for proper remuneration, Marsh will forever be tarred as one of the civil war's alleged baddies. Was it worth the sacrifice? Disdaining regrets as he does, the nod would almost certainly be a firm one.

Raymond John ('Ray') BRIGHT

b. Footscray, Melbourne, 13/7/1954
Victoria 1972–
Test debut 1977
11th Test
Test record to date:

I	NO	Runs	HS	50	100	Av	Ct
15	4	175	33	–	–	15.91	3

Balls	Runs	Wkts	Av	Best	5w/I	10w/m	SR
2262	834	26	32.08	7–87	2	1	87.00

When 'Candles' toured here in 1977, that prematurely receding thatch and thickset frame caused mouths to gape: not since Tom Veivers in 1964 had England glimpsed an Australian spinner with quite so roly-poly, so *Anglo rusticus* an appearance. Delivered with a twirling bustle that portends more venom than is generally realised, those left-arm slows have served his country as well as any post-war Australian equivalent (not that the competition has been terribly stiff). It is hard, mind, to avoid the conclusion that had doubts not been raised over Bruce Yardley's action, he might not be his country's first choice.

Having toured Sri Lanka with Australia Schoolboys (alongside Yallop, a fellow Vic), his Shield bow came against NSW the following season. He headed his state's bowling the next, securing a trip to New Zealand with the national squad. Twelfth man in three lands, it would be nearly four years before he made his Test debut at Old Trafford, as half of that most lesser-spotted of Australian pairings in Blighty, a twin-pronged spin attack. Grudging runs at under two per over and reaping three wickets in the first innings, he was excluded from the next match but returned at the expense of Kerry O'Keeffe's flightier, less rigorous leg-breaks for the last two, albeit sending down just six overs at The Oval. He also showed himself to be a stubborn, correct bat and an occasionally athletic gully.

More effective abroad than at home, he took 10 wickets in Karachi two winters ago but remains more inclined to restrain than confound. A WSC call, while welcome, succeeded primarily in making the trajectory flatter, the modus operandi meaner. To the travelling press corps, those four wickets he captured in the second innings at Lord's constituted a pleasant surprise, as Frank Crook admits: 'Not many among [us] thought Ray was up to it. We used to compare him to a rugby league player called Chris Anderson who was never a regular in representative sides but always seemed to be picked for the UK, but he did much better than we expected.'

Geoffrey Francis ('Geoff') LAWSON

b. Wagga Wagga, New South Wales, 7/12/1957
New South Wales 1978–
Test debut 1980
4th Test
Test record to date:

I	NO	Runs	HS	50	100	Av	Ct
4	1	40	16	–	–	13.33	–

Balls	Runs	Wkts	Av	Best	5w/I	10w/m	SR
541	222	11	20.18	7–81	1	–	49.18

A student in optometry at the University of New South Wales, Lawson's vision was clarified all the more on the opening two days of the second Test. Rumbling in with bounce and vigour for fully 43.1 overs, the sustained pace and hostility, allied to a modicum of swing and cut, brought him 7 for 81, four in the final spell as the last six Englishmen were toppled inside an hour. Pretty damned auspicious for a chap unknown outside New South Wales eight months ago.

The mantle of the new 'Thommo' had been in need of filling since the real McCoy relocated from Sydney to Brisbane, and Lawson appeared to fit the bill. Much was expected of him and, despite a disappointing 1978–79 season (22 wickets at nigh-on 40), he was summoned to India as a replacement the following autumn and remained on board for Pakistan. Thirty-one scalps at 20 left him fourth on the domestic first-class list and a Test bow against New Zealand beckoned, Bruce Edgar the first on a list of top-drawer victims that already encompasses Gooch (twice), Gower, Boycott, Woolmer and Botham. If England had sighed with relief at the pre-Lord's injury to Hogg, procurer of 41 wickets in the last Ashes series, Lawson's emergence (he bowled only eight overs at Trent Bridge) silenced those who deduced that the tourists' attack would be diminished.

Tall and menacing afield – if a mite nervy with willow in hand – he has already impressed onlookers and colleagues alike with his sharp, bone-dry wit and questioning mind. Jutting of chin and proud of nose, there is a glint in his eye that suggests he scoffs at the old saw about never trusting a fast bowler to lead a team. The nickname 'Henry' salutes the voice of the bush and (according to many) the national poet. Prominent among the original Henry Lawson's ballads is *Roaring Days*; judging by that performance at HQ, there should be oodles more of those in store for his namesake.

Dennis Keith LILLEE

b. Subiaco, Perth, 18/7/1949
Western Australia 1969–
Test debut 1971
51st Test
Test record to date:

I	NO	Runs	HS	50	100	Av	Ct
64	18	703	73*	1	–	15.28	13

Balls	Runs	Wkts	Av	Best	5w/I	10w/m	SR
13330	6130	262	23.40	6–26	18	5	50.88

Dean of the Mean, Master of Disaster, Laird of the Larrikins – you name it,

D.K. Lillee wears it well. Anything that encapsulates the demonic influence he has had on English blades (and untold others besides). Not since the heyday of Lindwall and Miller has an Australian set so many English hearts quivering by the mere act of marking out his run. On the verge of his 32nd birthday, despite not bowling as well as he can, he is as effective as ever. Not bad for a bloke who has been ailing since May.

Behind that record haul of Test wickets by an Australian, of course, lies the measure of the man. Having burst on to the stage with 5–84 against England on debut (plus a bit of argy-bargy with Jackie Hampshire), he brushed aside a World XI, Sobers, Lloyd, Gavaskar et al with 8–29 at the WACA the following winter, including a spell of 6–0 in 15 balls. The 1972 Ashes series was a personal triumph, 31 wickets in the five Tests, a new high for Australia in England, but on the 1972–73 tour to the Caribbean stress fractures were discovered in his lower lumbar vertebrae.

Not until the autumn of 1974 did he re-emerge, yet so intense and committed was his fitness regime, he returned a more complete bowler, albeit not quite so jarringly fast. Forging a ferocious partnership with Thomson, the duo shared 58 English wickets that winter. 'Ashes to Ashes, dust to dust,' as the contemporary ditty had it, 'if Thommo don't get ya, Lillee must.' The barrackers on the Hill at Sydney preferred a more erudite chant: 'Lil-lee, Lil-lee, Lil-lee, Kill, Kill, Kill.'

For Englishmen prepared to sit up all night with transistor glued to ear, and for all Derek Randall's jocular magnificence, there was a numbing inevitability about the 1977 Centenary Test. Greig's men, chasing an improbable 463, were sitting pretty on 346 for 4 before fatigue and rot set in, Lillee completing the job with his 11th wicket of the contest, ensuring that the 100th Anglo–Australian debate concluded in precisely the same manner as the first – hosts victorious by 45 runs. Rising just as effortlessly to the challenge of WSC, he nailed 79 victims in the Supertests, more than five per outing, matching that extraordinary official mean.

Leg- and off-cutters form an increasingly crucial part of the armoury nowadays, and if the haircut is comparatively subdued compared with the flowing mane of yore, the lovable scoundrel sports a natty headband to keep those locks in check, offending the easily offended – as is his wont and pleasure. He also knows how to get up Brearley's nose (and vice versa). Never a stranger to controversy (in his autobiography *Back To The Mark*, published during that 1974–75 Ashes rubber, he freely confessed that he aimed to hit batsmen and make them ponder the wisdom of persisting), during the 1979–80 series he flaunted an aluminium bat he was promoting until one clanging drive brought objections – albeit not from the ACB chairman, who for the life of him could not comprehend what all the fuss was about. The ensuing confrontation left the Laws looking daft, England's captain unusually petulant and Lillee the runaway winner of the mind game.

Those appeals, demands as opposed to supplications, remain as theatrical (and persuasive?) as ever, daring umpires to refuse him. The lift he gives a fielding side, in consort with his bosom buddy Marsh, is like no other. We may never see another like him. On that score, in English breasts at least, hope is certainly growing.

Terence Michael ('Terry') ALDERMAN

b. Subiaco, Perth, 12/6/1956
Western Australia 1974–
Test debut 1981
3rd Test
Test record to date:

I	NO	Runs	HS	50	100	Av	Ct
2	1	17	12*	–	–	17.00	2

Balls	Runs	Wkts	Av	Best	5w/I	10w/m	SR
542	251	11	22.82	5–62	1	–	49.27

To observe that pitter-pattering, easygoing, overlong approach to the crease is to wonder how he does it. He seems too genial, too gentle. Instead, after just two Tests, and much like Bob Massie in 1972, he has already reduced English bats to gropeful subservience. On debut at Nottingham he took 9 for 130, snaring Boycott in each innings. Lord's proved less obliging, yet he still confined the opposition to less than two-and-a-half runs an over while dismissing Woolmer and Willey. And how many wickets did Lawson glean as a result of the pressure inflicted by that metronomic accuracy and dastardly outswing? Australia can only pray that his body holds up better than Massie's.

What with dad Bill and brother John amply versed in first-grade cricket, and sister Denise playing Tests for her country, what choice did young Terence have? A leading light at St Aquinas College, he made his first-grade debut while still at school, and took five NSW wickets on his first-class bow. Able to flit smoothly between defence and attack, cut and swing remain the bywords, pace almost an afterthought. The appeal, trenchant and expressive, is the one concession to the Lillee School of Confrontation.

Although a bonafide No. 11 he is anything but typical of his breed in the field, being a fine asset to any cordon; the reactions were sharp enough to undo Boycott on the first day at Lord's when he caught a rebound knocked up by

Border. All in all, an inspired choice ahead of other compelling candidates such as Rod McCurdy, Carl Rackemann, Mike Whitney and Merv Hughes.

Trevor Chappell was taken aback: 'Back in Australia he never bowled long spells and, although he used to take wickets, he could be very expensive. Once he got to England he started bowling these 10, 15-over spells and being very economical.' Brian Mossop of the *Sydney Morning Herald* thinks he has a clue: 'When we played Warwickshire at Edgbaston Lillee spent a long time with him in the nets, showing him how to hold the ball. After that Terry swung it all over the place.'

If the Headingley pitch proves even half as favourable as predicted, Grecian 2000 profits may be booming by Tuesday.

Rodney Malcolm HOGG

b. Richmond, Melbourne, 5/3/1951
South Australia 1975–
Test debut 1978
Caps 21
Test Record to date:

Balls	Runs	Wkts	Av	Best	5w/I	10w/m	SR
4496	1869	81	23.07	6–74	5	2	55.51

'Hoggy, Hoggy, Hoggy' they roared on The Hill at the SCG, tinnies hoisted, expectations a-leaping, Poms a-baiting. 'Kill, Kill, Kill'. A shameless steal from the D.K. Lillee Songbook, granted, yet, for the duration of the 1978–79 Ashes series, the accolade was richly deserved.

No bowler since Victorian times has embarked on a Test career in such rampant fashion – 27 scalps in his first three outings, 41 in his maiden series – albeit to such little avail. Asthmatic he may be, but it was the England batsmen who were rendered breathless as they strove in vain to cope with the tousle-haired Victorian's accuracy, speed and skidding bounce. Nor did the Pakistanis fare any better as Hogg claimed his 50th wicket in his eighth Test: nobody this century has attained the landmark with such alacrity.

Somewhat inevitably, anti-climax ensued and, two-and-a-half years on, Hogg is struggling, those four wickets in the third Prudential Trophy match as deceptive as they were vital. Back trouble, no-ballitis and a tendency to pitch too short, exacerbated by the unexpected rise of Alderman and Lawson, have relegated him to the fringes. That he has not already been sent home encapsulates the faith of a management team keenly aware of the hold he exerts over the opposition, but the suspicion persists: perhaps English pitches simply do not suit him. The hosts have had scant else to console them.

Peter Ian PHILPOTT – Cricket Manager/Coach

b. Manly, Sydney, 21/11/1934
New South Wales 1954–67
Test debut 1965
Tests 8

Fighting off the twin disadvantages of a slight build and a congenital heart defect, Philpott became one of the leading state all-rounders of his day and, more recently, a vaunted coach. He had already retired once to concentrate on schoolteaching when, in the wake of Benaud's retirement, his leg-breaks finally gained recognition for the 1965 Caribbean tour. Now 32, he took six wickets on debut (including Sobers, Hunte, Kanhai and Butcher) and 18 in the series. A Lancashire League pro with Ramsbottom in the 1950s, this is his first official tour to England.

Frederick William Cecil ('Fred') BENNETT – Tour Manager
b. Petersham, Sydney, 5/9/1915
Vastly experienced NSW administrator who managed the 1975 squad, as well as parties to the West Indies, India, South Africa and Pakistan. During the Second World War he was a troop leader in New Guinea and the Solomon Islands, after which he served as secretary at Balmain CC for 27 years. Hailed as 'a meticulous organiser', he managed the 1970 tour of South Africa, the last such to the Republic; this is his sixth expedition. Bob Parish, the chairman of the Australian board, characterises him as 'a virtual permanent manager of Australian touring teams'. Sri Lanka's impending ascent to Test ranks will delight him no end; a passionate advocate of cricket on the subcontinent, he has long lobbied on their behalf.

Barrie John MEYER – Umpire
b. 21/8/1931
Keeping wicket for Gloucestershire from 1957 to 1971 while doubling as a professional footballer, this amiable son of Bournemouth totted up 708 victims, a county record, even if he was unlucky to peak while the shires were so amply stocked with quality glovemen. A useful inside-right, he scored one of the goals that helped Bristol Rovers humble Manchester United's 'Busby

Babes' 4–0 in the third round of the 1955–56 FA Cup, still regarded as the most memorable victory in the club's history. 'BJ' to one and all, he joined the first-class list in 1973 and has been a member of the Test panel since 1978. This is his seventh Test.

David Gwillim Lloyd EVANS – Umpire

b. 27/7/1933

Newly promoted to the Test panel, this cheery Welshman stood in the 1979 World Cup and is making his debut at this level. Born in Lambeth but raised near Ammanford, Wales, he joined Glamorgan as understudy to wicketkeeper Haydn Davies, winning the job in his own right in 1958. In 1963 he claimed 89 victims to beat Davies's club record, and in 1967 took six catches in an innings against Yorkshire to equal another of Davies's milestones. In all he amassed 558 dismissals before joining the first-class panel in 1971. Two keepers presiding over the same Test? Messrs Marsh and Taylor may be tempted to push for the empathy vote.

Part 4

<u></u>

The match

Brearley stokes phoney war before real battle

Hughes accuses Brearley of insulting Lillee

Mike Brearley is viewed by many as the best captain in cricket. But in one area he is even more talented. No Englishman, not even Douglas Jardine, has enjoyed such consistent success in getting up the noses of Australians.

The born-again England captain's view that Dennis Lillee should not be allowed to wander off the field to change his shirt whenever he wants was greeted with incandescent fury by the normally laid back Australian skipper Kim Hughes.

Prince Charles is apparently 'furious' that Archbishop Runcie has been telling the newspapers of the advice he gave to the Royal Couple on 'the importance of sex in marriage'. Hughes, too, obviously feels that Brearley is guilty of some dishonourable indiscretion.

The Australian captain claimed that Brearley has been underhand in not raising the matter with the tourists directly and claimed the English captain has 'insulted' Lillee by implying that he is 'a cheat'. Lillee, who has been suffering from pneumonia, was ordered by his doctor to change his shirt and vest after each bowling spell, Hughes claimed.

Brearley originally tried to play down the row, but then found himself warming to his theme, saying: 'To me it is a different game if a fast bowler is allowed to go off when he feels like it.'

The Australians are also due a stinging rebuke from the MCC for daring to use the home dressing room at Lord's when holding net practice last week.

Good God, did they think nothing of the impact of their antics on the annual Eton v Harrow match being played on the ground as they cavorted in such a vulgar fashion?! Lord Scarman, yesterday touring Brixton to investigate the recent riots, may have to be summoned.

Perhaps the MCC will follow the example of the All England Lawn Tennis Club, which has decided not to award the traditional honorary membership to new Wimbledon Champion John McEnroe because of his behaviour at this year's tournament, and make Australians as unwelcome as women in St John's Wood?

All these rows have as much to do with the third Test as the news that Ben, star of the Bird's Eye Beefburger ad, has been fencing stolen goods. However, they all help build the anticipation for what will be the crucial game in this six-match series. Defeat for England will leave them two down with three to play and the Australians two-thirds of the way to reclaiming the Ashes.

Emburey likely to play

Ben the Beefburger Kid is, of course, famed for his broad Yorkshire accent. His fall from grace will be a blow to the county, but it must brace itself for another.

The Headingley pitch appears even, but cracked, dry and with just a fine covering of greenish grass. As a result, England will probably resist the temptation to play four seamers and pick John Emburey ahead of Chris Old, despite the seamer's fine record on his home ground.

As Old knows, and regularly exploits, the atmospheric conditions at Leeds often encourage swing and there may be some unreliable bounce for the seamers. However, on this particular pitch, the spinners can expect to play a part too. The outfield is patchy in colour, but firm, well-timed shots will race to the boundary. Emburey's ability to keep the runs down could prove to be priceless.

His selection would mean only one change in the team. Woolmer, who has made just 30 runs in four innings, making way for Brearley.

Willis, with eight wickets in two Tests, and Dilley, with 12, look on paper to be in form. But the Warwickshire man, who bowled 32 no-balls in the second Test, has been suffering from a chest infection and has only played in a Second XI game since Lord's. Dilley's figures are even more misleading; his direction is inconsistent and he is not making the batsmen play at enough deliveries.

Both pacemen will know more consistency is needed if the selectors are not to turn to Lancashire's increasingly impressive Paul Allott. Sussex's Ian Greig, who is out-bowling Garth Le Roux and Imran Khan at Hove, will also be in the selectors' thoughts, as will Robin Jackman, Mike Hendrick and, of course, Old.

Middlesex's Simon Hughes and Derbyshire's Paul Newman both bowled well, along with Allott, against Sri Lanka in this week's trial match. A Test debut for either cannot be ruled out before the end of the series.

The word from the England camp is that the selectors were disappointed that Emburey did not get more success bowling into the rough outside the left-handers' off stump at Lord's. However, his match figures of 46 overs, 22 maidens, 2 for 59 prove his ability to operate as a stock bowler.

Derek Underwood remains the second-choice spinner, but he is being pushed hard by Nottinghamshire's Eddie Hemmings, who is proving that it's possible for a slow bowler to take wickets on Hadlee and Rice's Trent Bridge launching pad.

Despite the recent low scores, the batting has a much more settled look. Gooch and Boycott are the country's best opening partnership, a class above the most likely alternatives, the Northamptonshire pair of Wayne Larkins and the uncapped Geoff Cook.

Equally, Gatting and Gower are the two best middle-order players with Willey adding the necessary steel. There are few other options with Middlesex's Roland Butcher not making the grade in the West Indies and Derek Randall out of favour. Sussex's Paul Parker may get the nod later in the series if England want to replace one of their middle-order stroke players.

England's most desperate need is for a decent number three. Bill Athey and Brian Rose's Caribbean nightmare left a large question mark over their ability at the highest level and Kent's Chris Tavaré remains the most likely to break into the current side. However,

Worcestershire's Younis Ahmed – twice capped for Pakistan, but now available for England and the second man to 1000 runs this season – continues to argue – on and off the field – for a chance to restart his international career.

In this match Brearley will bat at number three. Brearley's deficiencies are well known, but he is in good form, with four centuries this season including one against the tourists.

Ian Botham, of course, remains irreplaceable. Leaving him out would require England to go into a match with four bowlers or a bits-and-pieces player like Geoff Miller batting number six. But Brearley will find Botham a much less commanding player than the one he handed over the reins to in 1980. His bowling has lost both snap and late, sharp swing. Equally his batting lacks the calculated exuberance and technical correctness of his early Test career. In three out of the four Test innings he has played this summer, Botham has been bowled or lbw early in his innings hitting across the line.

Gloucestershire captain Mike Procter today claimed that Botham should get the captaincy back at the end of the series, but only if he is given the guidance of a full-time 'football-style' manager. Procter suggested either Surrey's Mickey Stewart or Yorkshire's Ray Illingworth.

Whatever happens in the future, Brearley's influence on Botham in this match will be vital. Brearley has another, nearly as important, task – that of selecting which of eight possible candidates will field in the slips. The Headingley pitch is likely to encourage edges, especially early on, and England's recent close-catching performance has been woeful – probably costing them the first Test and Botham his job. Only Boycott and Willis will definitely not be asked to join Brearley in the slips, but few of the others – even Botham – have looked like hanging on to much.

Australia have the edge

Australia's great strength is their pace bowling. Lillee, though ill, has taken 11 wickets at an average of 24 and Lawson 8 at 19. Alderman has been a revelation with 11 victims at 23. His team-mates claim he has added a yard of pace since landing in England.

With England's pace bowling out of sorts, the weather predicted to be overcast until Saturday at least and Headingley, therefore, likely to live up to its reputation for helping the quick men, Australia seem to have the crucial advantage.

Australia are likely to go into the third Test unchanged, despite the temptation to pick Rodney Hogg and revert to the four-man pace attack that proved so effective at Trent Bridge. Hughes is likely to want the variety that slow left-armer Ray Bright brings to the attack.

Bright bowled roughly the same number of overs as Emburey at Lord's and took twice as many wickets. Despite this he remains unconvincing as a Test cricketer and the English batsmen must make the most of his spells.

Since beating the Australians in 1977, rain has ruined all three Headingley Tests – and the forecast for the next few days is not great. However, the spectators will at least have a new distraction if the heavens open.

Headingley has a new, electronic scoreboard. No doubt, many will react with the same horror as displayed by the tabloids on learning that the St Paul's choristers will each earn £1000-plus for singing at the Royal Wedding, but most, it is to be hoped, will welcome it as a rare sign of progress at the home of Yorkshire cricket. Brearley, though, didn't like it, saying it looks ugly – it was probably designed by an Australian.

One potential problem with the new scoreboard is that a bright sky sometimes makes the figures hard to read from the middle.

Further confusion may arise from the playing conditions. This match, unlike the first, fourth and fifth Tests, will feature the traditional Sunday rest day. Play was also due to begin at the usual time of 11.30 a.m., but tickets have been issued bearing an 11 o'clock start time. It was felt unfair to ticket buyers to revert to the original time so, like the second and sixth Tests, we'll be kicking off half an hour early.

England have not won a Test in 12 attempts. This equals their previous longest stretch without victory, recorded nearly 20 years ago between July 1963 and August 1964. That drought was finally broken in the first Test of the 1964–65 tour of South Africa. One G Boycott contributed 73 to the victory. How he would love to do the same at Headingley this week.

Eyewitness

Barrie Meyer: In 1981 the umpires were instructed by the then Test and County Cricket Board to report to the ground authority on the eve of a Test match. David Evans and myself did this and while at Headingley walked to the middle to have a look at the pitch. We agreed that the cracks in the pitch would suggest that batting first would be a huge advantage. Win the toss and win the game, we thought.

Mike Brearley: I commiserated with Ian [Botham] over the way he had been pursued by the press. I said he would probably score a century and take 12 wickets in the match – which would make up for it.

Peter Willey: There wasn't a lot of preparation for a Test match then. We just turned up on Wednesday and had a net and then an evening team meeting which 'Both' always wrecked. He'd tell us how he was going to bowl everybody out, slog a hundred, then he'd throw a few bread rolls around and that was it – we were off to bed.

Mike Brearley: At this stage we were not thinking in terms of four seamers. That idea grew gradually as we reflected on the parallels with Trent Bridge, as well as on our uncertainties about Botham and Dilley. Boycott said that he normally preferred a balanced side, but would be tempted to rely on Willey for spin. Botham and Gooch, on the other hand, reckoned that the dry crust on the pitch would allow spin from early on. Old was convinced that the seamers would be helped more than the spinners. I went to bed totally uncertain on this crucial issue.

Yorkshire CCC Secretary David Ryder: The old wooden scoreboard was rotten and unsafe. The replacement was going to be offered to the Rugby Club sponsor Scottish & Newcastle Breweries as an advertising opportunity. Their retail director knew of somebody who had been doing some digital displays for their pubs and it evolved from there. It was a completely new concept.

We had a few teething problems, particularly converting the cricket scoring system into a computer program. But then the head of Computer Science at York University, who was a Yorkshire member, offered his services. After he rewrote the program, everything was OK.

During the Test we worked out that the sheet of perspex which protected it from rain was reflecting the sky and making the scoreboard difficult to read. After the game we took away the perspex and replaced it with a roller shutter.

John Woodcock's pre-match prediction in *The Times*: No one will benefit from Brearley's presence more than Botham. If either side wins it will, I believe, be England.

Dyson grinds England down

Brearley blunders over Emburey's omission

Australia have scored 203 for the loss of three wickets

Animal lovers will have been cheered by the news that the Save the Whale march scheduled for Sunday has been given the go-ahead by the Metropolitan Police. Lovers of English cricket, another endangered species, will be concluding that rallying in Hyde Park may be the only way left to raise their own spirits.

The first day of the third Test at Headingley was a dispiriting one for English fans. The home side had little luck and deserved even less. At the 7 o'clock close of a rain-interrupted day which belonged to mid-April rather than mid-July, Australia were sitting reasonably pretty on a helpful pitch and have taken a confident stride towards regaining the Ashes.

The returning Brearley has a reputation as a skilful and lucky captain. Here he was neither. First Hughes called heads and won the toss – then it was revealed that England had left out Emburey from their eleven. Australia preferred Bright to Hogg and the 11 tidy and successful overs that Willey bowled (with an injured hand) demonstrates who made the right decision.

A doctor has been fined for stealing seven pairs of knickers from the Oxford St Marks & Spencer's, despite having £7000 in his wallet. On the embarrassment scale Emburey's omission might not rank so highly, but

Brearley must surely be thinking, 'They haven't brought me back for my batting'.

The pitch itself was white-ish in colour, which suggested it was dry and would not therefore encourage excessive seam movement. But there were more cracks than are usual on the first day of a Test match, meaning that the pitch will either bounce unevenly or break up to help the spinners.

The first passage of play lasted less than two overs as the scowling clouds plunged Headingley into semi-darkness. The new electronic scoreboard's illuminated display provided a navigational aid as the players groped their way back to the dressing rooms.

A strong wind was blowing, making the poplar trees at the Kirkstall Lane End sway drunkenly. The clouds blew away and the players were out again surprisingly quickly. Although the conditions could not have been more different from those in Graeme Wood's native Western Australia, the opening bat played some attractive shots which sped across the fast outfield.

Dyson, on the other hand, was living down to the reputation of a man who, until now, had scored just one Test 50. The tall right-hander invariably played the moving ball with the inside edge and appeared lucky to survive when a short-pitched delivery from Willis hit his wrist and was taken by Gatting, one of two short legs. Given more deliveries to play at he would have struggled to last the morning session.

Willis opened the bowling from the Rugby Stand end. It meant labouring up the Headingley slope, but the wind was at his back and it guarded against Willis's tendency to no-ball. Brearley picked Old to be Willis's opening partner, trusting the Yorkshireman to make best use of the local conditions. Old did a good job, initially bowling down the slope from the Kirkstall Lane End into the cool breeze and averaging just 1.77 runs an over during the day. His bowling was a reminder of his astonishing performance in the '78 Headingley Test against Pakistan when he bowled 41 overs for just 41 runs.

The Yorkshire seamer grew a fine, full beard on the West Indies tour. In fact, five of the English players have beards – Gooch, Gatting, Willey and Botham being the others. In contrast, no fewer than seven of the Australian team have moustaches – Wood, Chappell, Yallop, Border, Marsh, Lillee and Alderman. Most are of the strokable, luxuriant Zapata-style made popular under the Chappelli, although Alderman's looks as if a malnourished hairy caterpillar has decided to end its days beneath his nose. It's as if the two teams were sponsored by rival barbers.

Bright, of course, has a beard, but then slow left-armers have always been a law unto themselves.

English disease not catching

Brearley was the same as ever, the familiar mix of reserve and donnish decisiveness. The contrast of Brearley and Taylor's greying heads and – relatively – frail physiques with the hulking black-bearded bulks of Gooch, Gatting and Botham in the slip cordon was like a textbook illustration of cricket's much-quoted need to embrace both muscle and mind.

The returning captain appeared nervous about introducing his predecessor into the action, especially with Wood playing so positively. But when Australia passed the half-century mark without loss he finally brought Botham on as second change. Almost immediately he took Wood's wicket, a sharp inswinger trapping him plumb in front. Gooch, Taylor, Brearley and Gatting ran to hug the big man, whose victory leap suggested relief as much as celebration.

Wood, who had scored 34 from 55 balls, left the crease, taking with him any sense of adventure. The heavens wept at the prospect of a stand between Dyson and Chappell Minor and play was again halted at 12.25. Until yesterday Yorkshire had been suffering from a three-week-long drought. The power of international cricket to influence the weather remains uncanny.

Rain meant the afternoon session did not get going until nearly three o'clock. By 4.30 most spectators would have wished they were still snug under their umbrellas. Dyson ground on, mostly playing off the back foot, but sometimes lunging stiffly forward. Whichever foot he played off, the result was usually the same, a single squirted down to long leg or third man. Chappell, meanwhile, looked so out of his depth that you could imagine Greg back home in Australia feeling pangs of guilt about letting his little brother try to fill his vast boots.

Not that England could do anything to take advantage. With the exception of Old, the seamers bowled too wide and failed to take advantage of conditions in which deliveries regularly bounced awkwardly and moved, sometimes alarmingly, both through the air and off the pitch. The four slips, who on this sort of pitch might have expected a chance every other over, were an irrelevance.

Until, of course, with Chappell on three, Botham got a delivery to catch the edge of his bat and thence fly straight into third slip Gower's left hand and out again. Botham, no doubt, was wondering why a side not exactly bursting with natural athletes had their best outfielder in the slips, when Chappell, now on seven, gave another chance, this time off Willis, and the Somerset hero could only watch it rebound off his chest and onto the ground.

Brearley revealed in yesterday's *Sun* that he makes daily visits to a psycho-analyst, often getting up at 6.00 to fit in appointments before games. It might be worth his while taking England's slip fielders along for a group session on his next visit.

At tea Australia were 97–1, Dyson 43. Chappell had made 11 in an hour and a half. His move to the number three spot, after having batted at number five for the first two Tests, appears to have more to do with Yallop's poor form (23 runs in four innings), than with Chappell's prospects of forging a Test career at first drop. His lack of technique was cruelly exposed by the moving ball – at least on the rare occa-

sions that the English bowlers actually managed to pitch the ball up to him.

Brearley's debt to Willey

At the five o'clock start of the greyish evening session, Chappell and Dyson began, finally, to try to take the initiative. Chappell is, at least, a skilled and experienced one-day cricketer and he hustled his partner through for a series of quick singles. On two occasions he was almost too ambitious and Gower, freed from his servitude in the slips and once more a predator in the covers, nearly ran out both batsmen. Gower's fielding skills are well known to the Australians, but they always seem to be surprised when this Little Lord Fauntleroy lookalike sweeps in low to whip the ball back towards the stumps.

Dyson reached his 50 in a shade under two hours. He then started to open up, revealing some previously unseen, authoritative off-side shots off the back foot to complement his assured legside play. He looked a better batsman with every passing over, angular stiffness slowly giving way to assured correctness. He is similar in style to Kent's Chris Tavaré, who would also have battled hard on this pitch.

On 57, Dyson tried to square drive Dilley and the ball flew to Botham, who had just replaced Gatting in the gully. He got both hands to a difficult chance, but dropped it. By now the ground was about two-thirds full and the crowd started to taunt the former captain. He is the people's favourite no longer. Life as Scunthorpe centre-half has probably never looked more appealing.

Willey did a good job of ensuring

that England did not suffer too badly from Emburey's absence. He was able to spin the ball using his second finger and, bowling tightly from the Kirkstall Lane End, he sometimes got both turn and bounce. After tea, he came on at the Rugby Stand End and Chappell, making room to force a long hop into the off-side, got a top edge and was caught by Taylor for 27. His stand with Dyson had lasted two hours and 41 minutes and realised 94 runs.

In the breezy evening sunshine Hughes and Dyson tucked into the tiring English bowlers, the opener playing past cover point with something approaching flair. Together they added 47 runs in an hour. Compared to what had come before, it was like Coe and Ovett sprinting for the finishing line.

Dyson reached his century half an hour before the close and found himself being hugged by an effusive Hughes. The crowd celebrated too, not particularly over Dyson's century but more because Geoff Boycott was bowling.

Dyson's ton had taken nearly five hours and 234 balls. He had hit 14 fours.

Boycott sent down three overs. His cap turned back to front, the comic Ying of his bowling in perfect balance with the sober Yang of his batting. He swung it too – just two runs coming from 18 deliveries.

Fifteen minutes before the close Brearley gave Dilley one last go down the hill from the Kirkstall Lane End. With Dyson already looking forward to having an asterisk by his name overnight, he tried to force off his legs and was yorked leg stump. Nightwatchman Bright and his captain saw Australia through to the close.

England will have to make good use of the new ball first thing in the morning. A score of 300 looks like being a match-winning one.

Australia first innings

J. Dyson b Dilley	102
G.M. Wood lbw b Botham	34
T.M. Chappell c Taylor b Willey	27
K.J. Hughes not out	24
R.J. Bright not out	1
Extras (lb5, w2, nb8)	15
Total (3 wkts)	203

Fall of wickets: 1–55, 2–149, 3–196

	O	M	R	W
Willis	16	4	44	0
Old	26	11	46	0
Dilley	13	3	39	1
Botham	3	4	33	1
Willey	11	2	24	1
Boycott	3	2	2	0

Eyewitness

Australian commentator Alan McGilvray: Kim Hughes knew I had very strong feelings about the Leeds wicket going back over many years. We decided to go and have a look at this one before breakfast on the first day and I said that, whatever the match brought, he should do all in his power to avoid batting in the final innings.

Mike Brearley: Marsh asked if our omission of Emburey had been a bluff to get them to put us into bat.

Ray Bright: Three seamers were enough on that pitch.

Mike Brearley: I knew I wanted the reliable Old, plus Botham as all-rounder, and Dilley as a strike bowler. Bob

Willis, who probably imagined that Old would be left out if Emburey played, opted – uncertainly – for four seamers. Finally I too came down, with equal tentativeness, on the same side. The selectors inclined the other way, but let me have the side I preferred.

Peter Willey: I had a bad spinning finger. But I could bowl just a little bit, so they played me instead of John Emburey. If I had been unable to bowl, Embers would have played.

John Dyson: After the first 15 minutes I realised that anyone was going to need a bit of luck to survive on this pitch. Early on I played a French cut for four which could have easily gone straight into the stumps and I decided this could be my day.

If I was beaten I just forgot about it and concentrated on the next ball. If anything the ball did too much, it was beating everything.

I was a bit disappointed to get out just before the close, but mainly I was ecstatic at getting my first Test century.

Barrie Meyer: John Dyson and Kim Hughes both played very brave innings. Balls were jumping and hitting them on the knuckles and chest. They had a lot of fortune, but they got behind the ball.

Trevor Chappell: John Dyson's innings should have been a match-winner.

Mike Brearley [to umpire David Evans]: If all went well you could bowl a side out for 90 on this pitch.

Graham Dilley: People ask why we bowled so badly. Well, just look at the seamers we had. Both had just resigned the captaincy because he could hardly score a run or take a wicket; Bob Willis had to play in a Second XI game to prove his fitness, so it wasn't like he'd had a lot of cricket and was coming into the game on the back of a stackful of wickets; and I didn't want to be there.

Three out of the four had a question mark over them – we weren't in great form.

There were times, when you got it right, that you could see it was a huge struggle for the batsman to cope with what was happening. Really extravagant bounce, lack of bounce, sideways movement. But none of us pitched it in the right areas often enough to exploit that.

A Turn for the Worse

'The scientists fail us,' Colin Cowdrey bemoaned whimsically a few years back. 'They cannot do anything to supply men who are born to be groundsmen.' Perhaps this is why Australians refer to these put-upon creatures as curators. After all, it is their unfortunate lot to tend ancient pastures and museum pieces that, in Headingley's case at least, deserve to be dug up, stuffed and mounted as an example of how not to prepare a cricket pitch.

It is all too easy, of course, to blame Keith Boyce, Yorkshire's devoted if understandably neurotic turf-tender. Mere humans, after all, can only do so much to combat the wilfulness of soil, grass and elements. All the same, even though the Australian score is already assuming dreadnought proportions, the bottom line is unavoidable: this surface promises an even battle betwixt bat and ball in much the same way as Larry Grayson promotes butchness.

Peter Philpott was candour personified. 'We were crawling around on our hands and knees trying to work out what the wicket would do,' divulged Australia's agreeable coach. Mind you, it takes a fair old leap of the imagination to picture D.K. Lillee crawling anywhere other than along the floor of The Old Bull and Bush.

Fred Trueman, as is his wont, made no bones about it. 'Somebody,' he asserted, 'has badly read this wicket.' Trevor Bailey, his *Test Match Special* comrade-in-nostalgic-arms, nodded his assent; the pitch, he reckoned, would be taking 'quite a bit' of spin come the fifth day. Which will do little to console

John Emburey, for all that the Middlesex offie acknowledges that, since returning from the Caribbean, he has found it difficult adjusting to the slower pitches, hence the frequency with which he found himself being cut and pulled at Lord's.

'Half an hour before the start I found out I was 12th man,' this quintessential pro said ruefully. 'I wasn't expecting it. There was a little bit of moisture in the pitch for the seamers but I still thought I should have played. Shortly before lunch, Peter Willey bowled a couple of overs and made the ball turn, one or two quite a lot. Mike [Brearley] came up to me at the interval and said, "I made the wrong decision," which pissed me off even more. The conditions were helpful but we didn't bowl well.'

But oh, those muffed catches. The electronic scoreboard blinked on and off all day yet, by comparison with the England fielders, it was the soul of efficiency. Vast expanses of Mike Brearley's hair are already a distinguished silvery-grey: such cack-handedness can only hasten the extinction of black. To combat the return of the Amazing Dancing Brears, one can only assume that Kim Hughes phoned Harrods and ordered some top-grade green kryptonite.

Caribbean comedown

England do not underestimate these Australians, insists Emburey. Still, he readily concedes that the hosts' lame form thus far may be attributable to the sense of release that followed their

Caribbean exertions. 'After playing them [WI] in back-to-back series, there was a huge relief. The general feeling was, "Thank God we've seen the back of them."' What, though, is worse: being pounded to a pulp by demonstrably superior opponents or being subjected to the Chinese water torture John Dyson in particular appears to specialise in?

When Greg Chappell announced that he would not be touring, more than a few English hands were doubtless rubbed with glee. This was on a par, the bowlers may well have reasoned, with dispatching *The Victory* to Trafalgar without Nelson. On pitches such as this, set alongside Greenidge, Haynes, Richards, Gomes, Lloyd and Kallicharran, the tourists' top six pose all the threat of a de-clawed moggy.

Given that they have racked up 21 Test hundreds between them, Messrs Wood, Hughes, Yallop and Border may well take exception to such dismissive characterisation, and would be eminently justified in consulting their lawyers. Yet the unpalatable truth – for home supporters – is that England's attack foundered here on the tentative if stubborn blades of Dyson and Chappell, who between them had hitherto mustered 409 Test runs at 18.59 with a high of 53. That the latter's modus operandi has even less in common with his brother's silken authority than Jack Charlton's had with Bobby's is almost as galling as Dyson's emergence as this series' first centurion. What, pray, were the odds on that?

'A bank clerk going to war,' was Clive Taylor's immortal description of Northamptonshire's David Steele, improbable star of the 1975 Ashes series. Dyson is the pacifist drafted into the front line. There is nothing remotely violent or aggressive about him. As befits a schoolteacher, he has an air of thoughtful sobriety. At times, indeed, one half-expected the stiff breeze to bowl him over. Old nearly did the trick, striking him in the midriff; Dyson fell to his haunches and dropped his bat, eschewing the gum-mangling machismo so beloved by peers and forebears. When he hooked at Botham after forcing him square for four – and missed – the shock was comparable to seeing Angela Rippon flaunt her legs on *The Morecambe and Wise Show*.

To my nigh-on certain knowledge, Rickie Lee Jones, the gifted young American responsible for that cool-fizzin', finger-poppin' hit of a couple of years back, *Chuck E's In Love*, has never ventured to Headingley. There is, though, a track on her new album called *Traces of the Western Slopes*, the words to which may well carry a special resonance for Dyson: 'If they give us any flak/If they come up on our ass/We'll just give 'em the go-by …' Maybe the meek shall inherit the Earth.

The Australian Broadcasting Corporation, the Auntie of the Antipodes, was unaccountably remiss in terminating transmission before play began, depriving the black-coffee-and-matchstick fanatics of their fix. At the end of a day that Trevor Bailey saw fit to describe as 'rather mundane', it was sorely tempting to advise the Beeb to follow suit.

Botham's back, but England look doomed

Australia total 'worth a thousand' – Hughes

Australia have declared at 401 for the loss of nine wickets. England are seven without loss

The narrowness of Roy Jenkins' defeat in Thursday's Warrington by-election convinced the SDP candidate that he was the real winner of the contest, and he spent much of Friday waving from the back of a Landrover on a 'victory' tour of the constituency. The vehicle should be immediately driven across the Yorkshire Moors and put at the disposal of Ian Botham.

The all-rounder's performance, in what now looks like a lost cause, was the one positive aspect of another depressing day for English cricket. The Humber Bridge, opened this week by the Queen, was not the only towering achievement worth celebrating. Botham's spell of 5–35 late in the afternoon, accomplished with a right arm injured just above the elbow during a fall while fielding on the first day, suggested that England's finest cricketer is getting back to his best.

Friday's play turned out to be even more gloomy – though a little warmer – than Thursday's, with the same fierce wind. Umpire Evans's comb-over was whipped from his scalp and provided a handy guide if Brearley or his bowlers needed to check the wind direction.

Nearly two hours were lost to rain and what play was possible took place in the sort of weather normally reserved (ordered?) for Roses contests.

The Australian batting, too, would have had Cardus talking of Makepeace and Hallows who 'scored slowly not because they could not have scored faster, but on principle.'

The English bowling, Botham apart, was often as threatening as the bouquet of roses given to the Queen by cub scout Gary Henson. Gary's impromptu gift sparked a minor security alert; for most of the day the Aussies had no similar cause for alarm.

Australia declared just before close of play, having added 198 in 72 overs. Gooch and Boycott survived an over each from Lillee and Alderman.

The bounce in the pitch has become even more uneven, but although the Aussie batsmen took some sharp knocks on the thighs, the English bowlers failed to take advantage. Yorkshire pace bowling maestro Bill Bowes, watching from the main stand in the company of fellow legendary Tyke Johnny Wardle, must have despaired at the waste of such an opportunity.

England's slip catching also continued to deteriorate, Gooch missing a painfully simple chance off Botham when Hughes was 66 and Brearley failing to grasp a much harder half-chance off Old when Yallop was 22.

The new ball became available after

three overs of the morning's play and Brearley chose Dilley to replace Willis as Old's opening partner.

Neither bowler repaid his captain's faith. The left-handed Yallop is in terrible form, but Old and Dilley could not make him play enough to expose his lack of confidence. The Headingley crowd, unsurprisingly, chose to overlook the performance of their own man, who admittedly had bowled well on Thursday, and started to get stuck into Dilley.

Dilley responded by first hitting Bright in the box and then, next ball, ripping out his middle and off stumps with an outswinger. However, the bowler's gesture of contempt towards his tormentors in the crowd when he took the wicket suggested that their jibes and catcalls had got under his skin and that his concentration was shot. It was also, of course, the second time in the series that Dilley has reacted in this way after taking a wicket.

A blond southerner is always likely to get a rough ride up north and Dilley will have to toughen up mentally if he wants to survive for long in international cricket. He will also need to sort himself out technically; his high-kicking, foot-dragging action certainly looks impressive, but he lacks the accuracy of Australia's Lawson, who bowls in a similar way.

Bright had done his job well, scoring just seven, but surviving for nearly three-quarters of an hour on a far from friendly pitch.

Hughes obviously, and rightly, concluded that runs count for double on this pitch – he later said the Australian total was 'worth a thousand'. The Australian captain reined in his attack-

ing instincts, scoring only 22 runs in the 95-minute morning session, and shepherded Yallop back into form. Their stand of 112 in just over two-and-a-half hours could be the match's decisive passage.

One delivery in particular illustrated how England were wasting the advantageous conditions. When Hughes had reached 43, a vicious lifter from Willis had him flailing like a marionette with its strings caught in a ceiling fan – both feet off the ground, arms outstretched and head jerked back. His cap almost fell onto the stumps.

Willis did, in fact, bowl with fire in the morning session. But the blaze died down much too quickly for a Test match bowler. Unlike Lillee, who is the same age, the Warwickshire man seems unable to bowl his second and third spells of the day at anything approaching full pace.

By lunch, with 25 minutes lost to rain, the Australians had reached 250 and England needed to take the remaining wickets in a hurry if they wanted to stay in the match.

The return of the prodigal son

England bowled better in the afternoon session. However, Hughes and Yallop weathered the storm, figurative and literal – there was a 70-minute rain break – and went into tea still together. At 309–4, their job was almost done and Hughes was looking forward to arguably the most atypical, but valuable Test century of his career. He was also finally beginning to get into his stride, his collar turned up as he turned on the style. He pulled one boundary high over mid-on in thrilling style and began whipping the ball through the covers in a way reminiscent of his batting during the Lord's Centenary Test a year ago. Yallop too seemed to recover some of his form, reeling off a series of smooth leg-side shots.

Then – seemingly out of nowhere – Botham suddenly remembered he loves bowling to Australians. Brearley had given Botham just nine overs before tea and had not allowed the all-rounder a spell longer than four overs since the start of the match. Given the ball after the interval he did not relinquish it for 16 overs. Perhaps he had spotted shot-putter Geoff Capes in the crowd and wanted to remind everyone that he too is one of England's sporting strongmen.

This was the Botham of old; running briskly to the wicket, his momentum uninterrupted by the little sideways jump he has used recently to get him close to the stumps. As a result his bowling action has real fluency again.

Botham plunged towards the bowling crease with purpose, heavy arms swinging to build up speed. He leapt into his bowling stride, rather than stepping into it as before, then hurtling the ball through with a twitch of those enormous shoulders. Botham's action can sometimes seem almost touchingly innocent, the left hand raised palm up in front of the face, like some schoolboy trying to imitate Lillee. But the Somerset star is, of course, no novice, as Australia were about to be reminded.

A Botham delivery hit Hughes in the groin. The Australian captain doubled over in pain, but then hurried back into his stance. The very next ball he aimed to leg, turned his bat too early,

got a leading edge and sent back the easiest of return catches to Botham, who caught it and flung the ball to the heavens. Hughes, it seemed, had fallen victim to the Australian desire not to show weakness in the face of their opponents.

Botham is a genius at seizing these moments of fortune and he stood impatiently at the end of his run-up as Hughes was applauded from the ground.

The Australian captain made 89 in four-and-a-half hours. He received 208 balls and hit just eight of them for four. He also demonstrated great concentration for such a natural stroke-maker whose innings was interrupted five times by interval or weather breaks.

Border top-scored for Australia in the first two Tests, but this time he lasted just 20 balls. Botham, going wide to slant the ball across the batsman, beat him with a big inswinger to win his second lbw decision, although it was one that many less bowler-friendly umpires would not have given. Three runs later Yallop waved his bat at an innocuous Botham delivery and edged it to Taylor. Yallop had made 58 in three hours and 28 minutes and had squeezed five boundaries from 167 deliveries.

It is astonishing to see the effect Botham can have on batsmen's shot selection when he really runs in. He had taken three wickets for eight runs and the crowd, a couple of thousand stronger than on Thursday, began to cheer him. To Botham it must have sounded like the singing of angels.

Australia declare

Friday was Bob Taylor's 40th birthday and he still appears to have regular access to the adrenaline elixir available only to the best wicketkeepers. The side effects have not driven him as barmy as Alan Knott, but his star-shaped leaps and full-on appealing still look odd when delivered by a man who would appear more at home as a Grace Brothers' floor walker. The floppy white sun hat does nothing for his dignity either.

Lawson came in to join Marsh and for 45 minutes the Australians regained the upper hand. As a light rain fell Lawson kept the bowlers out and Marsh hit five boundaries, mostly straight down the ground. The wicketkeeper's batting has declined in recent years, his technique shaken by the unremitting fast bowling he faced in Packer cricket. But Marsh still punches the ball away with the same gusto when he gets going, freeing his arms in an uninhibited swing when the bowler pitches wide or short. The tempo rises whenever he comes to the crease; he remains a squat, bustling figure full of competitive intent.

The pair added 39 from 45 deliveries, but Botham was not to be denied. First he softened up Lawson with a bouncer, before digging in another short delivery, which the batsman was only able to fend off, the ball looping slowly into Taylor's gloves. Then, eight minutes later, Botham emphatically yorked Marsh for 28 with another inswinger.

Botham's reaction to this sixth wicket appeared significant, a half-hearted punch of victory perhaps suggesting that he knew he had left his charge too late – alternatively, he was probably just knackered.

Hughes declared just as Alderman stepped onto the pitch. Botham's spell had given him figures of 6–95, the first time he has taken five wickets in an innings since the Jubilee Test in Bombay over a year ago. That was, of course, also the last game before he took over as captain.

Gooch and Boycott had to last just two overs, but with the light fading fast they would not have relished the prospect. Luckily for them both Lillee and Alderman tried to bowl too quickly and as a result sent down three no-balls and a wide between them. Boycott had to play five Lillee deliveries from around shoulder height. Nasty stuff late in the day, but the sort of length which allowed Australia to score 400.

However, Alderman did bowl one awesome delivery which ducked in towards Gooch's bat before flying up off a good length, rocketing past the outside edge and causing Marsh to launch himself in front of first slip to save four byes. There will be plenty more deliveries like that on Saturday.

England closed at seven for no wicket, with Gooch on two and Boycott yet to get off the mark. The last time the Yorkshire opener faced the Australians in a Test at Headingley, he recorded his 100th first-class century and went on to score 191. As the batsman with by far the best defensive technique in the side, he will have to equal that achievement if England are not to lose this match.

Australia first innings

J. Dyson b Dilley	102
G.M. Wood lbw b Botham	34
T.M. Chappell c Taylor b Willey	27
K.J. Hughes c&b Botham	89

R.J. Bright b Dilley				7
G.N. Yallop c Taylor b Botham				58
A.R. Border lbw b Botham				8
R.W. Marsh b Botham				28
G.F. Lawson c Taylor b Botham				13
D.K. Lillee not out				3
T.M. Alderman not out				0
Extras (b4, lb13, w3, nb12)				32
Total (9 wkts dec)				401

Fall of wickets: 1–55, 2–149, 3–196, 4–220, 5–332, 6–354, 7–357, 8–396, 9–401

	O	M	R	W
Willis	30	8	72	0
Old	43	14	91	0
Dilley	27	4	78	2
Botham	39.2	11	95	6
Willey	13	2	31	1
Boycott	3	2	2	0

England first innings

G.A. Gooch not out				2
G. Boycott not out				0
Extras (b1, w1, nb3)				5
Total (0 wkts)				7

	O	M	R	W
Lillee	1	0	1	0
Alderman	1	0	1	0

Eyewitness

Graham Yallop: It was a tough pitch. I've never played on another one like it. You had to grind it out, carefree abandon was not the order of the day. We batted well above ourselves to get 400.

Ian Botham: I said to Mike: 'Give me the ball, keep me on for a long spell and I'll get five wickets for you.'

Mike Brearley: Ian was running in more slowly than he had eighteen months before. Moreover, just before reaching the crease he stepped in towards the stumps, which reduced his momentum. The purpose of this manoeuvre was to swing the ball more by getting his left shoulder round. But the outcome was only gentle swing. I encouraged him to come straight in, to bounce in, as lively as he could. I started to ridicule the jink in his run-up, calling him 'the Side-step Queen'.

Australian coach Peter Philpott: Botham looked both more relaxed and more angry ... and when he was riled he was a nasty proposition.

Graeme Wood: Botham usually bowled well at the tail. He was very unpredictable, which unnerved lower order players.

Ray Bright: Botham had picked up a yard or two in pace since Lord's.

Brian Mossop, *Sydney Morning Herald*: The '400 is worth a thousand' quote was typical of Hughes. He tended to make bold statements that weren't always hugely intelligent.

Graham Dilley: We knew that the game was over once they got 400. There was no way in the world that we were ever going to get back into the game. The pitch was doing so much and when we looked at their bowling attack – which had quality bowlers who were bowling well – we knew if everything went right for them they could bowl us out for double figures.

Trevor Bailey on *Test Match Special*: The batting has been workmanlike rather than distinguished. The bowling pretty ordinary. We haven't had a distinguished Test to date.

Hughes and Yallop Lay Ghosts of Ashes Past

'She says I'm not leader enough for her,' lamented the lovelorn Fielding Mellish in *Bananas*, one of Woody Allen's 'early funny' movies. 'Who's she looking for, Hitler?'

There must have been times on this tour when Kim Hughes has felt tempted to echo those sentiments. Nevertheless, having put his side firmly in the box seat, Australia's führer has every right to thumb his nose at his detractors.

That Graham Yallop should have been his stoical accomplice for nearly half the day's laborious, often enervating proceedings, making Mike Brearley squirm impotently until Ian Botham's late surge, seemed entirely apposite, for aficionados of poetic justice as well as Australians. Revenge, however partial, seldom tastes quite this sweet.

In 1973, Yallop and Brearley played in the same MCC side against Scotland. Their paths next crossed as opposing skippers in the 1978–79 Ashes series. 'Perhaps it will be like 1958 when everyone thought May's bunch would wallop us and the Poms were hammered 4–0,' mused Yallop, the scion of a well-to-do Melbourne family, whose links with Blighty extend to a brief stint with Glamorgan's Second XI and a wife from the Valleys. Indeed, at his inaugural press conference, despite being handed a side left threadbare by Kerry Packer's piratical raids and boasting just 55 caps, he ventured a step too far, forecasting a 6–0 stroll. Reality socked him in the jaw with all the finality of a Larry Holmes uppercut.

After the opening Test at the Gabba, scene of the first of five English victories, it was noted with some consternation that the total attendance of 42,523 had lagged behind the gate for a World Series night game in Sydney. 'I was fighting wars on two fronts,' Yallop recalled. 'And I couldn't really win either of them.' On the eve of the fifth Test he asked Bob Hammond, a respected Aussie Rules coach, to give a pep talk, prompting Christopher Martin-Jenkins to wonder: 'Was it not the captain's own job to inspire his men?' The trouble, remarked the fast bowler Alan Hurst, was that 'you couldn't look up to him – basically he didn't want the job, and he didn't have the experience or the personal manner for the role.'

As they strove in vain to save that Brisbane Test, Hughes and Yallop shared a liaison worth 170, their centuries towering Sears-like beside the contributions of nine colleagues who collectively cobbled together just 72. Confounding those convinced that he was all crash, dash and rash, Hughes expended six-and-a-quarter hours scaling three figures, the most sluggish to date by an Australian against England. Today's admirably stoical effort was cut from the same determinedly unnatural cloth.

Artisan 1 Artist 0

A sublime square drive off Dilley brought Hughes to 50, and one pull through midwicket off Willis was positively lordly, but what we beheld here was more artisan than artist, more grim than Brothers Grimm. Having seen John Dyson plant a foot squarely on the Poms' windpipe, he was in no mood to release the pressure, even if it meant boring the pants off everyone. While scorning a helmet bordered on the foolhardy, the message it imparted was as unequivocal as it was invigorating. 'There is probably a greater premium on temperament for a batsman,' opined Don Bradman, 'than for any player in any branch of sport.' Short of declining a box, Hughes could not possibly have done more to stamp his character on this contest.

If anything, it was even more excruciating watching Yallop. Normally so fluent, if less impetuous than Hughes, he took an hour and a half to reach 20, almost three for his 50, and made five singles from his last 36 balls. As with his skipper, the lives, edges and misses comfortably outnumbered the flourishes, not that there was any shame in that.

Much as a working journalist should never confess to knowing such things, there is on our commercial TV schedules an afternoon children's programme by the slightly risqué title of *Now for Nookie*. On this occasion it most assuredly wasn't. It was time to grimace and bear it, to grit teeth and wait patiently for a ball that was far enough from harm's way yet close enough to reach. For Yallop and Hughes it was a case of survival of the flintiest, a job for the ornery.

Yallop eased one early boundary off Botham, and later came a delicate open-faced glide through third man, but expositions of that trademark withering cut were sparse; that the stroke eventually undid him reinforced his wisdom in keeping it sheathed on such a capricious track. Spared by Brearley, fortunate not to get a touch to Chris Old's peach of a leg-cutter on 29, his contribution when the fifth-wicket alliance attained 100 – only the second century stand of the rubber, and Australia's first – was barely a third. Calling Hughes for a quick single as the pair quickened the pace, he was obliged to run across the pitch in order to circumvent three fielders. Nothing came easy.

Harpo and Groucho

They make a decidedly odd couple, less Lemmon and Matthau than Harpo and Groucho. Hughes struts and gestures theatrically, that mass of curls cherubic and cheeky; Yallop, angular and elongated of torso, has the stooping stance and the pantomime moustache. Neither was so much as a mischievous glint in his father's eye when Australia last won a Test on this ground 33 summers ago, when another lefty–righty pair, Arthur Morris and The Don, propelled those voluminous verdant caps to an unprecedented 404–3. In the circumstances, Hughes and Yallop's painstaking self-denial could well prove just as decisive.

The one cause for home cheer was Botham's return, if not to the swagger of yore, then at least to an approximation of his erstwhile ebullient self, with the ball if not in the slips. 'He definitely seemed more relaxed,' said Emburey, 'as if a great weight had been lifted from his shoulders. Ian can't manage himself. He needs someone to lead him.'

In he came, almost as an after-thought, bounding in with renewed zest to nick the rewards and plaudits more richly deserved by the persevering but luckless Old. 'I hope Botham gets five wickets,' declaimed Brian Johnston on *Test Match Special* when the out-of-sorts Midas had four to his name, the partiality as unabashed as it was touching. 'And no doubt when he goes in,' added the ever-effusive Johnners, 'he'll get a hundred.' Judging by Graham Gooch's narrow squeak against Terry Alderman shortly before

stumps, he has about as good a chance of fulfilling that prophecy as the Queen Mum has of winning *The Krypton Factor*.

Precedent, at least, is in the home corner. Hughes's closure marked the fourth time since 1948 that Australia have declared in a Test on these shores; on the previous three occasions they were unable to force a victory. Optimism, for all that, should be severely tempered. 'Tom Graveney told me he thought 400 was "impossible" on that pitch,' revealed Peter Philpott. In terms of squaring the series, England's mission, should they choose to accept it, probably feels even less feasible.

Australian bowlers plunge England into the depths

Botham's resurgence continues, but England follow on

England made 174 all out in their first innings. Following on, they have scored six for the loss of one wicket. They trail Australia by 221 runs

On Monday morning Environment Minister Michael Heseltine will set out for Liverpool, charged with investigating the reasons behind the Toxteth riots. He should be waylaid in the Midlands and rerouted to Leeds. The problems of English cricket might pale beside those of our inner cities, but to be at Headingley on Saturday was to taste despair as deep as it gets in sporting circles.

The day ended in farce with the umpires unable to restart play after 6 o'clock despite the ground being bathed in the brightest sunlight we have seen for three days. The capacity crowd booed and threw cushions onto the playing area. Two spectators staged a lie-down protest in the middle of the pitch. Many thought they had expired from grief; how we envied them.

Oh yes, and Yorkshire were bowled out by Notts at Trent Bridge for 104. 'Newcastle Bitter', said one of the boundary advertisements. Too right – and Sheffield, Bradford, Leeds ... 'Truman's Steel', said another, how they needed that now.

If it had not been for the news that Japanese car giant Nissan is to bring 5000 jobs to nearby Humberside by building a factory at Grimsby, the whole county would have had to join Mike Brearley in therapy.

Many of the Headingley faithful will wish they had spent their £8.50 more wisely. Eighty miles north of Headingley at Gateshead, 20,000 people gathered to watch England's athletes take on one of the sport's world powers, the Soviet Union. Coe, Ovett and Cram were the biggest draws of course, but when a young javelin thrower with the glorious name of Fatima Whitbread beat her Russian opponent, the crowd roared their approval.

What with one athlete winning a photo finish because she had bigger breasts ('You have to carry them all the way round,' the winner later said in justification), and a 1500 metre runner recovering from being hit by a javelin to take third place behind Coe and Cram, the meet had everything.

English athletics may not have cricket's traditional support base, but it clearly has the talent. There was little argument that England are fielding close to the best XI they can muster at Headingley. They are just not good enough. Could it be that in these Thatcherite times Britain only breeds sportsmen and women with a taste for individual events rather than team games?

For the second day running Ian Botham was the only Englishman to provide any hope. He top-scored with 50 and played with much of his old panache. The rest was a procession, hastened by a competent, sometimes exceptional, bowling performance on a pitch that is providing more help for the fast bowlers every day. The cloudy conditions conspired to make batting even more hazardous.

Lillee, his bushy mane kept out of his eyes by an orange headband, bowled the first over to Boycott and it must rank as one of the worst he has ever sent down. One delivery was signalled a wide, another resulted in four leg byes.

Lillee, especially by his own sky-scraping standards, bowled awfully in the morning session, sending deliveries wide down both the leg and off side. At that point it seemed that his recent bout of pneumonia had taken more out of him than we had thought. Brearley reckoned that if Lillee had bowled as well as he can, England would have only just scraped past 100.

But for the first time since Thomson's terrifying pomp, Lillee was not the Australian bowler likely to do the most damage. Despite the fact that he is playing in only his third Test match, Alderman has become a master of exploiting the sort of conditions encountered at Headingley.

The day was the warmest of the match so far – although that's not saying much – the humidity helping the ball to swing. Alderman cruised in from the Rugby Stand End under a leaden sky. His first ball was pitched on leg and middle, but swung back and Gooch was lbw playing across the line. Brearley nearly went the same way first ball.

Alderman – the king of swing

Alderman, like Lillee bowling to a field containing five slips, a gully and a short leg, also had Boycott regularly groping for the ball. Once he cut the ball back so sharply that it squeezed through the gap between Boycott's bat and pad that many county bowlers believe is just a myth.

Alderman has surprised even his team-mates. His run to the wicket is little more than a controlled trot and he often seems no more than medium-paced. The benign impression is accentuated by the fact that he appears to smile as he delivers the ball.

The batsmen rarely have anything to smile about. Alderman is a big man with powerful shoulders and as a result his deliveries surprise opponents with their pace and bounce off the pitch. But Alderman's greatest attribute is his line and length. He gets so close to the stumps that he regularly leaves the field with bloodied knuckles, having disturbed the bails during his follow-through. His textbook action, the right arm finishing ramrod-straight down his body at the end of his follow-through, means the ball will inevitably swing little but late, pitch in the danger area and search out pad or edge.

For most of the English batsmen Alderman is a puzzle, compared to which tackling one of the new Rubik's Cubes is as easy as answering the questions on *Bullseye*.

The tousle-haired Alderman bowled

so well, did so much with the ball, that it aroused the suspicions of umpire Evans. He asked to inspect the ball in the middle of an Alderman over, perhaps suspecting that the seam had been picked to make it behave in an erratic manner. He plainly found nothing to report and tossed the ball back to the bowler, who continued to make it talk.

Boycott was clearly relishing the battle, concentrating harder and harder as the ball jumped and sometimes shot. He was constantly hit on the hands and must have been thankful for his new gloves which have small strips of fibreglass protecting each finger.

Brearley's innings must have been exquisite torture for the England captain. Arguably the most intelligent and tactically astute cricketer ever to play for England, he would have known exactly what Alderman was doing with the ball and how, in theory, to counter it. His technique is not bad, although it lacks the refinement of a Boycott. He times his drives well and can accumulate when the bowlers are on top through a range of nudges and pushes. However, at international level, it is – ironically – his mind that seems to let him down. Doubt often clouds his stroke selection, his defensive shots appearing to feel for the ball.

The morning was still and grey. The crowd remained almost totally silent (well, people don't feel it right to make a noise at funerals, do they?) as Brearley took 15 minutes to get off the mark, finally dribbling a single to square leg off an inside edge. He narrowly escaped lbw shouts from Lillee and Alderman. The boyish Hughes crowded both batsmen with seven close catchers, plus Marsh, which at least allowed them to collect runs by pushing the ball through mid-on and mid-off.

The score had reached 40 just after 12 o'clock when Brearley was out. A half-hearted push at a lifting ball from Alderman giving Marsh the simplest of catches. England's number three batsmen – Athey, Rose, Gatting and Brearley – have now made 74 runs in 15 innings.

As Brearley walked off, he was followed by Lillee. Aware of the controversy over his regular trips to the dressing room, the crowd whistled and teased. Lillee just smiled and waved as he climbed the dressing room stairs. News from the two dressing rooms suggests that the matter has been settled peacefully enough, but it is just like Lillee to let everyone know that he has come out on top by accompanying his defeated persecutor off the field.

The lanky Geoff Lawson replaced Lillee. The New South Welshman is training to be an optician and Boycott may want Lawson to check his contact lens prescription, because he didn't appear to see the ball that bowled him. The truth is that it was a virtually unplayable delivery. It pitched just short of a length outside off stump before cutting sharply in. Boycott clearly expected the ball to bounce waist high and attempted to turn it to leg; instead it kept low, clipped the front of the batsman's left pad and went on to remove the leg bail. Boycott's 12 runs had taken an hour and a half.

A banner, referring to Ian Botham's latest TV commercial, was waved aloft by one spectator as Sir Geoff left the field. 'Geoff Boycott can eat three

Shredded Wheat', it read. Maybe so, but the diet is clearly doing more for the man from Somerset if the events of this match are anything to go by.

Gatting came out to join Gower and the two 24-year-olds began to rebuild the innings. It was not until 10 minutes before lunch that Gower started to play his shots, on-driving Alderman to deliver England's first boundary off the bat. Emboldened by this success, he played a flowing cover drive later in the same over and then caressed Lawson through the offside. After the attritional approach of the Australians – a brief glimpse of the real Kim Hughes apart – it was a relief to see a batsman dispensing such largesse.

Gower, as ever, trusted to his eye rather than using his feet to get into line. He was the picture of relaxation, but the tightrope he walks in every innings looked particularly frayed as the ball swung and spat. Gower went to 21, out of 71, and became the first batsman to pass the extras total. Gatting, a Falstaff to Gower's Prince Hal, joined in, punching the ball through extra cover.

It looked as if England's fortune was beginning to change, especially when the atrocious quality of slip fielding in this series was continued by Graeme Wood, who floored a chance given by Gatting off the returning Lillee with the batsman's score on nine.

Test record for Marsh

England lunched at 78–3, with Gower 24. During the interval the widely held view was that for England to make a game of it, Gatting and Gower would have to bat through the afternoon session and into the evening. However,

they were both gone within minutes of the resumption of play.

First Gower was dropped by Dyson at fourth slip off the distinctly sharp Lawson. However, with the very next ball the bowler produced a delivery that reared up from just short of a length and cut away from the left-hander. It clipped Gower's glove and Marsh took the catch two-handed high above his head. Gower and Gatting had added 42 runs in just 50 minutes, a rate much quicker than anything achieved by the Australians. Astonishingly, the scoring rate was to get even more frenetic; so, unfortunately, was the fall of wickets.

Gatting and Willey added six before Lillee, now bowling like his old self, trapped the Middlesex batsman lbw as he played forward – a big breakback hitting pad then bat. The score was 90–5 and England were sinking fast.

Botham, whose walk from the wicket at Lord's was made in sepulchral silence, was cheered by the crowd. The former captain showed his appreciation, and perhaps recognition that his luck is beginning to change, by launching a prodigious drive at Lillee and edging him high over the slips. Up on the players' balcony Brearley gestured that he should have tried to hit it even harder. Botham smiled hugely – amid the carnage it was an uplifting sight.

A single brought up the England 100 in the 36th over; extras were the equal highest score with Gower's 24.

Twice Botham thrashed Lillee to the boundary off the back foot, but refreshing though it was, it meant little. Botham and Willey had added just 22 runs when a yorker from Lawson hit the Northamptonshire batsman on the foot, with the ball then crashing into the stumps.

At this stage Lawson had taken half the wickets to fall. He is fast – quicker than Lillee – in his first spell and probably the sharpest bowler available to either side.

Taylor knows better than to try to bat like Botham and he concentrated on keeping the Aussie bowlers out, taking 35 minutes to get off the mark. In that time Botham played a series of thrilling and powerful shots, particularly off Alderman. One shot was fielded on the boundary by a black spectator, sadly a rare sight at Headingley and therefore easily identifiable as Mr Griffiths, the railway clerk who travels to all England's home games.

Taylor finally got off the mark and immediately drove Lillee straight for four. He then pushed at a ball wide of the off stump and was caught behind by Marsh.

Saturday was Lillee's 32nd birthday, but it was his fellow swashbuckler Marsh who collected the biggest present. The catch to dismiss Taylor meant that Marsh equalled Alan Knott's record of 263 Test victims. For a player who began his career labelled as a mere 'stopper' the achievement is wondrous. The fact that Lillee, who has provided Marsh with almost a quarter of his victims, helped deliver the record, was as perfect as it seemed inevitable. In the press box *The Times* correspondent John Woodcock mused that the man who will beat Marsh's record is probably still to play his first Test.

England's third 50 had taken less than 10 overs. Hughes, though, kept cool. The Australian captain crowded Botham as he neared his half-century,

which he reached at the rate of a run a ball. It was uninhibited, refreshing batting, but better still was the spirit which Botham brought to the middle. He was full of life again, laughing and joking with Lillee as they traded blows. It was a great duel, one even worth missing Big Daddy v Giant Haystacks on ITV's Saturday afternoon wrestling for.

Botham had struck eight boundaries and made exactly two-thirds of the runs since coming to the wicket. It was his first half-century in 22 innings, his last being 57 against the West Indies in June 1980 during his first game as England captain.

Once again English celebrations were cut brutally short. Botham leant back to square cut Lillee, but the ball leapt at the batsman who could only glove it to Marsh. Botham, spinning round in shock and alarm to confirm his fate, was out, England were finished and Marsh had the record all to himself. Given that Sunday is a rest day, the chances of there being any lager in Leeds on Monday are slim.

Marsh may not have the exactness of Taylor or be able to match the quicksilver reactions of Knott, but he has never let Australia down. Despite his wide crouch and low stance, gloves like flippers dangling close to the ground below his walrus moustache, the enormous strength in his trunk-like legs means he can still accomplish his trademark flying takes.

England 500–1 Australia 1–4

Dilley played some nice off-drives, but was quickly deceived into checking a shot, providing Lillee with a straight-forward caught-and-bowled. The

England innings then ended with a miraculous event, a slip fielder holding onto a catch.

As England crumbled, Brearley watched from the balcony, sitting next to selector Brian Close. It is thought that Close favoured giving Botham one more Test in charge. He is probably now musing that England could hardly be in a worse position if they had.

Lillee had the best figures of 4–49, but Alderman, 3–59, and Lawson, 3–32, had bowled better. Hughes had rotated them cleverly, and slowly, the Australians averaging just 12 overs an hour compared to England's spin-assisted 15. However, the hosts' lack of fight meant that Australia's potential weakness in not having a fourth seamer was never in danger of being exposed.

Extras were the second highest score after Botham's 50 and accounted for 20 per cent of the total. England had scored at three-and-a-half runs an over, Australia at two-and-a-half. It is obvious which tactic is the more effective on this pitch.

The decision to enforce the follow-on, taken during the tea break, was not a simple one; the pitch is deteriorating fast and batting will become more and more hazardous. But with a lead of 227 and with a rest day in which Lillee, Alderman and Lawson can recharge their batteries, Hughes decided to go for the jugular.

Gooch lasted longer during his second innings on Saturday than he did in the first – two balls longer. The third ball of Lillee's first over swung away late from just outside off stump and was edged low towards the slips. Alderman at third slip again showed what a fine catcher he is by diving to his left to take a chance that would not have carried to the deeper-set second slip.

Gooch has now made 82 runs in six innings and would probably do better batting down the order at No. 4. However, there is no obvious replacement at the top of the order. Chris Tavaré is the closest contender, but an England top three of Boycott, Brearley and Tavaré would have all the watchability of a *One Man and his Dog* Telethon.

As Brearley came to the wicket, the batsmen were offered the light and accepted it with alacrity. The players were off for just over an hour.

Through the murk the electronic scoreboard flashed up Ladbrokes' latest odds: Australia were 1–4 to win, the draw was 5–2. An England victory? 500–1. A frisson of graveyard guffaws ran through the crowd. 'Ladbrokes love a bet', read a hoarding below the dressing rooms – at those odds I bet they do.

At five o'clock play briefly restarted. Two Lillee leg-cutters slipped past the outside edge of Brearley's bat, but he did manage to ease a half-volley away to the boundary for England's first runs.

During the fifth over the players went off for bad light. The crowd sat patiently, reassured by the knowledge that play could continue to 7 o'clock and by the sight of the cloud cover starting to break up.

Out came the umpires just before 6 o'clock with their light meters. The light was still poor, but rapidly improving. Ten minutes later the ground was flooded with sunshine, but there was no sign of the players. Eventually it was explained that the rules only allow an extra hour's play if conditions are good enough at 6 o'clock. If they are not but then quickly get better, as happened here, bad luck.

It is a stupid rule, both captains said so, and a thoroughly pissed-off crowd were sent away from Headingley thinking that English cricket is played by incompetents and administered by imbeciles. It is hard to disagree.

Unlike at Lord's, the umpires were not to blame. They were only following orders. However, this is a meaningless explanation to most spectators. An angry crowd gathered in front of the pavilion as umpire Meyer tried to explain the unexplainable. He was shouted down.

Four men shouldered their way into the pavilion demanding to see the umpires. Perhaps they wanted to complain about the evening's farrago. Alternatively, they may have been Alec Bedser and his fellow selectors – heavily disguised – ensuring that England would suffer no more that night.

If you're coming to Headingley on Monday don't forget your sackcloth and ashes.

England first innings

G.A. Gooch lbw b Alderman	2
G. Boycott b Lawson	12
J.M. Brearley c Marsh b Alderman	10
D.I. Gower c Marsh b Lawson	24
M.W. Gatting lbw b Lillee	15
P. Willey b Lawson	8
I.T. Botham c Marsh b Lillee	50
R.W. Taylor c Marsh b Lillee	5
G.R. Dilley c&b Lillee	13
C.M. Old c Border b Alderman	0

R.G.D. Willis not out	1
Extras (b6, lb 11, w6, nb11)	34
Total	174

Fall of wickets: 1–12, 2–40, 3–42, 4–84, 5–87, 6–112, 7–148, 8–166, 9–167

	O	M	R	W
Lillee	18.5	7	49	4
Alderman	19	4	59	3
Lawson	13	3	32	3

England second innings

G.A. Gooch c Alderman b Lillee	0
G. Boycott not out	0
J.M. Brearley not	4
Extras (nb2)	2
Total (1 wkt)	6

Fall of wickets: 1–0

	O	M	R	W
Lillee	3.2	2	4	1
Alderman	2	2	0	0

Eyewitness

John Dyson: Alderman was much more successful than the English seamers because he bowled a tremendous line and moved the ball just enough.

Christopher Martin-Jenkins [on BBC TV]: A wonderful sight to see Botham hitting the ball with the same old freedom. It really looks as if the shackles have dropped from his shoulders.

Graham Dilley: Botham's change of mood was obvious to everybody. It was almost as if you'd taken a child – made him an adult for a while – then allowed him to go back to being a child.

Ian Botham: When my luck turned, people said it was obvious that responsibility had ruined my game. It was rubbish. Even Brearley said I was happy again and that I was laughing hugely. If I was laughing it was because I was in form again.

Mike Brearley: Brian Close, sitting beside me on the balcony, reckoned that Ian lost concentration after making 50. I didn't agree. If you set yourself to attack on such a pitch and the ball behaved oddly you had to be lucky to miss it.

Richie Benaud [on BBC TV]: Quite rightly, Kim Hughes has asked England to bat again.

Peter Philpott: We discussed batting again in the dressing room. But Kim and the senior players all thought that England looked so broken that now was the time to rub it in. Enforcing the follow-on was the last thing their batsmen would want us to do.

Dennis Lillee: When it was decided to make England follow on I immediately had my doubts, because I felt it would be very hard to bat on that wicket on the last day. Also, I didn't think England would bat as badly again.

Mike Brearley: We were not surprised when Hughes invited us to follow on. The Sunday rest day meant his exhausted bowlers could rest. My view is that as a captain you may hesitate before enforcing a follow on; but you do it.

Graham Dilley: Nobody was surprised when we got bowled out for 174. Some of us thought we'd done quite well.

Things were taking their natural course towards a defeat. The control of the game had been taken away from us. It was up to the Australians when the game was going to finish. Because, as well as we might play, we were never going to get into a position from which we were going to win the game.

Graham Gooch: I went in late in the day and was caught at slip by Terry Alderman off Dennis Lillee. Then they immediately came off for bad light. The light hadn't deteriorated during the over – so I had been dismissed in unfit conditions. I wasn't best pleased.

I was always very critical of my own performance. If I wasn't playing well or not contributing to the side I used to get upset with myself. When I got back into the dressing room I remember telling Peter Willey that maybe I should take a break from Test cricket.

David Ryder, Secretary Yorkshire CCC: When the umpires called off play for the day because of bad light, we had a stream of people trying to get hold of them to protest about it. We had to put some stewards to block the stairs up to the umpires' room.

Mike Brearley: I was certain that we would lose unless it rained for a day or more.

Frank Crook, The [Australian] *Sun*: On the Saturday evening Patrick Eagar took a picture of the Australian press men standing on the pavilion balcony. We were all grinning and smiling. I look at the picture now and think: 'Jeez, it was all downhill from there.'

Dennis the Menace feeds Rod the God

At least an end to the suffering is in sight. They'll probably still be plaguing Poms the winter after next, but come July 1985, when the next Ashes debate in England has run half its course, Dennis Lillee will be 36 and Rod Marsh 37. It is reasonably certain, therefore, that this summer will mark the last hurrah in Tests on these shores for cricket's most dynamic duo. Sentimental as the English can be, they will not be missed, at least not until a decent period of respite has elapsed – say a decade or two. Never in the history of Anglo–Antipodean conflict, after all, have so many been bullied by so few.

On Saturday they struck nine times between them and twice in harness, their 73rd and 74th collaborations. As Ian Botham made for the pavilion, Lillee clasped his pal around the head, removed his cap and threw it in the air. The ball before, ironically, Marsh had conceded four byes, a rare blemish. The crowd bit its lip and did the decent thing, although the applause did seem more out of gratitude for that brief sighting of the chap we used to call Beefy.

Were they asked to choose between doing without the elder Chappells or the joined-at-the-hip WA boys – at least one of the quartet has been on each of the five Ashes tours since 1964 – the Australian selectors would hum and haw and eventually plump, one trusts, for FOT and Rowdy. Given the ACB's frequently-aired disapproval of Lillee and Marsh, which the end of WSC did little to subdue, it is not as if they lacked a motive to dispense with their services. That the board recognised how crucial those services are, and were prepared to overlook their prejudices (albeit not so far as the captaincy goes), speaks volumes even Motorhead would blanch at.

Knott v Marsh

Nevertheless, there were many of the 14,600 at Headingley – and not solely Kent fans – who will maintain that, both as specialist gloveman and all-rounder, Alan Knott is Marsh's superior. They cannot be dismissed lightly. 'Knotty' is definitely defter standing up to the spinners, although the fact that approximately three-quarters of his 93 Tests have seen him conspire with Derek Underwood and/or Ray Illingworth has, admittedly, given him that much more opportunity to hone his touch. Marsh's most regular abettor in this respect, Ashley Mallett, played his 38th and farewell Test last year, taking only 32 wickets in his last 15 outings; rarely indeed did he have the luxury of a partner.

Knott also boasts a higher batting average and more centuries. Only three keepers to date have ever emerged from a Test series brandishing 250 runs and 20 dismissals: South Africa's John Waite (263 and 26 v New Zealand, 1961–62), Denis Lindsay (606 and 24 v Australia, 1966–67) and Knott (364 and

Day one

Grey Day – Proceedings at Headingley begin in characteristic manner, with ball moving sideways and clouds shifting bucketloads. Spectators would be somewhat less amenable when play finished early on the Saturday, hurling cushions as well as abuse.

... Botham, Taylor and Hughes look on as John Dyson plays Peter Willey to leg during his painstaking but invaluable century.

Day two

Above: **Take It On The Run** – The dangers of the pitch are apparent as Bob Willis inconveniences Hughes with one barely short of a length. Australia's captain went on to grind out a gritty 89 – a far cry from the attacking batsman who lit up the 1980 Centenary Test.

Left: **New Life** – Returning to the ranks, Botham grabbed five wickets as Australia moved towards a declaration, then scored 50; his first such all-round contribution since he inherited the captaincy, a job many felt he should never have been burdened with.

Day three

Piece of the Action – Geoff Lawson, junior member of Australia's pace trio, claimed three key victims as England folded 227 behind, among them Boycott, bowled by an extraordinary delivery that pitched well outside off. Still, it was the old warhorse, Lillee (below), who did the most damage with his 4 for 49 and garish headband.

All Stood Still – Lillee and Marsh appeal successfully against Mike Gatting, lbw as usual. Eyes lit up in unison when Australia's finest double act saw the 500-1 odds against England glaring from the electronic scoreboard.

Day four

You Might Need Somebody (revisited) –
England follow on and crumble again as
Boycott (left) almost loses his head to Lillee ...

... and David Gower edges
Alderman to Allan Border:
37 for 3.

Stray Cat Strut – Graham Dilley's motto, 'If it's on stumps block it, if not, welly it,' lifted
the gloom. 'The highlight of the series to date,' said Trevor Bailey on *Test Match Special*
of his alliance with Botham. 'Yes,' retorted Henry Blofeld, 'but it's not going to alter the
result ...'

One Day In Your Life – Prodded into action by Dilley, Botham began to chance his arm, the frequent mishits and edges only just eluding fielders ...

... but as partnership grew and deficit shrank, so he grew in authority, seldom attempting (right) to disguise his pleasure ...

... and abracadabra, come evening (below), he was still in command, itching to secure the strike for the following morning.

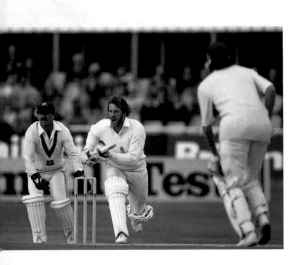

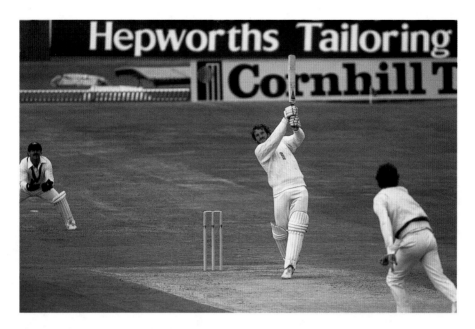

I Don't Need This Pressure On – 'Botham's innings was one of such astonishing aggression it must be wondered who he was actually thrashing,' mused Allen Synge. 'Could it be that Ian had (Chairman of Selectors) Alec Bedser in his sights?'

Spellbound – Botham celebrates his century: 'I had no idea whether we were ahead or behind. I batted like a maniac because our position was so hopeless. I suppose someone who isn't a gambler would not have dared so much, but more fool them.'

Lay All Your Love On Me – Hero and public at stumps, reality suspended. That the match was going into a final day left David Ryder, the Yorkshire Assistant Secretary, in a quandary: 'We had told most of the turnstile operators and stewards they needn't bother turning up.'

23 v Australia, 1974–75). To try to imagine any keeper bringing more lustre to his art than Knott did in the 1970–71 and 1977 Ashes series is to ask too much and expect nothing. Yet Marsh, arguably, has done more for the collective effort, rousing nobles and rabble with equal aplomb.

Rugged, roly-poly and roughneck, in demeanour as well as physique, he is more the archetypal village stumper than a suitable heir to the dapper likes of Don Tallon and Wally Grout. 'Forearms like coalminer's and legs like bollards', as Paul Sheahan so eloquently put it. Loyal to the last but definitely no kowtower or forelock-tugger, he looks as if he'd be happiest cradling a pint of Greene King, a wad of Old Holborn and a stash of Rizlas at the ready. There is a lot of the Staffordshire Bull about him, notably the bark.

'I'm this side of the line, you're that side and never the twain shall meet,' he pointed out tersely earlier in the tour when a spectator strayed inside the boundary and fielded the ball. 'If they do, I'll break your (blankety-blank) teeth.' As a cheerleader, nobody can touch him. Where Knott is a Jack-in-the-box, popping up as if on a spring and always pristine, Marsh is a scrum-half, a Sid Going, forever sniping and harrying and exhorting, grass-stains guaranteed. Never mind the language, feel the energy.

Bundled out for 77 by Queensland on a Perth greentop, WA, led by Marsh, were facing certain elimination from the 1976–77 Gillette Cup. The visiting order, after all, numbered not only Greg Chappell but Viv Richards. Marsh plotted Chappell's demise. Signalling for Lillee to bowl a bouncer down the legside, he took up a position

best described as widish leg slip and pouched the ensuing edged hook, leaving the batsman slack-jawed. Lillee, meanwhile, softened up the Antiguan, earning a warning for three consecutive bouncers, defiantly flinging down another, then bowling him two balls later when Richards missed a straight one. Queensland ultimately subsided for 62, pick-pocketed by a couple of rogues Fagin would have loved to have had on his payroll. They had also been out-thought by two of the galaxy's foremost cricketing brains.

Dedicated follower of passion

Lillee, himself on the brink of becoming the most prolific bowler in Ashes history, cites his initial inspiration as Wes Hall. He was 11 when, in 1960, he jumped the fence at the WACA to watch the Barbadian hurl his lightning bolts. He recalls being 'struck almost dumb by his awesome approach to the wicket and the way he could make the ball fly so fast and so far'.

Unusually, Lillee and his father have been 'mates' rather than the conventional *fils et père*, which may well account for that palpable absence of fear for authority figures. That notwithstanding, Len 'Pop' Halifax, his maternal grandfather, exerted the more profound influence. It was Pop who took part in all those front-lawn 'Tests', and whose motto took root in young Dennis's mind: 'If you can call up a second wind and be in control of your body, then your mind will be free to cope with the job ahead.' Those were the words that spurred the teenage Lillee to run laps after practice while his muckers mucked about, the first step on the road to the game's most scintillating action since … well, since Wesley Winfield Hall's medallion stopped flapping in the breeze.

Pop's homespun wisdom also ensured that, after his back rebelled in 1973, Lillee whipped himself to a virtual standstill before pronouncing his body fit to return to the fray, just as Marsh had worked out incessantly to divest himself of those spare tyres. Of necessity, that flowing, chillingly co-ordinated run-up was cut and the mechanics adjusted. The dedicated follower of passion became more upright, less leonine. Gone were the jiving elbows and jutting bum that made him appear to be dancing a new version of 'The Twist'. Gone, too, the rhythmic sway of the shoulders. Where once he rocked, now he rolled.

As a consequence, he was able not merely to survive, but to dominate. Only eight bowlers have taken 100 or more wickets at a rate of five per Test: England's Colin Blythe, Bobby Peel, George Lohmann and S.F. Barnes, Australia's Clarrie Grimmett, Bill O'Reilly, Charlie Turner – and Lillee. Of these, only Lillee and O'Reilly have been capped since 1936, and 'Tiger' was history by 1946, well before Test cricket became a truly competitive sport as opposed to an Anglo– Australian stitch-up. Aside from Lillee, furthermore, none of these worthies purveyed their wares at above medium pace. And none came within even 60 victims of the 278 currently bulging Lillee's jolly swagbag.

He has not, it is true, come within a metric mile of his best either here or at Lord's, where that first-innings return of 0–102 was as unflattering as any he has sustained. Squint long enough at that infernal headband and he turns into one of those ageing New Yorkers who thinks it hip to jog around Central Park with a pacemaker. Yet, ailing or not, he continues to hold Englishmen, batsmen especially, in complete and utter thrall. Even though it threatened neither body nor stumps, Botham was drawn towards the ball that gave Marsh his historic 264th dismissal as if magnetised, as if he had no say in the matter. When desires as strong as Marsh and Lillee's fuse, what chance those of even fractionally less passion?

Mike Brearley, on the other hand, may be relieved he had no say over the day's major bone of contention, namely the follow-on. Peter Philpott, on *Test Match Special* betrayed doubts. 'It's hard to throw away the advantage of the follow-on,' he acknowledged, 'but I don't think I'd like to be batting last. The last day could be very unpleasant. One hundred would be gettable, 150 would be impossible and anything in-between would be interesting.'

Not-so-smart Alec

Alec Bedser reminds us of the heard-but-never-seen doorman in the American sitcom *Rhoda*, blunt and annoyingly savvy. He may have turned 63 a fortnight ago but the advancing years have not brought any discernible mellowing of that we–did–it–better–in–my-day crustiness, or any diminution of that disarmingly guile-free fondness for plain speaking. After more than a decade as chairman of selectors, during the course of which he has overseen a decline of almost Roman proportions, who, in all honesty, can blame him? The pitch is a good one, he insisted; his boys simply hadn't been up to scratch. Agreeing with the latter, though, is a good deal simpler than justifying the former.

The ball from Geoff Lawson that did for Geoff Boycott was a viper of a thing, creeping and hissing its way to the stumps after pitching outside off; this was not the act of a trustworthy surface, hence Philpott's fears. For Gower and Co. to fuel them further, nonetheless, they will first have to bat out of their proverbial skins. On recent evidence, this seems only marginally more likely than Robert De Niro playing one of the principals in the rumoured Michael Winner-Lou Grade remake of *Little Women*.

Drowning sorrows

Epworth is a village outside Scunthorpe, best known for being the birthplace of John Wesley.

It is also Ian Botham's refuge from an increasingly hostile world and the venue for his traditional barbecue held on the Saturday of the Headingley Test. Since Sunday was a rest day, hair could be let down and pints sunk without worrying, too much, about how you'd feel in the morning.

Botham, ever the convivial host, had invited the Australian as well as the English players to join his family and friends, many of whom were Epworth locals. The event required much organisation, with guests, as David Gower remembers, being 'billeted out at Both's sister-in-law's, the nanny's sister's place, what have you'.

The Australians arrived cock-a-hoop according to Peter Willey: 'Oh yeah, they were in a good mood all right. They expected game, set and match on Monday really.' Kim Hughes's men had other reasons to celebrate too. It was Dennis Lillee's 32nd birthday and Rod Marsh had just broken the record for Test dismissals by a wicketkeeper. The record-breaking victim was his host for the evening.

The England players were, in contrast, as happy as Marvin the Paranoid Android, sullen star of the new radio hit *The Hitchhiker's Guide to the Galaxy*. Despite that, once the wine and beer began to flow, even the Englishmen began to enjoy themselves. Willey's memory is of 'a very good night' where 'everybody had a fair amount to drink and the food was good'.

Likewise, Gower recalls the 'enormous barbecue' and, 'as is usually the case when Ian is entertaining, enormous amounts to drink'. He also remembers spending his time 'attempting to forget three dreadful days', and how refreshing it was 'to have different people around'.

'The mood was fatalistic,' he adds. 'We thought we might as well enjoy ourselves, enjoy the night.'

Bob Willis and his wife, Julie, also found the party 'a thoroughly sociable event'.

As the party got into full swing, all kinds of Botham-inspired mayhem kicked off. A video of the event shows one guest weaving through the throng pushing a wheelbarrow with another enjoying the ride. Willis recalls dancing with Botham and the first part of the evening ended with the England and Australian players locked in a huge rugby scrum on the lawn.

Around midnight most of the Aussies, having enjoyed what Graeme Wood claims was 'a very friendly atmosphere', headed back to their hotel. Allan Border and his wife, Jane, stayed and would have watched and listened as many of the England players contemplated their futures.

According to Willey: 'There were quite a few England players there who thought Headingley would be their last Test match. They thought that if they didn't do anything in the second innings, that would be it. I was one of them. I expected to be dropped.' The bowlers were particularly depressed, knowing that their chances of having another go at the Australian batsmen were very slim. 'Willis knew this Test was make or break for him,' says Willey.

Gower remembers the drinking going on until three or four in the morning and that Botham was, as usual, the last to bed. Wayne Larkins, who had replaced John Emburey as 12th man in the squad, remembers little. 'It's all a bit of a blur really,' he admits. 'We downed pint after pint and most of us could not even remember where we flaked out.'

Graham Dilley awoke with a splitting headache, but a desire for adventure. 'Some of Both's neighbours had these quad bikes,' he recalls with a guilty grin. 'I can remember nearly driving this thing into a great big ditch full of water. That would have looked good, wouldn't it?!'

Most of the other partygoers had more peaceful pastimes in mind for the rest day.

Chris Old had invited Mike Gatting to his home for Sunday lunch. The plan seemed doomed when Chilly's wife had to go into hospital to have a cyst lanced, but Old's mother-in-law stepped into the breach. Afterwards, a replete and happy Gatting dozed in the armchair, dreaming no doubt of dodgy lbw decisions and second-innings heroics.

Back in Epworth, the late sleepers stirred. 'We had a quiet, typically English Sunday,' recalled Willis. 'A couple of lunchtime pints in the local followed by a roast lunch and an afternoon nap. The Test was hardly discussed, although when the subject did arise we were unanimous in thinking that it would be over well before the end of Monday's play.'

Botham inspires awe, but not victory

Australia still favourites

England have scored 351 for the loss of nine wickets in their second innings and lead by 124

On the day the Manx judiciary defied the European Court of Human Rights to order the first birching on the Isle of Man for five years, Ian Botham attacked the Australian bowling with such savagery that Kim Hughes could also reasonably look to Strasbourg for salvation.

But just as the 16-year-old Scottish youth facing the birch is forecast to receive a less medieval sentence on appeal, so the Australians will expect justice to deliver them victory on Tuesday in a match they have dominated for all but two of its 24 hours.

The 120 minutes of English supremacy came after tea in a session which had about as much in common with the rest of the match as a night out in downtown Toxteth does with the school run in Slough.

At the end of play, Botham, 145 not out, ran from the field mobbed by boys all apparently wearing the same brown-striped tank top and cheered by a crowd frantically waving Royal Wedding Union Jacks. However, the air of surreal euphoria couldn't disguise the fact that England are still only 124 runs ahead of Australia with one wicket left to fall. The odds on an England victory may have shortened from the Ladbrokes quote of 500–1, but they are still longer than those on

Charles and Diana spending their honeymoon sightseeing in Afghanistan.

The day had started under cloudy skies with drizzle in the air and a muggy atmosphere promising swing for the Australian bowlers. The ground was sparsely populated. The 2000-odd anorak-and-jumper-clad spectators were subdued, rugs wrapped around knees, the Monday-morning blues not lifted by the prospect of a day off work. If you closed your eyes, you would have sworn you could hear the strains of this week's number one single, The Specials' *Ghost Town*, drifting spectrally across the empty acres of the Western Terrace.

Boycott and Brearley faced the inevitable opening attack of Lillee and Alderman. The Yorkshireman lives for this kind of situation and he began to carefully construct his innings, encouraged by quiet mutterings of approval from the Headingley faithful. Brearley, too, looked like he might stick around, but after 15 minutes' play and with England's score on 18, he pushed forward to a nasty lifting delivery from Lillee which cut away from him and was caught low down at third slip by the ubiquitous Alderman.

Weird is the best word for Gower's innings. After spending more than half an hour on nought, he took nine from a Lillee over. He then played a firm-footed square push to the first ball of the next over from Alderman and was caught by Border, the second of the bowler's five slips. Gower had survived countless jaffas from Lillee and Alderman, but could do little about this delivery. It pitched on middle-and-leg and moved a foot to take the outside edge. Initially it looked like a typical Gower dismissal – fishing outside the off stump – but this time the bowler should take most of the credit.

With the ball swinging like a jazz band on Bourbon Street, Gatting was always a likely lbw candidate. Alderman knew this, of course, and bowled a sharp in-ducker, which was doubly difficult to play when it scuttled through low. Gatting moved forward too early and, misjudging the line, placed his left leg too far outside off stump. Because of this misjudgement he could not swing his bat through the line of the ball and was forced to play across it. The ball hit him on the back pad and he was on his way – lbw for the fifth time in the series. Gatting expressed surprise at the appeal, but as he was bent double, legs spread wide, feet pigeon-toed and with his bat facing towards fine leg, his attempt to influence the umpire carried little authority. The ball might well have been slipping down leg side, but if so the decision was still a victory for aesthetics as well as good bowling. England were 41–4 and a pall of despair settled over Headingley in a familiar, comfortable fashion.

With nearly an hour to go before lunch, the crowd began to wonder what delights Leeds city centre might offer on a Monday afternoon. Willey was nearly caught at slip first ball, but then began to bat well. He has the tenacity if not the technique of Boycott and when he plays at his very best, as he did in Antigua earlier this year, he has the buccaneering swagger of a Greenidge.

Willey managed to keep Boycott company until 1 o'clock. He played a couple of trademark cuffs through the offside, the jut of his jaw and his muscular forearms making him look like a cricketing Popeye. Even the raised left leg as he cut gave the impression of a man batting on the tilting deck of a ship.

At lunch, England were 78–4, still 149 behind. Boycott had made 35 during the session, Willey 12 in 52 minutes.

Lillee snares Ashes record

After the interval Boycott and Willey took their stand past the 42 added by Gower and Gatting in the first innings – until then the biggest partnership between English batsmen in the match.

As the partnership grew, spectators were diverted by the bizarre sight of the England captain chatting animatedly to Rodney Hogg on the players' balcony. Perhaps the sight of his skipper clearly enjoying the company of the man who had so tormented English batsmen two-and-a-half years ago disturbed the normally implacable Willey too?

First he glanced Lillee for four, no mean feat for a man with a stance facing towards mid-on, before cutting a short delivery over the slips for another boundary. In Lillee's next over, the bowler placed Dyson at fly slip, two-thirds of the way to the third-man boundary. His next delivery was short outside the off stump, cutting into the batsman. Willey played another upper-cut, but was cramped by the late movement and could only chip the ball straight into Dyson's hands. If Willey was capable of blushing he would have left the field redder than Toyah's latest barnet.

Willey's dismissal gave Lillee 142 wickets in Ashes matches. This broke the record held by the Australian Golden Age off-spinner Hugh Trumble, whose 141 Test wickets all came against England – the last in 1904. Trumble took 31 Tests to reach his tally, Lillee 25 to go one better.

Lillee bowled much better than on Saturday. His low, raking run to the wicket still gets the blood surging, the action is as beautiful as ever, the chest hair bursting through the unbuttoned shirt is even thicker and his roof-raising appeals forever the most dramatic. However, this fearsome image is a little spoilt by the hair spilling up over his headband – which makes him look like a particularly angry shaving brush – and a taste for flared flannels.

The talk around the ground was all of Boycott getting to 95 and therefore passing Colin Cowdrey's total of 7624 runs to become England's highest scorer in Tests. The Yorkshireman was in a world of his own, his partners' indiscretions and failures throwing his own success into ever sharper relief. As ever, Boycott's whites were immaculate and his concentration absolute. He rode Lillee's short-pitched deliveries, left elbow high, and was solidly behind Alderman's snaking swingers. Self-absorbed? Yes, but this time it suited his team.

At 2.15, 35 minutes into the afternoon session, Botham strode to the crease. His arrival at the wicket raised the first English cheer of the day, but there was little chance to play to the gallery with Boycott taking most of the strike. Fitzwilliam's finest must have reckoned that the chances of Botham deliberately running him out for scoring too slowly – as it is alleged he did three years ago in New Zealand – were pretty slim in the circumstances.

Eventually Botham did get going, striking three boundaries in reaching 22 from 31 balls as the England score increased by 28. Then, disaster. Alderman snapped yet another delivery towards Boycott's pads and appealed as it struck his left leg, the batsman's forward movement for once a little indecisive. 'Leg-side, leg-side', the hushed mantra ran through the crowd, but Meyer didn't agree – Boycott lbw 46 after three-and-a-half hours of almost flawless defensive batting. He had hit just one boundary, but will be reasonably pleased with his scoring rate of a run every third delivery on such a devil of a pitch and against such skilled opponents. He will be less happy with the umpire's decision.

Well before the crowd, now grown to around 5000, had even begun to get over the shock, Alderman got yet another ball to jump alarmingly from a length. Taylor tried to fend it off, but simply succeeded in dollying it into Bright's hands at short leg. England were 135–7, 92 runs behind with three wickets left.

And then, with half an hour to go before tea, something strange happened.

The mood of the match suddenly lightened. The weather brightened and the Australians relaxed, confident of an easy victory and a day off. The crowd – freed from the exquisite torture of willing Boycott to the Test record – decided to loosen up. The batsmen too – mindful of Hughes's words on Sunday that 'sooner or later the pitch will get you' – decided to have a dash. In the words of the latest TV catchphrase, everyone was 'game for a laugh'.

Dilley ignites the fuse

It was Dilley, curly blond hair spilling out from under his blue helmet, who responded first. Planting his front foot around middle stump he swung with all his might at anything pitched on the off. His first few attempts met nothing more than thin air, but he kept trying, perhaps egged on by a grinning Botham at the other end. When Dilley did make contact, thumping the ball through the covers, Botham leant on his bat and laughed out loud. They were shots straight from the pages of *Boy's Own*, stand and deliver thwacks which had the ball pinging off the boundary boards.

Not a lot is expected of Dilley with the bat; his record of 11 runs in 7 innings during the recent West Indies tour is often quoted against him. But he knows how to play against anything except extreme pace and entered this match averaging 40 for the series.

Of the first 27 runs the pair added, the left-handed Dilley made 22. But Botham, bareheaded and with his collar rakishly worn outside his sweater, was warming to the task. On 32 he escaped a hard chance to Bright in the gully as he unfurled a sledgehammer square cut.

A few minutes later a mix-up had the non-striker Dilley stranded halfway down the pitch and Botham dithering just outside his crease. In the confusion the livewire Chappell swooped and unleashed a fierce throw at the striker's end, missed the stumps and saw the ball disappear over the midwicket boundary. A gentle lob to the bowler's end would have seen Dilley out by 10 yards. For a fielding specialist it was a bad mistake. Dilley and Botham met in the middle and laughed about their mutual escape.

On the players' balcony, Brearley and Hogg went their separate ways. England at tea were 176–7, still 51 runs behind. Dilley had contributed 25 to a stand of 41 in 36 minutes.

When play resumed Botham and Dilley junked the logic of the match and sailed into the Australian bowling. In the 30 minutes following the interval they scored at two runs a minute, Dilley driving with due flair and abandon and Botham seemingly willing to dislocate his shoulders every time he played a shot, such was the force of his strokeplay. Botham reached his second 50 from 57 deliveries. Next ball, a thick outside edge screamed to the third-man boundary and England took the lead.

Dilley was not to be outdone. He all but went down on one knee to cream Lillee through the off side for four. The incredulous bowler marched back to his mark and came racing in again, only to see the ball vanish in near identical fashion, this time a little squarer. Tired of this latest piece of styling, Dilley instead leant back at a crazy angle to drill a couple more boundaries into the offside boundary boards.

The Australian bowlers maintained a consistent line outside the off stump, appearing to believe that the lift and movement they had generated all match was bound to eventually defeat the batsmen. Instead, good-length balls simply disappeared back past the bowler or through midwicket. Dilley missed the short-pitched deliveries, but Botham sliced them over the slips, crashed them square and once even played the most delicate of late cuts.

These were showman's shots, the best coming when Botham charged Alderman and slammed a respectable length delivery over mid-on for six. As the ball rebounded onto the outfield, the ground rocked with awed laughter. Botham's wife Kathy looked on beaming, revelling in her husband's resurrection. Her two companions looked much less happy, but that's probably because they were Jane Border and Angela Wood.

Botham's power, too, was awesome. One attempted hook hit the splice and still landed one bounce where a deep mid-on would have been standing. Even more astounding was another hook that ended up going for four through mid-off. The match's imaginary theme tune had changed from *Ghost Town* to *Chariots of Fire*.

Dilley flayed Lillee through extra cover to bring up his first Test 50, his innings developing the momentum of a runaway train. Alderman then decided to go round the wicket to cramp Dilley's expansive off-side shots. It worked. Dilley, playing one vast drive too many, was bowled off his inside edge, the ball just trimming the bails. He had made 56 from just 75 balls,

nine of which he hit for four. He and Botham had added 117 in 80 breathless minutes, England rushing from 150 to 250 in just 14 overs. The stand was seven runs short of the English record for the eighth wicket against Australia, but for the purity of its hitting and its sheer unexpectedness it was in a class of its own.

Alderman was by now clearly exhausted, but he was rewarded for his marathon spell with a five-wicket bag, the second in a three-match Test career.

Botham's century

Surely the match was over now? With an hour-and-a-quarter's play still remaining, England were just 25 runs ahead with two wickets left.

But Old is an uncomplicated and talented striker of the ball – with seven first-class centuries. Like Dilley he is also a left-handed batsman and the constant need to switch their line undermined the effectiveness of the Aussie bowlers, especially as they began to tire. Like England on the first two days they began to pitch too short. Some in the press box also thought the pitch's uneven bounce was disappearing, but again this was probably a product of the weary bowlers being unable to put their back into most deliveries.

By now Botham was playing like a man possessed (possibly by the spirit of Gilbert Jessop), and blazing a trail towards his century like the US Space Shuttle on afterburner. The only man who appeared to be taking it all in his stride was Lillee, still attending to his fan club down on the third-man boundary, reeling off autograph after autograph.

With Botham on 95 and the crowd roaring, Somerset's pride and joy hit Lawson for consecutive boundaries. Pandemonium. As Botham raised his bat towards the England dressing room and his applauding team-mates, Brearley stopped clapping and began jabbing his finger towards the century-maker. The message was clear: 'Stay there.' Botham, grinning, flicked an impudent V-sign at his skipper. He was not going to let up for anyone.

Botham's 103 came from 87 balls and took two hours and 35 minutes. The 64 runs he had scored since tea included 14 fours, a six and just two singles. His second 50 took just 30 balls and 40 minutes. Only one other man has ever scored a century and taken five wickets in an Ashes Test – the Australian Jack Gregory at Melbourne in 1921. It is the fourth time in his Test career that Botham has made 100 and taken five wickets in an innings, twice as many as any other player has managed ... and he's only 25!

Old's reputation is as a destroyer of medium pace and slow bowling who gives himself too much room on the leg side, exposing his stumps, against the quicks. But his determination to stay in line and support Botham was clear from the start. Soon he too was picking the right ball to hit and almost keeping pace with Botham.

As the lead passed 50, the romantics in the crowd (and press box) began to speculate on what England might need to make a game of it. The general consensus was that a target of around 180 would be challenging. Realists suggested that England's best chance was to establish a lead of around 150 and rely on the unsettled weather forecast for Tuesday to scrape a draw.

With the score at 309–8, Bright, the man who had dismissed Botham first ball the last time he had bowled to him, was introduced into the attack. The pitch was now producing puffs of dust when the ball pitched in the bowlers' footholds, but this does not suit the slow left-armer as much as the pace-men. Bright's selection ahead of Hogg appears, with hindsight, to have been a tactical blunder.

However, Hughes should have brought Bright into the attack sooner, especially when it was clear that Botham and Dilley had targeted the still relatively inexperienced Alderman. Dilley, as a left-hander, in particular would have been vulnerable to the spinner pitching the ball into the rough outside his off stump.

The Australian skipper must have been mentally kicking himself when, at Bright's second delivery, Botham took an almighty swing only to see the ball miss both his off stump and Marsh's gloves by a fraction. The ball ran away for four byes – Bright's hands in the air and Marsh staring at the ground in a frozen tableau of disappointment.

Alan Knott sent Marsh champagne on Saturday when he beat the Kent man's Test dismissals record. Assuming it's still unopened – and with Marsh of course that's a big if – it will have to stay on ice a little longer.

Lawson's beamers

Once again the atmosphere in the ground changed. The crowd's carefree enjoyment of the audacious, sometimes reckless batting was replaced by thoughts of avoiding defeat that most scarcely dared to express. The boundaries were still cheered by the increasingly hoarse spectators, but their appreciation of Botham's defensive technique, which remained classical between the butchery, was growing as quickly as England's lead. When, with his score on 109, a mis-hook was finger-tipped by a leaping Marsh, hearts vibrated alarmingly in a thousand ribcages. The catch was a hard one, but the Aussie keeper will regret not trying to increase his reach by going for the chance one-handed.

With the lead closing in on 100, Old finally returned to his bad habits and retreated towards square leg as Lawson ran in. Cleverly, Lawson delivered a slowish yorker and Old's leg stump went for a walk. Old had made 29 from just 33 balls, hit six fours and together with Botham added 67 in 54 minutes. With only Willis to come and England just 92 ahead, any miracle escape for the home team seemed likely to be stillborn.

But the Australians' mood had changed too. Their wry amusement at the Botham/Dilley stand had given way to frustration with a batting assault which appeared a direct challenge to their dominance of the game and the series.

The Australian attack was now coming apart at the seams. The bowlers could not hide their exhaustion and Hughes, more than ever, looked like an eager but frightened young officer trying vainly to rally his tough but weary troops for one last effort. He pointed and gesticulated, walked with the bowlers back to their mark delivering advice and held conferences with the stern-faced senior NCO Marsh. Until this last session, Hughes seemed to have an easy rapport with his bowlers. But no longer. The irritated look on Lillee's face as he turned away from Hughes and his advice said it all.

For the final 20 minutes of the day, the crowd held its breath. Botham was now playing with the assurance of a Hammond or a May, although the starstruck crowd probably saw him more as a combination of Flash Gordon and Magnum PI.

The Tom Selleck lookalike kept the majority of the strike, while continuing to slaughter the stunned Australian bowlers. Willis had to face just five balls. Botham powered on to 145, lifting himself onto his toes and sometimes off them as his shots took on an even greater majesty. Seven Australian fielders were forced back onto the boundary. The only scare came from the last ball of the day when Botham called Willis through for a risky single to retain the strike, and the fast bowler hesitated in mid-pitch like a startled giraffe before lurching home.

By close of play Botham and Willis had added 32 runs, the latter's contribution a solitary single. England finished 124 ahead. In the two hours after tea they had added 175 runs, with Botham scoring 106 of them, in just 27 overs – a rate of six-and-a-half runs an over. In all, Botham hit 26 fours and that performance-defining six from 137 deliveries. All the Australian bowlers, apart from Bright, had disappeared at a run a ball or more. It was Botham's seventh Test century, his second against Australia and his highest score in 38 Tests, beating the 137 he made against India on the same ground two years ago.

Botham ran from the field as quickly as he had sprinted the few singles that had been necessary during his three-and-a-half hours at the crease, the crowd surging around him as if England had already won the game. The Australian players dodged and shouldered their way back to the dressing room, their body language betraying the impact of Botham's onslaught. However, they are still strong favourites to win this match. To stop them it will take a lot of rain or another extraordinary performance to match Monday's. Once again, all eyes will be on Botham.

In the early evening sunshine the crowd gathered below the England dressing room, cheering and calling for their hero. When he emerged they sang, 'For he's a jolly good fellow' – and so say all of us!

England second innings

G.A. Gooch c Alderman b Lillee	0
G. Boycott lbw b Alderman	46
J.M. Brearley c Alderman b Lillee	14
D.I. Gower c Border b Alderman	9
M.W. Gatting lbw b Alderman	1
P. Willey c Dyson b Lillee	33
I.T. Botham not out	145
G.R. Dilley b Alderman	56
C.M. Old b Lawson	29
R.G.D. Willis not out	1
Extras (b5, lb3, w3, nb5)	16
Total (9 wkts)	351

Fall of wickets: 1–0, 2–18, 3–37, 4–41, 5–105, 6–133, 7–135, 8–252, 9–319

	O	M	R	W
Lillee	24	6	93	3
Alderman	34	6	131	5
Lawson	23	4	96	1
Bright	4	0	15	0

Eyewitness
Before Botham

Willey c Dyson b Lillee 33
Peter Willey: I was going quite well. I was in with Boycott, we had put a few on and we were getting a bit of control back. I felt in quite good form and I was hitting the ball well. Then Lillee set a sort of bouncer trap and I hit it straight down short third man's throat. I was going to play the shot anyhow, but it swung in on me a little bit. Of course, I looked an absolute prat. They set everything up and I chopped it straight down his throat. I didn't say much to Both as we crossed, just: 'Good luck'. It's not what I'd said to him in the past when he had played shots as stupid as the one I'd just played. Nobody in the dressing room was very nasty, but I was very down.
Richie Benaud [on BBC TV]: Hughes's decision to put Dyson at short third man is one of the best pieces of tactical thinking I've seen in a long time.

Boycott lbw Alderman 46
Barrie Meyer: Boycott was a bit upset that I gave him out lbw. He still reminds me about it 19 years later. But I've seen it lots of times since and it's still out.
Allan Border: We could smell the Ashes.
Mike Brearley: I decided to pack my bag and change. However, feeling that a striped shirt might be seen as too blatant an admission of defeat, I changed back into a cricket shirt.
Test Match Special **producer Dick Maddock:** Tea is over. I return you, for the last time I suspect, to Headingley.

Brian Johnston: What do you mean for the last time Madders? Only 51 to make Australia bat again. Cheers for the two England batsmen coming out.
Trevor Bailey [on *TMS* as England top 300 and Botham reaches his century]: This has been the highlight of the series to date.
Henry Blofeld: Yes, but it's not going to alter the result of the match.
Trevor Bailey: Well ... another 50-odd runs ...

After Botham

Peter Philpott: The Australian players were psychologically damaged by England's fightback – particularly by the way the tail showed no respect for bowlers like Lillee.
Allan Border: We were a bit stunned, but hardly demoralised. We reckoned if Botham could make 140 on his own, all of us should be able to make 130.
Bob Taylor: I went into the Australian dressing room that night. I needed to get some bats signed – the usual kind of request that every team complies with automatically. The air was thick with swearing and general abuse at life and I could sense a feeling of defeatism. One of their players took it out on me: '**** off with your ******* bats.'

I reported back to the England lads that they seemed very down. I felt that the psychological balance had tipped our way.
Graham Dilley: The longer the England innings went on, the more it began to dawn on people that there was a chance that things might happen. But even so, if we bowled anything like we bowled in the first innings then it

wouldn't matter.

My mind kept going back to the first Test when they needed 130-odd to win. I managed to pick up a couple of wickets and they were struggling at one stage, but then they came through and won.

I thought: 'The way things have been going it's more likely that the same thing is going to happen again. We might pick up a few wickets, but getting the runs should be no problem the way we're performing.'
Pat Gibson [in the *Daily Express*]: The amazing Ian Botham had the mourners dancing in the aisles at Headingley last night with the greatest comeback since Lazarus.
Allen Synge: Botham's innings was one of such astonishing aggression it must be wondered who he was actually thrashing. Could it be that Ian had Alec Bedser in his sights?
Yorkshire CCC Secretary David Ryder: We had told most of the turnstile operators and stewards that they needn't bother turning up on Tuesday. We spent much of the evening doing a pretty swift ring-round. Not all of them were on the phone, so we were doing things like ringing neighbours and getting them to pop next door.
Chris Old: I left the ground and went to my village pub for some hand-pulled Tetleys. It was jam-packed. 'Now then, Chilly lad,' said one bloke, 'we've had a sweep on England and 20 per cent of the winnings will be there on the bar for you.' I'd been on a high but I was coming down and I didn't want to talk about it. After two-and-a-half hours of mental pressure, I needed to get away from it.

O Lucky Man

'You really are *unnecessarily* beautiful.' Thus did a teaching colleague bitch to Jenny in Kingsley Amis's *Take A Girl Like You*. In addition to being extraordinarily talented, Ian Botham, it could be argued, is an unnecessarily lucky young man. All the same, having spent the past 13 months plunging and plummeting, only a curmudgeon of the highest rank could begrudge him his braces-twanging fun.

One shot above all others encapsulated the mood of the Fates. In came Alderman, serving up a fullish-length ball a smidge outside off and swinging in, the self-same delivery that had yorked Botham so comprehensively at Trent Bridge. On that occasion he swiped across the line; this time he aimed a lavish off-drive, an even woollier effort. The ball skewed through midwicket for four, bringing him to 50. And so it went on, bowlers fried and battered by strokes from the textbook but mostly beyond, logic and context smithereened. Ironic at first, the cheers gradually rose in authenticity until they scaled Mount Hysteria. The slow burn was perfectly understandable. Even before England's second-innings spiral, *Sunday Observer* billboards were bragging the news all over Melbourne: 'Ashes Come Home'.

For a further précis, try the over from Lawson that spirited Botham to three figures. The first ball found him going forward, thinking about a quick single but wisely desisting as the bowler darted in. To the second he heaved and middled the breeze, playing well outside the ball; those three men manning the offside boundary were asking for it. The third saw him unwind for another ya-hoo only to be struck on the pads, the ball plopping in front of him. Now the field retreated further, to ensure Old remained on strike for the next over. The fourth ball produced a brutal pull, denied its due by Wood's sprawling dive. Cutting at the fifth, he bisected the fielders with a geometrist's precision, freezing the field and surging to 99. The next was carved with a trainee butcher's expertise, the ball screeching behind gully for four. Rupert Pupkin's maxim in *The King of Comedy* sprang to mind: 'Better king for a day than schmuck for a lifetime.' Kris Kristofferson, though, put it best: 'Freedom's just another word for nothing left to lose'...

As serendipity would have it, who should have been at the microphone on *Test Match Special* when Botham came in to bat but Henry Blofeld, the very chap who had accused him of bodily assault at Bermuda airport three months ago. 'He plays in such a way, he could be the man to get a biggish score and set Australia a target tomorrow,' intoned Blowers, more out of something positive to impart than any genuine faith. Then again, making monkeys of professional seers is the man's stock-in-trade, and the tea party that followed would have been far too populous for London Zoo to handle.

Into the confectionery stall

On the box, Christopher Martin-Jenkins, too, tempted fate. 'What a triumph it would be for him,' he said as

Botham marched in, 'If he could still be batting at 6 o'clock this evening.' Across the nation's motorways, otherwise sane men monitored events on their Blaupunkts and hoisted thumbs at each other. 'There's no point looking for that, let alone chasing it,' recommended Richie Benaud after one six. 'It's gone straight into the confectionery stall and out again.' Indelible memories are made of this.

Nit-pickers may be interested to learn that when Bruce Taylor, another strapping jack-of-several-trades, reached his century for New Zealand against the West Indies in 1969 off 83 balls, he had been in for 86 minutes. Botham, on the other hand, received one more ball yet had been at the crease for almost twice as long. Time, though, was a glorious irrelevance. To all intents and purposes, it had stopped. The final session was dreamlike, chimerical. Onlookers were suspended in a state of pure imagination, floating around on some surrealistic pillow, chortling at every blow. It was as if Kim Hughes had suddenly turned soppy, and agreed to relieve the meagre throng of its pain by inviting Brearley to play a benefit match for English cricket.

To suggest that Dilley and Old were mere appendages, that Botham could have done it without them, is, of course, poppycock. It ignores the not unsalient fact that cricket, unlike baseball, never lets a man bat on his own (and thank goodness for that: Bradman might have averaged 200). If anything, the junior partners seemed more secure. It could well be that Old peered down the pitch while Botham was flailing away and found himself gazing, not at the captain who hadn't wanted him in his team, but at the player he could have become, should have become – had he been favoured with a tad more luck and/or self-belief. Both he and Dilley undoubtedly suffer from a shortage of the latter, but Botham followed their lead. Yet had he not been there to inspire by reputation, front and bottle, to inject them with a dose from that bottomless reserve tank of conceit, would they have summoned the gumption to act as they did?

A bit of a giggle

What, then, of Hughes? Keeping the cordon well-stocked and leaving third man vacant may in retrospect seem like folly, yet – the way Botham and Dilley were playing – edges always seemed imminent. That they never came – or at least not in a guise that gave anyone other than Twizzle a hope in hell of intercepting them – is something no captain can bargain for. Even if he had summoned Bright earlier, that was scarcely a foolproof solution. The force, indubitably, was with the batsmen.

That feeling of impotence, however, will surely fade on Tuesday, even if English super-optimists are doubtless busy drawing encouragement from the way the tourists stuttered when set 132 at Nottingham. Even so, no matter how secure captain and crew feel about the final outcome, no matter that those raspberries blown at the laws of probability were essentially a bit of a giggle, a temporary distraction, they could easily leave scars on the collective psyche.

True Original

'Did he walk the 64 miles from Cowley to Southampton for a trial, carrying his bat, pads and all his personal belongings in a cricket bag on his shoulder? Could he tear a pack of cards across with his bare hands? Did he keep wicket for England wearing motor-cycle gauntlets? Was he one of the most savage strikers of the ball cricket has known? Did he once ride a motor bicycle at speed down the steps to the Bournemouth promenade? Did he once pull his bat away and breast down a bouncer from one of the fastest bowlers in the country? Did he once seize a well-known Yorkshire player by the front of his jacket with one hand and hold him over the well of a six-storey spiral staircase until he apologised for an alleged insult?'

John Arlott was thinking of George Brown, that Hampshire he-man of the 1920s, when he asked those self-pinching rhetorical questions in the latest issue of *Wisden Cricket Monthly*. What a pity he wasn't up in the *TMS* box to pay similar homage to another true original from the shires.

It was Brown who orchestrated that wondrous victory over Warwickshire in 1922, when Hampshire, hustled out

for 15, followed on 208 behind and piled up 521 thanks primarily to the keeper's 172, then dispatched their hosts for 158 – still the most miraculous *volte face* the game has ever witnessed.

Eerily enough, another Brown, Yorkshire's Jack, loomed large in the greatest escape in Test annals, second-top-scoring with 53 as England ran up 437 after following on at Sydney in 1894 and ultimately won by 10 runs. Botham, the owner of another singularly English name, reckons his side needs another 50 to make things 'interesting' – dare we anticipate such sorcery now? Come now, let's not get all Disneyfied. Besides, why be greedy?

Above and beyond transforming the course – if not the destination – of this match, Botham achieved something immeasurably more significant and more memorable. Not only did he erase those ingrained frowns, he gave Poms of all hues a reason to smile. And my, amid all this not-so-summery doom and gloomery, how we needed that. Top that, Chuck and Di.

'Let's give it some humpty'

It was never going to be 'we'll get 'em in singles'.

But when Graham Dilley walked out to bat at four minutes past three on that Monday afternoon, he found Ian Botham was not even thinking about the possibility of victory.

'Both asked me: "Have you checked out of the hotel yet?" I hadn't, because I thought it would be the wrong thing to do. He just looked at me and said: "I have, but I forgot to pay the extras bill, I hope I don't have to go back." I was, like, "Alright Ian, what are we going to do then?" "Play shots," he said. "The game's gone, just enjoy it. One ball or 20 balls, just enjoy it."'

Enjoying it was certainly on Botham's mind as he had strode out to bat 50 minutes earlier with what Mike Gatting remembers as 'a peculiar look in his eye'. Umpire Barrie Meyer takes up the story.

'When Botham came to the wicket at 105–5, I was standing at the bowler's end. One of his first shots was an edged drive over the heads of the slips for four. A little later he played a drive behind square for four, another drive – no contact – and then took a single to my end. As he arrived I suggested that it might be a good idea to have a look for a while. "That's what I've just done," he said.'

In contrast, enjoying himself, as you'll read elsewhere, wasn't big on Dilley's to-do list back in 1981. He was expecting, even hoping, to be dropped for the next match. 'When I wandered out in the second innings,' he remembers, 'I thought, "Well, this is it. This is the last time I'll be doing this for some considerable time."'

In that frame of mind, and with England in a hopeless position, Dilley was in no mood to hang around. Not that he expected to last long anyway. 'By the summer of 1981 I was a genuine tailender,' he claims, 'and if I did score runs against the Aussies it was more by luck than judgement.

'When I went to the crease at Nottingham in the first Test, Mike Gatting was batting well and for most of the hour I spent with him I simply tried to push a single as early as I could in each over. When he departed and Bob Willis followed first ball there was only Mike Hendrick left. I started to wind up since I knew the innings was not going to last much longer.

'It was one of those days when the slogging came off as we added 26, but I do not deserve any credit for my strokeplay, and to suggest that I could have become an all-rounder was well wide of the mark. But it did set the tone for how I was going to play in the rest of the games – it was just a case of carrying that on.'

As the England second innings at Headingley crumbled, Dilley had agreed a simple strategy with Chris Old on the players' balcony: 'If it's on stumps block it, if not, welly it.'

Out in the middle, Dilley followed

the plan to the letter and, with the ball threatening first feet, then forehead, Botham upped the ante even further.

'Come on,' he said to Dilley. 'You don't fancy hanging around on this wicket for a day and a half, do you? Let's give it some humpty.'

Dilley took him at his word and in their first half-hour together, the Kent man scored 25 to Botham's 16. At tea Botham joked that after his violent start he was now playing for a not out. Few believed him and after the interval he slammed into overdrive. 'Picca kept on hitting so I decided to join in,' related Botham.

However, Dilley reckons that the onslaught was sparked by Botham's realisation that his partner was catching him up – 'I don't think he was that pleased.'

But soon everybody was having fun, as Botham recalled: 'My golf clubs were in the boot. There was no pressure. Picca and I tried to see who could play the most idiotic stroke. He hit two booming off-drives off the inside edge to the boundary, real Chinese cuts. He laughed and so did I. We felt like men in a play, following a script someone else had written. Everything had a dreamy feeling about it, particularly since it happened so quickly. It was like a mad interlude in a serious drama.

'For four days batsmen had hardly been able to survive, Balls were lifting, cutting and shooting. You could be out at any moment. Suddenly we swiped and the score rattled up. We scarcely knew what we were doing. An air of unreality hung over it all. I had no idea whether we were ahead or behind – it was confusing. I batted like a maniac

because our position was so hopeless.

'I suppose someone who isn't a gambler would not have dared so much, but more fool them. Angels wouldn't have won that game for England.'

Dilley, too, recalls the air of unreality: 'For a period it became more like a benefit match, because what you did didn't matter. There was no game plan, just to see who could hit the ball the hardest. The lesson I learned was that you can perform better when you have a more relaxed attitude ... though I think I often went a little too far on the relaxation front.'

As the Botham and Dilley stand built, Hughes turned to his quickest bowler, Geoff Lawson. Dilley asked his batting partner for advice. 'I remember saying to Both, "Lawson is going to bounce me." He said: "Well, what are you going to do?" "Get under it?" I suggested, but he was having none of it and told me: "Nah, have a go at it".

'Lawson ran in and bounced me. I was all set up mentally to have a go, but when I hooked the ball it just missed my nose. I was wearing a borrowed helmet that didn't have a visor. It went through to Marsh and there were a few comments from behind. I thought, "There is no way that I'm trying that again."

'Richie Benaud said on the commentary: "I think he was through a little bit early on that one." It was the only time the great man has got anything wrong.'

With the partnership in full flow, Dilley saw the opposition begin to wilt. 'The Australians had got to the stage mentally where they thought, "This game's over." They thought I might come in and slog a quick 20, but that wasn't going to make any difference. They relaxed a little bit and once they'd done that it was difficult to get back into top gear. It wasn't obvious though – Lillee wasn't suddenly bowling 20 m.p.h. slower – but that was my impression.

'At the start if I had a waft and missed there were some fairly big smiles behind the stumps. You could see them thinking, "It's going to come soon, he's going to nick one in a minute." But as our partnership developed, if we missed one it was, "Jesus!" – hands going everywhere.'

Botham noticed the change in attitude too: 'They were bowling faster as they got angrier, but they started to lose control.'

From the commentary box one of Australia's greatest captains began to see things going badly wrong. 'It seemed to me that the Australians had no real plan for bowling to Botham,' said Richie Benaud. 'Botham is always at his best when he is given room for the stroke outside the off stump, never quite so certain when he is cramped for room with the ball moving in at him from short of a length and slightly outside off stump.'

According to Alec Bedser, the same criticism applied to the way the Aussies attacked Botham's partners. 'Lillee bowled like an idiot to Dilley and allowed him to get 50,' Bedser claimed. 'It makes me wonder about Lillee. Why did he keep bowling outside the off stump?'

Dilley himself agrees that the bowlers made it easier to counter-attack: 'There weren't that many deliveries that were that straight. There was always a little bit of width on them.'

John Dyson is less critical, but admits that the Australian attack was at fault: 'Botham and Dilley established a rhythm as the innings went on and we didn't try hard enough to break it up.'

Up on the players' balcony was the next man in, Old, sitting virtually on his own, watching Botham and Dilley tear the attack apart. His increasing nervousness was not helped by the antics of his captain. 'Brears was very upbeat, rushing round, getting very excited. I just wanted him to go away,' Old sighs.

Out on the field emotions were equally mixed.

'We still didn't think that we could win the game,' remembers Dilley, 'but we sensed that there was just a chance we might make them bat again. The change in the way the Aussies were reacting made you think something was going to happen. But nobody really pictured what actually was.'

With a crashing extra-cover drive Dilley brought up his first Test half-century. 'I didn't know what to do when I got to 50. It was a very quick bat up in the air, bat down again. The crowd were still clapping when I was taking guard for the next ball. I thought: "I really don't know what to do, I better get on with the game."'

Dyson looked on ruefully as the England No. 9 dismembered his team's previously dominant attack. 'Dilley wasn't good enough to nick the good balls, and he played some great shots to put away the bad ones.'

Once past the 50 mark, Dilley couldn't help but wonder about the chances of getting a hundred. 'I definitely thought I could go on,' he claims. As he pondered, Alderman decided to come round the wicket to the left-hander to restrict Dilley's freedom to swing his arms and continue to clout the ball through the off side. 'My biggest regret was not running down the pitch to Alderman's first ball round the wicket and trying to slog it. I didn't want him to go round the wicket, I had to find a way to get him to go back over. I thought about running down the pitch, but I didn't have the confidence to do it. I should have gone and asked Both.'

Dilley stuck to swinging from the crease, but Alderman's new line was more difficult to hit. At 4.44 a full-length ball slid past Dilley's scything bat and bowled him. He and Botham had added 117, of which Botham had made 57 to Dilley's 56.

'The game was still over,' recalls Dilley. 'We'd gone out there and slogged the Aussies around, scored a lot of runs very quickly and given people great entertainment. It had been great fun, but that was it.'

In the press box, much the same was being thought.

'We were pretty patronising about Botham's innings,' admits Frank Crook of the (Australian) *Sun*. 'Once he'd got 50, we were thinking – "Good innings, Both, but that's enough". Botham was just hitting everything and we thought, "This can't last." '

Over in the England dressing room Willis exhorted Brearley to 'make Chilly play!' Dilley and Old passed each other on the field. 'Great innings,' said the Yorkshireman. 'Thanks,' replied Dilley, 'You do the same.'

Old was certainly going to try. 'I felt we could win,' he states. 'Lillee,

Alderman and Lawson weren't as dangerous now and I just had to stay in for a while and give the strike to Ian as much as I could. If we set them a tough target – 150, maybe 200 – it would be an interesting game. At the end of every over, even after a boundary, I'd go down the wicket and say to Ian, "C'mon, keep going". I told him not to try to hit every ball but to pick it about a bit.

'I probably had a harder job calming him down than keeping myself calm. Brears was making all these signals from the balcony and Ian wanted him to shut up.

'It was one of the hardest innings of my career. It was the end of the day and I wanted to keep the momentum going but the key was staying in. Having fought back and gone into the lead, it was a great feeling. It was a matter of total concentration.'

Old was well known for backing away against fast bowling. Peter Willey, watching Old settle into his stance on the dressing-room TV, took a bat and wedged it against the Yorkshire captain's bottom to keep him in place.

But Willey need not have worried. Old was soon on his way, pulling Lawson for four – 'down legside, in the slot and it went,' he grins.

So what did Brearley's signals from the balcony mean? The guru himself is not so sure: 'At the moment in the BBC highlights video when Ian is acknowledging the applause for his remarkable century, the camera pans to the players' balcony, and focuses on my gesture to the batsmen. I am pointing in an angry, insistent way. What did this mean?

'In his commentary, Richie Benaud generously gives me the credit for telling the batsmen to play their shots. I think what my gesture meant was more complex, less simply right. I was in favour of that, but I also wanted Old to rivet his back foot before it made its involuntary jerk backwards.

'I wanted Ian too, not to stop hitting or to take himself too solemnly, but to see that we had this real, though outside, chance of an extraordinary reversal. It's as if I was saying: "This is now serious, not just an enjoyable but ultimately useless frolic in the face of defeat, like that of the sailor in the war film who raises his hat and bows with mock gallantry at the instant before his ship sinks and he disappears forever beneath the freezing Baltic."

'But serious in what sense? If I am honest it was not so clear a message as Benaud suggests. I fear that my gesture betrayed a more restrictive attitude.'

Botham certainly began to play with more care once he had reached his century, but his strokeplay remained brutal. The deterioration in the Aussie attack which Dilley had first noticed was now reaching crisis point.

'We had a message system at Yorkshire,' reveals Old. 'You'd give two knocks on your bat if you could see opposition struggle. After about 10 minutes I knocked. Lillee, Marsh, Hughes, Alderman, they were all signalling different fielders to go to different positions. They were in disarray.'

Willey is quick to point out that England's all-out attack had other benefits as well. 'Both took the pressure off Graham and Chris. The Australians wanted to get Both and didn't concentrate as much on the two fellows at the other end.'

Lillee and Alderman were nearly out on their feet, having bowled for most of the day. It was to prove a costly tactic according to Aussie coach Peter Philpott. 'Hughes overbowled his Western Australian team-mates, Lillee and Alderman. He left Lawson out of it for too long. He took an almighty punt on keeping them going so long and he bowled them into the ground. When he did rest Lillee and Alderman, Botham was flying and he was forced to bring them back on before they could recover.

'I could see the temptation to keep Lillee and Alderman on – the wicket suited them, they'd been so successful and getting Botham's wicket would have meant victory. Out in the field it's the captain's game, but part of me was thinking: "We're stretching these boys too far." The way Chris Old – never the best against pace – batted was indicative of how tired the bowlers were.'

Graeme Wood, another Western Australian, says his captain eventually acknowledged the mistake. 'I've spoken to Kim about this a lot. In hindsight we should have tried something different. Brought Bright on earlier, given Chappell a try. But the fast bowlers had done the job until then.'

Even the possibility of using a stand-breaker like Chappell appeared to be completely ignored. 'Hughes never spoke to me about bowling,' says Chappell. 'In fact, I didn't bowl at all in the series.'

At least Bright did eventually get on – if only for four overs. 'We needed to take some of the pace off the ball,' remembers the spinner. 'The quick bowlers were trying to bowl faster and faster and Botham used that pace in his shots. I made a few unsubtle hints about wanting to get on, but they did me no good. At the end of the day Kim said: "We should have got you on earlier." '

In the eyes of Bob Willis, Hughes' decision to keep Bright out of the attack may have proved to be one of the turning points of the match. 'They should have bowled Ray Bright earlier,' he insisted. 'Against the spinner Botham would almost certainly have perished to a catch in the deep.'

Botham would no doubt have backed himself against Bright, but he concedes Willis's point: 'Hughes kept the fast bowlers on for too long before trying to tempt me with a spinner.'

Peter Willey puts another spin on it: 'It was the macho thing wasn't it? Lillee and the other fast bowlers against Both. They bowled to his strengths.'

As the Botham/Old stand built, Lawson bowled two beamers in one over to the English centurion. Botham was in no doubt that this was a sign that the Aussies were rattled. 'Geoff Lawson lost his rag to such an extent that he actually sent down two beamers,' he wrote in his autobiography. 'I could accept one as an accident but two had to be more than coincidence. I stored them away in the memory banks for future reference.'

In *Phoenix From The Ashes*, Brearley is equally vehement in his denouncement of Lawson: 'The Australians' desperation was highlighted by two beamers in an over from Lawson to Botham, after which umpire Evans spoke to Hughes. The beamer has been universally condemned by cricketers as an unfair delivery since the best batsmen have been unable to pick them up even in bright sunshine when well set.'

Lawson, however, reckons he had a good excuse. 'I tore a back ligament during the afternoon by putting my front foot in the deep footholes created by the bowlers in their follow-through,' he explains. 'I pulled up suddenly, and at a strange angle.' But since he was warmed up and therefore able to play through the injury, and his side was under the cosh, Lawson continued to bowl. 'That's when I bowled the supposed "beamers" to Botham,' he claims. 'They were in effect very slow inswingers that were extremely painful from my end. Let's face it, if I had bowled a proper beamer it would have hit him.

'It took me six weeks of full-time treatment when I got home to recover. I could hardly walk on the last morning of the Headingley Test and batting was not an easy task.'

With the score at 319, and with England 92 runs ahead, Old was out. 'Lawson got me, yorked leg stump. I picked it up late. The sightscreens were a bit funny at the Kirkstall Lane End – his hand came out of the background of the trees and I lost it. I was unhappy because the lead we had by then didn't seem enough. Had all that hard work been wasted?'

By this stage, with Botham in total command, the England balcony was crowded. 'Ian was one of those batsmen – and at that stage of his career he was in his prime – we all used to watch bat,' remembers Graham Gooch. 'He was a devastating batsman and he'd sometimes do the most unexpected things – hitting opening bowlers back over their heads, hooking and cutting from the word go. It was compulsive viewing.

'Most players don't watch [the play] all the time, but Botham was the kind of guy who'd make you go out onto the balcony thinking, "What's he going to do today?" There was always something happening.'

However, even by Botham's standards that Headingley Monday was special, as David Gower recalls.

'We had all given up. Beefy too. He wasn't playing seriously any more. It was bizarre and unfortunate for Australia. They might have had a better chance if we'd been slightly ahead before Ian's innings.

'It was a totally carefree knock. There was never a question of a downside – there was nothing whatsoever to lose because we'd already lost the game. In the early part it was a case of who gives a s***? It didn't really matter what happened. In the end it became almost sadistic.'

Bob Willis agreed: 'I am convinced Ian began batting the way he did as little more than a bit of fun. It was high-class slogging – the description cannot be avoided. He was very fortunate in having two partners who adopted very similar tactics and played above themselves.'

Bedser dismissed any thoughts that the innings had been inspired by the return of Botham's mentor. 'It's nonsense for people to suggest that Botham played an innings like that because of Brearley,' he snorted. 'Botham knew it was all or nothing.'

For Willey, one overwhelming impression remains: 'Just the power really. Both was a hell of strong fellow.

When he hit it, it stayed hit. I'd never seen him play like that in Test matches before, though I'd seen him do it in county matches. Everything went his way. Another day you could try to play like that and get out first ball. When he hooked the fast bowlers, half the time he'd have his eyes shut. He was lucky enough to get it far enough to clear everybody. You can't imagine anybody playing that sort of a knock now.'

It was the very carelessness of the innings that was the Australians' undoing, according to Gooch. 'As a captain you can legislate for somebody doing that and scoring 50-odd,' he recalls, laughing, 'but in the end they hit one up in the air. In Both's case it just didn't happen.'

Out in the middle, the Australians could only watch and wonder.

'I've never seen an innings like it,' says Graham Yallop. 'Botham must have thought that all his Christmases had come at once. The ball was dropping between the fieldsmen, flying over their heads or falling short. It was an educated slog. Both he and Dilley played some fabulous shots and had tremendous luck.'

John Dyson, too, was awestruck: 'Botham's was a fabulous innings. But the wicket took the pressure off him. Nobody expected him to last long; he had nothing to lose.'

Philpott is more direct: 'Botham's innings was an almighty slog. He stood up like a baseball player and swung from the ding.'

Surprisingly perhaps, Botham concurs with Philpott's assessment: 'Mine wasn't a great innings, it wasn't really an innings at all – just an almighty heave. I didn't put anything into it, I didn't walk out and say, "Right, we're in a mess and I'm going to sort it out". I was playing by pure instinct. If it was in the slot I drove and drove hard on the basis that even if I got an edge, more likely than not the ball would carry over the heads of the slips.'

However, Botham claims that although his innings owed plenty to luck it was also a product of his approach to the game, one shared by his great mate Viv Richards and few others. 'I was so well into the groove that I can't remember playing a defensive shot.'

Although he did in fact play some textbook defensive shots, the blows which brought his 28 boundaries are what everyone, including obviously Botham himself, remembers. But which was the best shot? The six off Alderman? Apparently not. 'The shot I remember above all others was a square cut off the back foot off Lillee which was probably the sweetest shot I have ever hit in my life.'

When Botham ran from the field on that Monday evening, 145 not out, the press were clamouring for quotes. But Botham was still sore at the media for the way they had treated him when he was captain. He refused all requests for interviews. Instead he sat in the dressing room, puffing on a contemplative cigar – trying, and failing, to make sense of the day's play.

On *Test Match Special*, producer Dick Maddock was signing off, telling his massively swollen audience: 'This is folk hero stuff. The sort of thing the England cricketing public has been waiting two-and-a-half seasons for. I think we're entitled to be a little bit euphoric.'

On television, Christopher Martin-Jenkins said simply: 'Botham has become a national hero once again.'

Meanwhile, Pat Gibson of the *Daily Express* was getting around Botham's refusal to speak by asking his wife Kathy for a reaction. She, not surprisingly, was overjoyed. 'It's like a fairytale,' she told Gibson. 'I'm so pleased for him, because we have all gone through a lot recently.'

Botham himself fled to his car, pursued by reporters, a towel wrapped around his mouth. He finally agreed to speak about his innings when the match was over and then revealed he had used a bat belonging to Graham Gooch. 'He hadn't used it much and I thought there were a few runs left in it,' he told the *Sun*. Gooch, of course, had scored just 2 and 0 in the match.

But, like many of the myths that have grown up around Headingley '81, it isn't exactly true, as Gooch explains. 'Ian and I were both with Duncan Fearnley, the batmaker. I had this bat, which was a slightly different shape from the normal ones. Duncan had scooped out a little of the back in the shape of his logo – a sort of V-shape. It was one of my spares that I was just knocking in. Ian pinched it off me, used it and I never got it back.'

Towards the end of the Headingley century, the bat – perhaps understandably – split. Tongue firmly in cheek, the Australian tour manager Fred Bennett commented: 'We would have been in trouble if he'd had a complete bat.'

Headingley '81 (slight return)

Four months after Botham and Dilley's rescue act, the two batsmen found themselves facing another crisis during the first Test against India at Bombay's Wankhede stadium.

'We were 50–6 in the second innings chasing 241,' remembers Dilley. 'I was batting with Both and he asked me:

"Do you remember Headingley?" and I replied: "Yeah, of course I do." "Come on," he said, "let's do it again."

'Two balls later my off stump was cartwheeling out of the ground.'

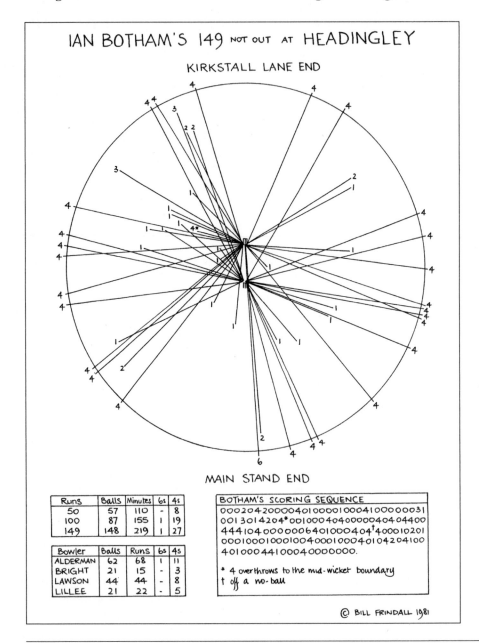

IAN BOTHAM'S 149 NOT OUT AT HEADINGLEY

KIRKSTALL LANE END

MAIN STAND END

Runs	Balls	Minutes	6s	4s
50	57	110	-	8
100	87	155	1	19
149	148	219	1	27

Bowler	Balls	Runs	6s	4s
ALDERMAN	62	68	1	11
BRIGHT	21	15	-	3
LAWSON	44	44	-	8
LILLEE	21	22	-	5

BOTHAM'S SCORING SEQUENCE

000204200000401000010004100000031
0013014204*00100040400000040404400
444104000000640100040404†400010201
0001000100010040001000401042042100
4010004410004000000.

* 4 overthrows to the mid-wicket boundary
† off a no-ball

© BILL FRINDALL 1981

England victory defies logic and lifts country

Willis saves England and career

England scored 356 all out in their second innings, setting Australia 130 to win. Australia in their second innings totalled 111 and lost by 18 runs

Leeds Royal Infirmary was reportedly dealing with a flood of self-inflicted injuries on Tuesday evening after scores of dazed spectators flooded in from Headingley having spent the day pinching themselves in disbelief at the events happening before their eyes.

The bald facts are that England won the third Test by 18 runs, with Bob Willis taking an international career best 8–43. But these statistics fail dismally to capture the sheer unlikeliness and heart-stopping drama of England's victory. With the match over, the crowd surged up to the pavilion and sang 'Jerusalem' at the top of their voices. Three days before they – or others like them – had stood in the same place and staged a noisy protest at England's incompetence and the intransigence of the umpires. In a country torn by riots, with unemployment hitting a record 2.85 million and the Royal Wedding edition of the *Radio Times* scuppered by industrial action, it was an astonishing sight.

Throughout the day, the players, spectators and, towards the climax, two entire countries were teased by a game which showed as much respect for sporting tradition as King Carlos of Spain did for court etiquette in announcing his decision to snub the Royal Wedding.

With the ground still buzzing from Botham's Monday massacre of the Australian bowling, the day began with an anti-climax which seemed to suggest that the miracle cupboard was bare.

The memory which gave hope to the English fans as they took their seats on a breezy but sunny Tuesday morning was Willis's three-hour stand with Willey against the West Indies at The Oval last year. If the Warwickshire captain lasted as long this time, England would be safe and Botham would have smashed every batting record in the book.

Some hope. Hughes took the new ball immediately and Botham cover drove Alderman for four, despite the Australians having seven men on the boundary. Willis added a single but was then snapped up at slip by Border from the third ball of Alderman's second over. Botham and Willis had added 37 priceless runs in 31 minutes, Willis facing just nine balls. Altogether the last three wickets had added 221, 40 per cent of the runs scored by England in the match.

Botham's eventual undefeated tally of 149 came from 148 deliveries. Just how selective and unmerciful his hitting was is revealed by the fact that his runs came from just 54 scoring strokes, 28 of them boundaries.

The Australian bowling figures were dominated by Alderman's Charge of the Light Brigade performance. He'd bowled 10 overs more than Lillee and 12 more than Lawson and taken the brunt of Botham's broadside. But he had also picked up six wickets which gives him 20 at 21.25 for the series; a great Test career is just beginning.

England were all out for 356. Australia had to make just 130 to go two up in the series. Few thought they would not succeed.

Brearley chose Botham and Dilley to open the bowling, the third new-ball pairing of the match, obviously hoping the duo would mesh as well with ball as they had with the bat.

Botham began as if Australia were chasing 330 not 130, with a long hop and a half-volley, both of which Wood hit for four through the leg side. At the other end Dilley, bowling up the hill and into the wind, looked diffident and ineffectual.

Then England got their first break of the day. In Botham's second over, Wood drove at another half-volley and hit the ground with his bat just as it appeared to make contact with the ball, which then flew through to Taylor behind the wicket. England's appeal betrayed doubts that the ball might have missed the edge, but Meyer sent Wood on his way. He was out for 10 and Australia were 13–1.

Dilley's second over was as poor as his first and as soon as it had finished he disappeared into the dressing room. Although he reappeared moments later, after having a suspected groin strain checked out, he did not bowl again in the innings.

Despite Dilley's heroics, and the fact that he is second to Botham in the series batting averages, he will be lucky to get a game at Edgbaston.

Brearley replaced Dilley with Willis from the Rugby Stand End. Many in the press box speculated that without something spectacular happening this would be Willis's last spell for England. Willis, no doubt, was thinking the same thing.

Dyson and Chappell picked up from where they left off in the first innings. Both mixed stubborn defence with the sort of luck needed against the new ball on this pitch. A third man kept the runs down as the edges proliferated, but the score mounted with, for English supporters, a sickening steadiness. With little cloud cover the new ball produced only gentle swing.

Australia lose three for two

Just over an hour into the Australian innings, Dyson and Chappell had taken the score past 50 – almost halfway there with just one wicket down. The biggest talking point was the whereabouts of Geoffrey Boycott and speculation as to when substitute fielder Wayne Larkins would resume his Test career.

Old replaced Botham and then, after five unremarkable overs, Willis made way for Willey. However, Brearley straightaway switched the Warwickshire fast bowler to the Kirkstall Lane End and gave him his first bowl down the hill and with the gusting wind at his back. Coming 20 minutes before lunch it was the decisive moment of the final innings.

Immediately Willis began to bowl

quicker. Knees pumping, eyes glazed and elbows thrashing away like a piece of agricultural machinery conceived by Dr Frankenstein, Willis clearly meant business. Behind him the clouds began to bank up on the horizon and the watery summer sunshine began to boil away into something much more threatening. Only blasting out the 'Ride of the Valkyries' over the tannoy could have filled the atmosphere with any more electricity.

The job of the Valkyries, of course, was to accompany the slain from the battlefield and they were soon in business.

In his second over from the Kirkstall Lane End, Willis catapulted the ball just short of a length towards Chappell's face. Chappell avoided expensive plastic surgery by getting the handle of his bat in the way and Taylor ran forward to take a gentle looping catch. As a statement of intent the delivery left little room for interpretation. Chappell was out for eight made from 56 deliveries. It was to be the second longest occupation of the crease by an Australian batsman in the innings.

Old replaced Willey from the Rugby Stand End. Dyson and Hughes, still bravely wearing a cap, dug deep in an effort to reach the haven of lunch. They nearly made it.

After 14 minutes, Hughes, still on 0, tried to repeat the steer to third man he had used so profitably in the first innings. But he failed to get on top of a lifting delivery from Willis and sent the ball flying low to Botham at third slip. Diving to his left Botham caught the ball arms outstretched, bounced to his feet and flung the ball into the stratosphere. The England slip cordon

exploded with delight and then started scanning the sky with wry grins for the rapidly descending ball.

Three balls later the celebrations were in full swing throughout the ground as Willis produced another cobra-like delivery which struck at Yallop's throat. Gatting at short leg was on his heels as ball hit bat, but he flung himself forward to take a breath-taking catch.

Gatting took the chance beautifully, snatching the catch off his toes. England are lucky that after swapping specialist short leg Bob Woolmer for the slip-fielding Brearley they have such a talented and courageous replacement. On a pitch where the ball is kicking as much as it did at Headingley, a good short leg is vital.

Since switching ends Willis had taken three wickets without conceding a run in 11 deliveries. He had also transformed the game from a victory stroll to an, at times, unbearably tense struggle for supremacy.

The rest of the players followed Yallop into the pavilion for lunch. Australia were 58–4 with the last two batsmen out for a duck but Dyson once again standing firm on 29. Few could even think about food as their butter-fly-crammed stomachs heaved and the 40-minute interval crawled past. Ladbrokes had Australia 5–2 to win the match, England 3–1 – some fall from Saturday's 500–1.

Brearley's masterful control

Of all the Australian batsmen it was Dyson and Border who had the guts and technique to put the target in perspective. Brearley reacted to this crucial period by sticking with Willis and

Old once play resumed.

There were concerns that Willis might stiffen up during the interval, but if he had, it made no difference to the ferocity with which he attacked the Australian batsmen. In his single-minded purpose to bowl fast, straight and short he overstepped a dozen times. But after every no-ball Brearley would make a point of clapping encouragement, geeing up Willis to bowl even faster and forget everything else.

Bowling with the wind at his back and downhill from the Kirkstall Lane End was obviously making it harder for Willis to hit the crease correctly, but switching him back to the Rugby Stand End was unthinkable. Willis appeared to be in a trance. He ignored the urgings of team-mates and shrugged off encouraging slaps on the back: he had surrendered himself to the moment. The Buddha of Brum was bowling to save England, to save his own career.

Once Brearley realised that Willis was the on-song bowler, the captain's performance was faultless. He stood at first slip throughout, moving Gooch, who had fielded there since the start of the series and dropped everything that came his way, to second slip. With Botham now at third slip when he wasn't bowling, Willey could move to his specialist position in the gully and the dangerous Gower was able to roam free at cover.

From his pivotal position next to the wicketkeeper and in the bowler's eye-line, Brearley kept England as calm and focused as any team could be in such a situation. He also exploited a myriad of psychological tricks to upset the Australian batsmen. For example, he started to blow on his hands and rub them together in an ostentatious show of readying himself for a stinging slip catch. Soon the entire English slip cordon was at it. Even if Botham had still performed as well as he did with bat and ball, England would have probably lost had he still been captain.

After 13 minutes, it was Old who made the vital breakthrough. A break-back caught Border's inside edge and ripped his leg stump out of the ground. As with those that preceded it, it was the sort of delivery that knocks the stuffing out of a batting side. It was also – astonishingly – Old's first wicket of the match. Between them, Hughes, Yallop and Border – the engine room of the Australian batting line-up – had lasted just 20 deliveries without scoring a run.

Old's contributions to the game, although not in the same league as the spectacular achievements of Botham and Willis, were significant. His stand with Botham allowed the England No. 7 to murder the tiring Australian attack and today he was a mean foil to the rampaging Willis.

Old gathers his arms around his chest as he runs steadily in before delivering the ball with a slightly incongruous whirling of both arms. The bounce and movement he generated here meant he gave away few runs, while producing countless painful smacks on the batsmen's gloves. Until Bright got after him in his last over, Old bowled 48 deliveries for just 11 runs.

In the over before Border's dismissal, Dyson had safely hooked Willis for four. Now he tried again and, playing the shot too soon, gloved a catch to

Taylor.

Dyson was out for 34, made from 83 balls in a minute short of two hours. Australia, at 68–6, were staring down the barrel.

Over the weekend the right-wing pressure group, Aims of Industry, issued a guide to Marxist theory for businessmen. 'Not even Cassius Clay would go into the ring with one hand tied behind his back,' said the author, a Dr Watkins from Sheffield University. 'Yet that is the position of the manager who is totally ignorant of Marxist theory.' The Australians facing Willis were in the same boat; they didn't have a clue.

Bright and Lillee fight back

To no one's surprise Marsh came out swinging. Off his ninth delivery he connected with a Willis bouncer and sent the ball spinning and swirling down towards fine leg for what most thought would be the first six of the innings. But waiting at long leg was Dilley, a hero on Monday, surplus to requirements on Tuesday. The Kent quick stood under the rapidly plummeting ball. With a seeming calmness he could not have felt, he ran backwards and gathered the ball feet from the boundary rope as it swirled down out of the gun-metal sky.

Australia were 74 for 7. It made as much sense as your average episode of *Tiswas* – the Phantom Flan Flinger played by one Bob Willis.

The injured Lawson was the next batsman. He had delivered two beamers to Botham on Monday and he hobbled to the wicket, displaying all the confidence of a PLO supporter at a barmitzvah. To Willis's first ball, only

the second he had faced, Lawson waved his bat at a delivery that lifted and moved away. The resulting edge gave Taylor his fourth dismissal of the innings.

Seventy-five for eight. Australia had lost seven wickets for 19 runs in two minutes short of an hour. Six of the wickets had fallen to Willis during the same number of overs for just eight runs.

Australia had 55 to make with just two wickets left standing. England were favourites to win for the first time in the game. Twenty minutes later they were back in the underdog's kennel as Bright and Lillee began to chance their arms.

Lillee is, when he needs to be, a resourceful batsman. The world's best batsmen have worked hard to try to combat his attack and Lillee has learned much in the process. He also, of course, has nerves of steel and when Willis nearly yorked him, he turned grinning to the slip cordon and raised a hand in mock salute to the baying English supporters.

Willis was bowling slightly short of a length, aiming for a spot on the pitch which often made the ball leap like a scalded cat. With the pitch's bounce so uneven, batsmen could not rely on the ball carrying over the stumps and had to play everything. When the ball moved in, defensive and attacking shots were cramped; when it moved away, the desire to reach for it was proving irresistible.

Lillee decided he could not worry about the bounce and stepped away to leg to uppercut the ball over the slips for four. Willey, of course, had done the same thing to Lillee on Monday and the great Australian bowler had responded by getting him caught at a specially positioned fly slip/short third man. Brearley tried the same tactic, but Lillee repeated the shot and beat Dilley on the boundary. Willis aimed for the yorker and Lillee clipped him in the air down to fine leg for three, before playing another cut. At the other end the bearded Bright, who has a first-class hundred to his name, whipped the equally bushy Old over midwicket for two boundaries. It was like watching Captain Birdseye take on his evil twin.

In four overs Australia had added 35 and were now only 20 away from victory.

Brearley was forced to loosen the tourniquet of close fielders: some went to the boundary, Gatting went from short leg to mid-on. Botham stood in the slips waving his arms in exhortation; Brearley gestured for him to calm down.

The match was slipping away from England. Willis, blowing his cheeks out with the effort, began to pitch the ball up. Lillee immediately found it much harder to score and eventually aimed a sketchy legside flick at a Willis outswinger. He made only partial contact and chipped the ball towards mid-on. As the ball skyed towards Gatting, and the ground held its breath, it appeared as if the fielder had misjudged the flight. Maybe, maybe not, but after first back-pedalling, Gatting suddenly launched himself forward down the slope, gathering speed like an untethered beer barrel before diving to take the catch inches above the ground. Lillee, 17 runs off 15 balls, was out and Australia were 110–9.

Willis ran to congratulate Gatting, but on reaching the fielder all he could do was limply throw his arms around the Middlesex man and lay his head on Gatting's shoulder. It was a surreal and moving sight. Willis had bowled himself into the ground and knew what Gatting's catch meant to both England and himself. Willis needed wickets to keep going and two barren overs were as much use as a Rich Tea biscuit to a heroin addict.

The last wicket

There was just one thing Brearley needed to do now and that was to bring back Botham to finish it all off. Old, the displaced bowler, went to third slip as Bright took a single and exposed Alderman to Botham.

The crowd was now producing one continuous roar which rose in pitch and intensity as Botham pounded in. Alderman – the bunny in the head-lamps – could only poke a sharp chance straight to Old … who dropped it. Around the ground heads plunged into hands, unable to watch. When they looked up they saw the tragedy repeated, although this time the chance was lower and harder. Could England be robbed of victory at the 11th hour? Too bloody right!

Then – at 2.20 on this unforgettable afternoon – it was all over. Willis's first ball of his 16th over was fast, straight and full. Bright went to on-drive, played over the ball and had his middle stump spun out of the ground. Willis flung both arms skyward in victory and wheeled away towards the pavilion. His team-mates, who would have shamed the Bolshoi with their simultaneous jump for joy, grabbed the stumps and followed. On surged the crowd,

Day five

Don't Slow Down – Beset by illness and knee trouble, Willis's future had been in doubt for some time, and now Brearley regretted his inclusion at the expense of a spinner. On the Saturday night, Willis assured friends he would never be picked again. Dyson is about to feel the backlash …

Above: **Dancing on the Floor** – Gatting tracks the ball en route to Taylor's safe gloves as Trevor Chappell, undone by pace and a nasty spot just short of a length, becomes Willis's first victim: 56 for 2.

Above right: **Ain't No Stopping** – Hughes looks back in disbelief as Botham gets happy after diving to catch him at slip off another Willis snorter: 58 for 3.

Right: **Good Thing Going** – Dyson's stoical resistance ends in a mishook off Willis, safely pouched by Taylor: 68 for 6.

Above: **Einstein A Go-Go** – 'On Friday I watched J M Brearley directing his fieldsmen very carefully. He then looked up at the sun and made a gesture which suggested it should move a little squarer. Who is this man?' (Letter to the *Guardian*)

Below: **In The Air Tonight** – Eyes to the rear as Marsh, still a dangerous hitter, sends a top-edged hook off Willis swirling high to long leg.

Left: **Wordy Rappinghood** – Dilley assures Botham, Brearley and Willey that there was never the slightest doubt about him dropping the catch: 74 for 7.

Above: **Rapture** – Taylor, 40 going on 20, pays due homage as the thickset Gatting moves heaven and earth to terminate Lillee's threatening assault with extreme pride and prejudice: 110 for 9.

Below: **That's Entertainment** – 'Wha'ppen?' wonders Ray Bright after Willis applies the *coup de grâce*, and still they reckon 111 is the Poms' unlucky number.

Above: **The Oldest Swinger in Town** – Gatting, Gooch, Willey and public try in vain to catch Willis as he dashes off, still immersed in that 'cocoon' of concentration. 'I'd have sworn he was drugged,' said trusty physio Bernard Thomas. 'I know he wasn't, and that concerned me even more. What do we really know about hypnosis?'

Left: **Reward** – Fred Trueman announces Botham as Man of the Match: 'A captain's performance that came one match too late ...'

Right: **Once In A Lifetime** – Botham takes a moment to drink it all in.

Left: **Can You Feel It:?** – Merlins in clover as 'Goose' pours and 'Beefy' slurps, the former's anti-media tirade forgotten. 'That's better,' sighed Willey who at last, in his 19th Test, had a proper excuse to partake of the bubbly. 'All the other stuff I've drunk has made me want to puke.'

Below: **Happy Birthday** – Twenty years on, the memories burn bright. The scoresheet is the handiwork of Stan Dawson, the mementoes courtesy of David and Keith Summerfield, father and son who attended all five days. Not a lot of people can say that.

swallowing up the Australian batsmen who stood shock still in the middle of the pitch. Up on the Australian dressing-room balcony Allan Border sat alone, head in hands.

The English players, racing up the dressing-room stairs, had to push past scores of photographers, who were not now focusing on Willis, Brearley or Botham, but on the mass of spectators invading the outfield – Headingley had never seen anything like it.

The Australian innings had lasted just 36 overs and taken only two hours and 49 minutes to complete. The playing time between Chappell's and Bright's dismissals was almost exactly an hour and a half. As in the first innings, Dyson had made the highest score. Bright, who had nearly snatched the game back for Australia, made his 19 runs from 32 balls in 50 minutes of the most pulsating cricket he will ever experience.

The winning margin of 18 runs may yet nag at the Australian captain. One wonders if, in the days to come, Kim Hughes will think back to his first-innings declaration, with the 10th-wicket pair of Lillee and Alderman yet to get off the mark. At Lord's, Lillee and Alderman had added 31, while at Trent Bridge on a wicket just as bad as Headingley's, Alderman contributed 12 not out to a 31-run stand with Border.

Dotted around the ground some spectators sat frozen in their seats. No doubt many felt like the British diplomats accused in a House of Commons report of having 'frankly rotten' language skills – they could find no words to express what they had just seen.

England's victory was their first in 13 Tests, ending the team's longest stretch without a win. The 12 unsuccessful Tests, of course, coincided with Botham's stint as captain. It was England's narrowest win over Australia since the fourth Test of the 1928–29 Ashes series, when they sneaked home by 12 runs.

Records galore

Willis's 8–43 off 15 overs and one ball were the best figures of his Test career and the best ever achieved in 82 years of Test cricket at Headingley. Willis had started his spell from the Kirkstall Lane End with the score at 48 for 1. In 10 overs and one ball he had taken eight Australian wickets.

But Willis was not the only English player to break records. When Bob Taylor caught Geoff Lawson he recorded his 1271st first-class catch – one more than Middlesex's John Murray. On Saturday it was said that the player who beats Marsh's Test record has probably not yet played his first international. With the number of county games declining and Taylor still some way from retirement his eventual tally of catches is likely to be as unchallengeable as Jack Hobbs's 61,237 first-class runs and Wilfred Rhodes's 4187 wickets.

Brearley chalked up his ninth win over Australia as captain, one more than W.G. Grace's record. If the press box scorer had announced that Brearley had been beatified and that Botham was replacing the Archbishop of Canterbury at next week's 'do' in Westminster Abbey, we would have blithely scribbled it down, so far had our credulity been stretched by firsts, longests and greatests.

Soon everyone was talking of the long forgotten first Test on the 1894–95 tour of Australia. England had won by 10 runs, the only other example of a team winning a Test match after following on. That match was dominated by Australian all-rounder George Giffen, who scored 202 runs and took 8–239. In this game Botham made 199 runs for once out and took 7–109. Then people started remembering the 500–1 odds against an England victory that Ladbrokes had set on Saturday. A small number of hopeless romantics had staked £52 between them and will now, no doubt, plunge their winnings into buying up Royal Wedding memorabilia.

But perhaps the most astonishing fact of all is the speed with which the game's logic was not so much upturned as eviscerated. By the finish, there had been less than six hours' play since Graham Dilley had walked out to join Ian Botham with England 92 runs behind and only three wickets intact.

This morning the biggest boost for the UK on the horizon was Ronald Reagan's decision to order cloth from a British textile mill for the suit he's having made to replace the one ruined by the would-be assassin's bullet. Now things are different. Don't be surprised if the unions suddenly decide to accept British Rail's 11 per cent pay offer or if Maggie pays Michael Foot a compliment. The world's a brighter place today and, for the first time since 1953, we can thank the England cricket team.

England second innings

G.A. Gooch c Alderman b Lillee	0
G. Boycott lbw b Alderman	46
J.M. Brearley c Alderman b Lillee	14
D.I. Gower c Border b Alderman	9
M.W. Gatting lbw b Alderman	1
P. Willey c Dyson b Lillee	33
I.T. Botham not out	149
R.W. Taylor c Bright b Alderman	1
G.R. Dilley b Alderman	56
C.M. Old b Lawson	29
R.G.D. Willis c Border b Alderman	2
Extras (b5, lb3, w3, nb5)	16
Total	356

Fall of wickets: 1–0, 2–18, 3–37, 4–41, 5–105, 6–133, 7–135, 8–252, 9–319

	O	M	R	W
Lillee	25	6	94	3
Alderman	35.3	6	135	6
Lawson	23	4	96	1
Bright	4	0	15	0

Australia second innings

J. Dyson c Taylor b Willis	34
G.M. Wood c Taylor b Botham	10
T.M. Chappell c Taylor b Willis	8
K.J. Hughes c Botham b Willis	0
G.N. Yallop c Gatting b Willis	0
A.R. Border b Old	0
R.W. Marsh c Dilley b Willis	4
R.J. Bright b Willis	19
G.F. Lawson c Taylor b Willis	1
D.K. Lillee c Gatting b Willis	17
T.M. Alderman not out	0
Extras (lb3, w1, nb14)	18
Total	111

Fall of wickets: 1–13, 2–56, 3–58, 4–58, 5–65, 6–68, 7–74, 8–75, 9–110

	O	M	R	W
Botham	7	3	14	1
Dilley	2	0	11	0
Willis	15.1	3	43	8
Old	9	1	21	1
Willey	3	1	4	0

Eyewitness
Before Lunch

Frank Crook, [Australian] *Sun*: I had breakfast with Kim Hughes. We agreed that the Aussies were bound to win this Test and probably the series. I asked him, if that happened, if he thought the Aussie selectors would replace him with Greg Chappell during the 81–82 season. Kim said: 'No, I don't think they'd dare.'

John Dyson: At the start of the day we were a little disappointed that we'd let the game go this far.

Ian Botham: The Australians were thinking overnight that they might not get us out and that they might have to get 200 – it preyed on their minds.

Peter Willey: I remember running out onto the field and there were goose pimples on my arm. The atmosphere, the noise – it was unbelievable.

Trevor Bailey [on *TMS*]: The England bowlers know their places in the Test side are in jeopardy. They will pull out all the stops.

Graeme Wood: I hit a couple of fours and then Botham pitched one in the footmarks that went through to Taylor. I didn't get within a bull's roar of it and nobody but Botham appealed, but Barrie Meyer still gave me out.

The climax

Graham Dilley: With four wickets down at lunchtime everybody started looking at each other thinking: 'What is going on? How stupid is this game that we can be in a situation where we can win it?' Then the buzz started and everybody got caught up in it.

Peter Philpott: The change in atmosphere was stark. For the first hour it was all hilarity and good humour. By lunch the mood had got very sombre.

Ian Botham: You could tell that something had happened to the Aussies. As we came out after lunch we looked across the balcony and saw the expressions on their faces: talk about rabbits caught in the headlights.

Peter Philpott: I still think that gutsing it out was the best approach. We didn't really have anybody like Botham who could go in and have a swing.

David Ryder, Secretary Yorkshire CCC: It was a strange day. To begin with the ground was only about a quarter full. There was no Teletext in those days and people used to ring the ground for the score. When they found out what was happening, they said: 'Right, I'm coming.' You could see the crowd growing minute by minute.

Allan Border bowled Old 0

Chris Old: At lunch we talked about Border being the key man, about how, if we got him quickly, we'd have an excellent chance of winning. I always enjoyed bowling to left-handers, and Brears knew it. If you can make the ball come into them, which I could, they had to play at it. And the tighter the line, the better your prospects. Brears put me on straight away. I bowled him a ball which cut back under his armpit and Taylor had to take it diving to his right. The next one pitched round about off, swung in, then left him a bit like an off-break. This time Taylor took it in front of Brears' face at first slip. The third ball was similar to the first, although it didn't cut back as much, and he played on trying to leave it. All of a sudden I saw the not very pretty sight of Ian Botham coming down the wicket to congratulate me. To have got Border so soon after lunch maintained the momentum.

Marsh c Dilley b Willis 4

Peter Willey: I was at fine leg most of the time and for some reason I thought I'd have a change and go down to third man. Next ball Marsh top-edged one and Dil was under it – and I thought 'Thank Christ for that'.

Graham Dilley: I remember every second of it. Willis was running in and I was thinking, 'Don't bounce him' – and he bounces him. And Marsh has gone for it, as he was obviously going to, and this thing has gone up miles – miles and miles – and the higher it's gone the more I'm thinking, 'Shit, it's not gone for six.' I had a pretty good idea where the rope was and, as I was moving backwards watching the ball, I knew I was getting close. The ball was coming down and I put my hands up to catch it Aussie-style, the back of my hands turned towards my face. When I took it, it pushed me back a little and I had to take one more step backwards. When I looked round I was about a foot from the rope. I felt absolute and utter relief that I had managed to catch it and I hurled the ball as hard as I could back up into the air. Both came racing down and put his arm round me. Then the bastard told me exactly what they'd said in the slips. As Marsh hooked the ball up in the air Brears had looked to see who was underneath it. And when he'd seen who it was, he'd turned round to the slips and said: 'Oh God, it's Picca.' Both could have come

down and said, 'Great catch, mate, well done' ... but, oh no. If you watch the highlights you can see me nodding and going, 'Yeah, thanks, Ian.'

TMS commentator Don Mosey: The Australians played shots they will be ashamed of for the rest of their lives.

Brian Mossop, _Sydney Morning Herald_: At the start of the day we were still quite complacent about victory. It wasn't a lot to get and up 'til then Australia had played reasonable cricket, even taking into account Botham's innings. But they didn't approach the last innings seriously. There was no plan, they just went out like lambs to the slaughter.

Fred Trueman ⌈on _TMS_⌉: I keep wanting to pinch myself to see if I'm still in bed. If anyone had mentioned victory for England this morning I would have laughed in their faces.

Christopher Martin-Jenkins ⌈on BBC TV⌉: A little before this time yesterday English cricket was being buried.

David Ryder: When Australia were seven wickets down we just threw open the gates. Even when the match was over, there were still people coming in. Just standing on the terraces, just wanting to be here. There must have been 15,000 people in the ground.

Mike Brearley: Umpire Evans had told Willis not to bowl bouncers at Lawson. I was amazed. 'Forget it,' I said. 'But don't bother with an out-and-out bouncer at first – short of a length, rib-height.'

Graham Dilley: During the Lillee–Bright stand my emotions were in turmoil. We'd staged a great fightback, but we were still going to lose. Not that we'd played ruthless cricket for five days or anything like that and deserved to win. You just thought, 'Why does it have to go wrong, why can't we as a team experience winning a game?' I'd never been in a winning Test side before and this game had turned into the best chance I'd had ... and now Dennis was going to take it away – with the bat. I thought that if I could score some runs on this pitch, anybody could.

Peter Philpott: I couldn't watch. I had to go for a walk.

Lillee c Gatting b Willis 17

Mike Gatting: Seeing Brears was about to switch the field around, I walked up to him and said, 'Why doesn't Bob just try bowling a *length* at Dennis?' Lillee, having faced a few good-length balls and looking decidedly uncomfortable, tried to chip one through midwicket, the ball straightened and I took the catch at mid-on. But it was a near thing because I lost my footing as I went for the catch and only held it as I was about to hit the deck.

Ian Botham: When Mike Gatting caught Dennis Lillee it was like watching the winning goal in the FA Cup final.

Chris Old [on dropping Terry Alderman]: The first one hit me on the shin. Didn't get a hand on it. The pitches kept low at Headingley then, so I stood closer, two yards in front of Taylor. If a dropped catch means getting a hand on it, it wasn't a drop. But I couldn't believe I dropped the second one. It took me the best part of 20 years to realise how I managed it: my left hand was on the floor, so there was

no give. 'I've got that,' I thought, then, 'Shit, what's happened there?' It was the last ball of the over and I went down to deep square, right in front of the Western Terrace, so I got quite a bit of bird. I heaved a huge sigh of relief when Willis got Bright with the first ball of the next over.

Ray Bright: Willis had picked up yards in pace since switching ends, but I knew we had to try to score some runs off him – take the momentum away from England. We were getting there – and then Dennis got out. Terry came in and was dropped twice in an over and I thought, 'I've got to get on with it.' I was expecting a short ball from Bob, but instead he bowled me one of the best yorkers I've ever seen. I can still hear the clunk as it hit the middle stump.

Richie Benaud on BBC TV: It's all over and it's one of the most fantastic victories ever known in Test match history.

David Ryder: When the last wicket fell, the spectators rushed on to the field and up to the pavilion. Some of them tried to get up the stairs to the players' dressing room. It had never happened before and I was frantically shouting for some police and stewards to stop them.

Victory and defeat
The English

BBC Sport presenter Peter West: Ian, you said last night that if you got another 50, that would make it interesting. You got another four.

Ian Botham: Well, that made it even more interesting.

Ian Botham: The Aussies had bought their victory champagne in advance. When we sent our dressing-room attendant into theirs to ask if we could borrow some, it was suggested to him in good old-fashioned Australian that he might consider leaving the room. Eventually the England management succeeded in negotiating a fair price for a few bottles and we downed the lot.

Peter Willey, who had only ever tasted winners' bubbly when it had been offered to him by the other side, said simply: 'That's better. All the other stuff I've drunk has made me want to puke.'

Graham Gooch: It was a one-off situation that I don't think will ever be repeated. Not to win from that position, but to win because of an innings like Ian Botham's – where he basically went out there for fun, with no pressure, just going for his shots.

Bob Taylor: The Aussies congratulated Beefy but they felt they'd lost it, as they always do. You'll never get an Aussie to admit he was beaten fair and square.

Ian Botham: The Australians deserved to win; in effect – on Monday afternoon – they'd already won.

Chris Old: We had a brief chat with the Aussies after the game, but they were so down, even more than I thought they'd be. Given the circumstances, what could they say? On the other hand, we were too happy to feel sorry for them.

I remember driving down the M1 and hearing the news on the radio: it registered a bit. But it wasn't until I was watching the highlights at a hotel in Sheffield – where I'd retired to bed with a bottle of champers and two pints of Guinness – that what had happened hit me properly. Thank goodness it rained for the next three days! I spent the whole Yorkshire v Sri Lanka match walking around like a zombie.

Peter Willey: We couldn't celebrate too much because most of us were playing in NatWest games the next day and had to drive to wherever the games were being held. I only stayed an hour or two.

The drive back from Leeds to Northants down the M1 was unbelievable. I had a sponsored car with my name on the side and every time somebody saw the name, they were tooting, waving and saying 'well done'. It was like winning a world war.

People you'd never seen before kept coming up and saying, 'Well done, well done.'

Back on the county circuit, all anybody wanted to talk about was Botham's innings. Apart from Botham, and maybe Willis, people don't remember who played in that match, but I was proud to be part of the game. It's the Test match that everybody remembers. It's my, 'What did you do in the war, Dad?' story.

Graham Dilley: It wasn't until you were driving down the motorway and people were beeping their horns at you and waving and giving you the thumbs up that you realised what had been achieved. It was then you started to realise what it meant to people, everyday cricket watchers.

It wasn't just our victory. Given the state of the country in 1981 it was something that people could latch onto to give them some escape. It had given them some hope.

Mike Brearley: A cable awaited me at Lord's when I returned to London, from

Spike Milligan, which read: 'Marvellous – have my ticket for the Wedding.'

The Australians

Kim Hughes: We did nothing wrong except lose.

Dennis Lillee: I remember thinking it was just a dream, one of those fairy-tales. I still can't believe we lost. I guess I never will come to terms with it.

Peter Philpott: We were shattered and exhausted. We'd been on a psycho-logical high – as illustrated by that stupid 500–1 bet – and then we'd been plunged into depression. It was awful.

Dirk Wellham: The power of the surging crowd's chant of 'Botham, Botham' bounced around the ground relentlessly, only relieved by the dirge-ful dittoes for bustling Bobby. Inside our dressing room there was profound silence – everyone remained unmoving, voiceless.

Graeme Wood: I don't think I ever felt as bad as that. We should have been two-up in the series, the Ashes nearly won and have caused the demise of two champion players in Botham and Willis. But we dwelled on the negatives for too long. We played the better cricket for three-and-a-half days. Hughes was too inexperienced to get us to focus on that.

John Dyson: It was a game we'd won – a nightmare.

Alan McGilvray: There was a general feeling of disbelief afterwards. And a certain awe. We had seen an Australian win butchered from the strongest pos-sible base.

Brian Mossop, *Sydney Morning Herald*: The Aussies were shell-shocked, they couldn't believe they had lost. But they also thought it was a momentary aberration and that England couldn't play that well again.

David Ryder: As the Australians' coach was leaving, they got some stick from some England supporters. Rod Marsh came charging off the coach and started having a go back. We quickly got him back on board and they were away.

The Rest

Barrie Meyer: We sat in the dressing room and tried to relax. David Evans uttered the first words: 'Gosh, I hope they're not all like that.'

David Ryder: One guy rushed back to his office with a couple of scorecards, got them typed up with the complete match details, raced back to Headingley and got all the England players to sign them. He's kept one and the other's hanging on the wall of our office.

C.A. Philbrick, Letter to *The Times,* **25 July:** Sir, The sight of Ian Botham, and on the following day, Bob Willis, having to make their undignified head-long dash for the safety of the dressing room was the only sad aspect of the exciting finish to the recent Test. It is a player's right to be allowed to walk back to the pavilion in the traditional manner after producing an exceptional piece of cricket. It is more moving and emotionally satisfying for the player and spectator alike. I should have felt cheated at not being able to stand and clap my hands for the full minute such an exit usually took years ago.

Dylan Tangled Up In Blue

Was this match won by the much-maligned if grossly exaggerated might of the fourth estate? Ridiculous as it may seem, this is entirely possible.

It did not seem unreasonable to expect Robert George Dylan Willis to be a teensy bit happy with life. A toss-up, perhaps, between dumbstruck delight and outright delirium. After all, he had just bowled England to the most astonishing comeback since the prince stole into that glade to give a comatose princess mouth-to-mouth resuscitation. His message to the nation suggested quite the opposite. One of the more improbable ditties ever to penetrate Radio 1's recent Top 40 is the smasheroonie by Kirsty MacColl, *There's A Guy Works Down The Chip Shop Swears He's Elvis*. Anyone for *There's A Guy Works Up The Cricket Pitch And I'll Swear He's Potty?*

Willis had just turned H_2O into Chateau Laffite, plucking his Test career from the fire, not to say his country's cricketing credibility. ITN would lead with the news on their 5.45 bulletin, ditto Radio 4's *PM*. One gander at the man alternatively known as Goose, though, and you just knew something was horribly amiss. What ensued was a resoundingly successful attempt to turn water into whine.

Peter West approached him, mike in hand, wonder and bonhomie in voice, old school tie tucked primly inside blazer. Good old Westie: to millions the acceptable, kindly, innocuous establishment mouthpiece. Wouldn't – couldn't – utter a nasty word to a soul.

He would have told the Nazis they were being bad sports and left it at that. The hero, regrettably, was in no mood for basking.

Perhaps he'd been listening when Fred Trueman read the last rites on *Test Match Special* the previous afternoon? 'I couldn't believe the bowlers could allow Australia to reach 400 on a pitch made for seam bowling,' Fiery Fred had blazed in full-on 'I-don't-know-what's-going-off-out-there' mode. 'We have possibly seen the end of one or two Test careers,' he continued as Bob Taylor fell, before adding a sensible rider: 'Who is there to pick?'

Or was Willis still miffed about the previous summer's encounter with West at Trent Bridge? The way the latter tells it, Willis had told him to eff off, whereupon West took him to task in a Lord's hospitality tent a few weeks later, for being 'rude': Willis fled 'in high dudgeon'.

Here, discreetly allowing the captain a few minutes' respite, West sought out Brearley soon after the players returned to the pavilion, seeking permission for a few words with the matchwinner on behalf of a grateful nation. 'Bob's in the bath,' he was advised. 'You can ask him yourself.'

Cue one of the more squirmish moments of West's eventful tenure as the Man from the Beeb. Knocking on the door of the England dressing room, he was bidden to enter. Stretched out in a bath ludicrously short for a fellow of 6ft 5in lay Willis, soothing his gammy knee and infected chest, steadying that pounding heart.

Or, as the would-be interviewer put it, 'Contemplating his navel'. West proffered his heartiest congratulations (strictly nouns and adjectives, including the odd 'tremendous'), then asked if the bather wouldn't mind awfully if he asked him a few questions on behalf of the great unwashed. Willis glared out from beneath a mound of soggy poodle curls. What about their, er, contretemps? 'Surely we can forget that,' replied West. 'It's been a marvellous day for English cricket.' Willis reconsidered. 'All right,' he consented. 'I'll be with you in five minutes.'

When he re-emerged on the balcony, Willis's long, lugubrious face was drawn and pallid. Almost bloodless. The crowd had seen fresher week-old milk. Those close enough to the presentation balcony – or drinking in the giddy, heady brew from office and hearth – could make out the eyes. Intense, glazed, blank. Perhaps he was still absorbing the announcement that Botham had pipped him for the Man of the Match award? ('A captain's performance that came one match too late,' decreed adjudicator Trueman with due poignancy and unusual sensitivity.)

What we all anticipated, demanded, craved, was a dose of good old-fashioned gushing. Tempered, naturally, with compassion and respect for the doughty efforts of the gallant losers (tee-hee). In short, as Tom Tom Club's latest slab of fab electro-poppery so eloquently puts it, some *Wordy Rappinghood*. Instead, we got *Desolation Row*. A full quotation seems both pointless and unjust. Suffice to say, the man of the hour, rather than inform us how parrotesque he had been feeling lately, and how far over the moon he'd just vaulted, proceeded to denounce the media as a cross between Jake La Motta and Kim Philby.

'Cheer up, you look like you just lost,' joshed one baffled member of the paparazzi.

'Some of you lot wish we had,' snapped Willis. The gist was plain: the assembled hacks were two-faced, insensitive, destructive, disloyal and generally unhelpful to the cause. Spirit had been undermined and performance deflated by knee-jerk responses and perpetual criticism, never mind callous invasions of privacy in search of 'small-minded' quotes at the expense of proper cricketing analysis.

Willis may well have been justified in a number of these insinuations, but this was hardly the appropriate time or medium. Why not save it for that *Wisden Cricket Monthly* column? Or, better still, for a *Sun* 'exclusive'? Then again, although he and Brearley are both understood to be peed off about that 'Test War' headline in the previous Thursday's Currant Bun, perhaps this righteous, ill-focused indignation was simply a matter of him sticking up for his chum? If anybody had cause to complain about receiving disproportionate helpings of the third degree from the fourth estate it is assuredly I.T. Botham Esq. Then again, if antagonising a bloke drives him to hitherto unimagined heights, so be it. One fellow hack suggested that, if this was what came of writing Willis off, he would dip his pen in vitriol more often.

West, not unnaturally, was taken aback by all this bile and spleen-venting. 'Bob,' he interjected, 'you've just won a Test match in the most remark-able circumstances. Can't we stick to a happier topic?'

Pausing mid-rant, Willis finally did the decent thing. And yes, he had pleaded with Brearley to switch him downwind. The reason? 'I'm an old man now.'

Unlucky Hendrick

Few worms have turned quite so rapid-ly. The man who beheaded six Australians in as many overs had sent down the best part of 200 balls in the first innings and emerged wicketless. When Alec Bedser rang him at Edgbaston last Saturday, it was to inform him that he had been dropped. Aggrieved that selectors and captain had assumed he would be unable to last five days, he argued his case forcefully and persuasively. Mike Hendrick's invi-tation to play was intercepted some-where between Lord's and Derby.

Thirty-two, as Lillee seldom tires of reminding us, is no age for a fast bowler – Brian Statham was 35 when he won his last cap, Trueman and John Snow both 34. By the same token, the Subiaco Superman, unlike the Sunderland Sunderer, has an action that is built to last. Willis ranks among the few members of the international cricket fraternity to be saddled with more than one nickname, namely 'Dylan' and the aforementioned 'Goose'. The latter stemmed from that unique, elbow-flapping run-up, a methodology that defies emulation (much as Gooch makes a brave stab of it amid that repertoire of impressions he saves for dreary days). The only odder approach belonged to John Price, the erstwhile Middlesex and sometime

England new-baller – curved run, two changes of gear followed by an exquis-itely co-ordinated flourish at release as he reared back then recoiled, before thrusting himself forward once more, arms flying hither and thither like some mad eruption of helicopter blades. Squint just a shade and the man from Harrow could have been bearing down on W.G., spotted a black widow in the undergrowth of that mangy beard, but decided to press on regardless. Price concocted it, he readily confessed, to stand out from the crowd. Competition was sterner 20 years ago.

It is hard to picture Willis, a chap with a tendency to clutch cards close to chest and disdain showmanship, being motivated by such considerations. He may be smarter than the average pro-fessional cricketer, and by some dis-tance, but how he conceived his modus operandi defies comprehension. Can you picture the scene in his bedroom 15 years previously? 'Righto then, I'll start by curving in a shade, then straighten up. Head down, chest out. Wiggle elbows as much as possible, pump knees vigorously enough to be in perpetual danger of chinning myself, and run like the clappers as if trying to scale a cliff. Oh, and get rid of the thing before running out of puff.' Colleagues have long remarked that, when in the groove, he occupies a galaxy of one.

In last month's issue of *Wisden Cricket Monthly*, Willis acknowledged that his 'unorthodox delivery puts amazing stress on both my knee-joints', and answered the misgivings expressed by a reader from Bangor, Bill Clutterbuck. 'I appreciate very much our reader's point,' he wrote, then explained that Arthur McIntyre, then Surrey's coach, had tried 'to get me to bowl like Alec Bedser', i.e. braced left leg and classical side-on delivery. Pace and line deserted him; after a few weeks he was talked into reverting to the original style by, among others, John Edrich – who now, of course, is a selector bathing in the reflected glow.

Cocoon of concentration

Yet who, in all honesty, can begrudge Willis his distracted outburst? Before the start of the Australian innings Brearley made 'a brief, exhortatory speech' to his troops, insisting on 'more aggression, more liveliness, more encouragement for the bowlers – *they're* the ones who are nervous now'.

Willis immersed himself in a 'cocoon of concentration I could not afford to disturb'. *Et voila* – a Red Admiral fluttered forth: 'I knew exactly what I had to do and, once I had begun to bowl well, I believed it could be done.' Even if Brearley had wanted to bring him off, Willis, totally entranced, would have required a poke in the eye or a yank on the collar to get the message.

Throughout his career, he will tell you, he has bowled at his best when left alone to operate in his own sweet way. There are few things he loathes more than being halted on that hike back to his mark by a frantically gesticulating captain keen to change the field or submit advice. Brearley came to know and respect this. Never – once he saw Willis was sequestered in his twilight zone – had he interfered, and at Headingley he was not about to start.

Taylor and Gooch supplied a regular stream of sweet nothings and supportive pats, the keeper almost invariably at the end of each over, yet Willis turned neither hair nor head, continuing on his blissfully impenetrable way. Taylor and Gooch strongly suspected that their words fell on deaf ears.

The switch from uphill labourer to down-dale destroyer was 'a final shot'. After five overs Willis told Brearley straight: he was 'too old for that sort of thing'.

The captain's response was sardonic, even irritated: 'You mean you've had enough of coming uphill and into the wind?'

At first Willis did as he was told. 'Okay,' he replied, grumpily, 'I'll carry on here then.'

During Old's next over, however, after consulting Taylor and Botham, who both believed he was looking 'our most dangerous bowler', Brearley decided to 'give Willis his head'.

What would have happened had Brearley decreed otherwise, as he had every right and cause to do? Instead, at 12.06, with Willis further emboldened by the skipper's reassuring suggestion that he needn't fret about overstepping, the last ball of that first over exploded off a length and threatened to decapitate Chappell. At which point Brearley decided it might prove an efficacious move.

Much as one is reluctant to accuse any Australian side of fear, were Hughes et al cowed less by that one delivery than by that sheer intensity, turbo-charged as it was by the certain knowledge that it was time for last orders in the Last Chance Saloon? Did they stare into those eyes in search of frailty and glimpse nothing but frozen steel? There have been murmurs about drugs, specifically cocaine; thus far, happily, they have had everything bar substance. (The cheque's in the post, Basil: it is Mr rather than Master Brush, isn't it?)

Zombiefied

'Everyone will tell you Bob was like a zombie for 40 minutes after the game,' said Bernard Thomas, England's doughty physio. 'I'd have sworn he was drugged. I know he wasn't, and that concerned me even more. What do we really know about hypnosis? Whether Bob's condition was a reaction to the game or as a result of self-hypnosis, I don't know. What I do know is that hypnosis can affect people in many ways. Personally, I'm afraid of [it].'

Geoff Lawson scoffed at the notion that he and his team-mates were petrified by a drug-addled monster: 'I think it was his haircut that scared us above anything else. Let's face it, you would have to be on a bad acid trip to let a hairdresser do that to your bonce.'

Some three hours later, Willis returned to his car, emotionally sapped. Turning on the radio, his ears pricked up at the unmistakably fruity tones of Henry Blofeld – not until that moment did he realise that Robert George Dylan Willis was now a national hero. Pink Floyd coined a term for it: comfortably numb.

At the time, Willis's future was far from certain. It was entirely possible that he would continue to defy the media's self-appointed arbiters of longevity. Some believed that, provided he persisted with that shrewd approach to county duties (i.e. play as infrequently as a captain can possibly

get away with), he could supersede Trueman's 307 Test scalps and maybe even give Lillee a run for his money. Conversely, those knees could just as easily decide that this was the final huzza after all.

All that could be said at the time with any conviction is that R.G.D. Willis could have picked up a BBC microphone there and then and spent the next 20 years being as bitchy to his heirs as he pleased, safe in the knowledge, the same knowledge that inures Trueman, that he would have been forgiven all. Which is rather more, in all probability, than could be said for Kim Hughes.

'Bob just went berserk'

Barrie Meyer: Bob started bowling at my end. I said to him: 'Don't you think you're on at the wrong end?' He didn't say anything, I don't know if he even heard.

John Dyson: Bob Willis developed these crazy eyes and began to bowl shorter and more aggressively. Then some of the deliveries started staying low as well.

Peter Philpott: By the fifth day, the wicket was a real bugger. Willis was producing some absolute bastard balls.

Trevor Chappell: Bob just went berserk. He bowled me a short one and I didn't have a clue what to do with it. It came straight at my head, hit the bat handle and looped over my head and into Bob Taylor's gloves. I was still waiting for the ball to drop into short leg's hands.

Frank Crook, [Australian] *Sun*: Willis was terrifying, he terrorised Yallop. He reminded me of Frank Tyson at Sydney back in 1954–55. It was the only other time I'd seen such a great piece of sustained fast bowling.

Ian Botham: It was the most magnificent spell of hostile fast bowling it has ever been my privilege to witness.

Peter Willey: Something just clicked in his brain. I've never seen eyes like it. I shouldn't say it – but you'd think he'd been on drugs.

Graham Dilley: I didn't notice Willis's 'trance' until he got the last wicket. We were both running off at the same time and I looked into his eyes and it was like there was nobody there. I know that Bob can be a little bit distant sometimes, that's just his character. But it really was like somebody had

hypnotised him. The eyes were open, but there was no life coming out of them.

He'd got himself into such a focus that nothing and nobody else existed. I found that quite weird. A bloke you know reasonably well and, when you look at him, it's almost like they're dead, because there's no life in their eyes.

Brian Mossop, *Sydney Morning Herald*: I think Botham's innings helped resurrect Willis's career. He was inspired by Botham. And, let's face it, Bob often goes into a trance even when he isn't bowling.

Part 5

We were there
(or thereabouts)

Witnesses to a miracle

I saw my first first-class match in 1957, the Test against West Indies at Headingley. I hitched from Newcastle: I don't think we realised that Peter Loader had taken his hat-trick.

Keith was five when I took him to his first Test, the 1973 Lord's Test against New Zealand. Being a quiet, contemplative type, I thought it would appeal to him. I'd had a long hiatus from the game. I was fortunate enough to have been there on that unforgettable final afternoon at Lord's in 1963 against the West Indies, but work had prevented me from going to Tests since then. As it happened, that day Keith met Cardus. He was sitting on a wall behind the pavilion, talking at us, pointing a bony finger. After that I'd pick Keith up from Hebrew classes at Edgware Reform Synagogue, pick up some salt beef sarnies and take him to Sunday League games at Lord's. He started reciting Sunday League scorecards and *Wisden* extracts at school assembly.

In 1981 I was working as a solicitor at Highbury Corner and living in Edgware. I decided the Headingley Test would be an ideal way to do all five days of a Test. We'd been to Lord's, Edgbaston and The Oval together and I worked out that it wouldn't be that much more expensive to become Yorkshire members and hence gain free admission. Keith was now old enough, and interested enough. We didn't have to book tickets; we just turned up and showed our membership passes.

One of the attractions was the fact that Brearley had been recalled. He was our hero. Keith used to send him birthday cards. When he left for the India tour of 1976–77 he sent Keith a postcard from the airport. 'Dear Keith,' it read, 'we're off.'

We sat behind the Berger Paints sign at the Rugby Stand End – third man to the right-hander. I can recall one woman member being there for all five days, too. She had a Benson & Hedges holdall from Australia and saved our seats every day. We got there on the Wednesday, booked into the Nordic Hotel, a B&B, and watched net practice, which was a bit of a ritual.

I kept score and Keith watched every ball, although he may have read the paper a bit during Dyson's innings! Neither of us listened to *Test Match Special* – I don't know why. It was probably that we were so thrilled to be there we didn't want any distractions. Mind you, we watched the highlights on TV every night – 'so that's what happened ...'

The best part was Dilley's stand with Botham. It was one of the most engrossing passages of cricket I'd ever seen. The sense of being on the edge of danger, of Australia's lead diminishing. Dilley lifted our spirits. I can recall thinking Botham was clever to keep the strike off the last ball of the day. After the close I went to the toilet and heard a Yorkshireman say, 'I think 'e'd be in contention for Man of the Match.' Yet through it all, all that was going through my mind was, 'What the hell are we going to do tomorrow?'

Only at 1.15pm on the Tuesday did we think there was any possibility of a tight finish. 'Bugger me,' I thought. 'We're going to get a full day's play.' That was still my main concern. I don't remember any frisson in the crowd. Dilley caught Marsh right in front of us. When Lillee started upper-cutting it was the first time I'd ever seen the shot played. I watched the last ball on binoculars – then took them away to make sure I believed my own eyes. I didn't realise Willis had taken eight wickets – and I was scoring!

At the end everyone else was leaping on the pitch but I had to finish scoring before the ecstasy set in. I was a bit surprised when Willis slagged off Peter West, not that we could hear much. We went to the original Harry Ramsden's at Guiseley to celebrate. The queue for the ladies was the biggest I've ever seen.

My eyesight is now deteriorating badly, and there are times when I wonder how much I recall through hindsight, from the TV highlights and the video. The match had more impact on me than the 1966 World Cup final because it was so unexpected. To have drawn it would have been a miracle. There is an element of 'we fortunate few' about having been there as well as at Lord's in '63. Those two last days were very similar; they had the unity of time as well as wickets and runs. It was pure fluke, but how many others went to arguably the two best finishes to a Test in England in my lifetime?

David Summerfield

The Edgbaston Test that followed was a much better contest, but I don't think there's ever been such an exciting game – for an Englishman. It was unusual for me because Jim Laker was ill, and I was doing TV, not radio. I'd just gone freelance after eight years as BBC radio correspondent, and although I enjoyed TV, I enjoy radio more.

The gloom on Saturday night, in every sense, had to be seen to be believed. When Botham came in on the Monday and I said it would be a triumph if he was still there at 6 o'clock, it was always in hope, never expectation. It took a fair bit of time to dawn that something so unforgettable was unfolding. I'd checked out of my hotel that morning. Only when Hughes went just before lunch, and Chris Old got Border soon after, did I really think it might happen.

Michael Fordham was scoring for us, quite a nervous little man. At one point he got so tense he asked me to take over while he went for a p***.

There was much more excitement than usual in the commentary boxes, regardless of the state of Michael Fordham's bladder. Richie Benaud remarked at lunch after Kim Hughes' dismissal that the Australian dressing room would be full of 'very anxious fellows'. I think we all sensed that something remarkable might be about to happen. I can't recall finding it harder to retain a state of journalistic objectivity.

Botham and Willis left equally strong memories: Willis couldn't have done it without Botham. Ever since then, in similarly dire circumstances, England have always been more likely than any other Test team to come back from the dead.

Christopher Martin-Jenkins, *The Times*

This was the best match on which I have ever commentated. There was a lot of very good cricket played, even without the astonishing fightback, and it was a good underlining of the fact that anything can happen in the game.

Certainly the match was to the benefit of English cricket. It is still talked about as one of the great victories in the history of the game and thoroughly deserves that rating.

Richie Benaud

My most cherished memory of the match is my surprise and pleasure at the victory and the way it was obtained. Blowers [Henry Blofeld] and I were on air as the final wickets fell but remembering what he said would have been difficult the following day, let alone 20 years later.

Trevor Bailey

During the Test I stayed at the Dragonara (now Hilton) Hotel. I spent most of the match wandering around the ground. The press box was lousy. You couldn't see too much, and it was cramped. You could walk round the cycle track then, and that's how I saw Australia bowled out, with Terry Brindle of the *Yorkshire Post* and, I think, Peter Smith of the *Daily Mail*, making notes on a cigarette packet. It probably heightened the enjoyment. There was a sense of seeing something special. And it was England–Australia. Mind you, I did see England win the Ashes five times, so I did get a bit blasé. And when we won we were every bit as patronising to their journos as they were to us when they won.

I don't know where the 'greatest comeback since Lazarus' line came from. I went to church in my young days, so I suppose I knew a lot about Lazarus. That was what it felt like before his hundred – mourners in the aisles. I've seen the line so many times since, I'm not even sure I wrote it any more. I probably ran it past my sports editor, Ken Lawrence, before committing myself. I was quite pleased with it. I did the main report – at least 30 paragraphs, roughly 1000 words – another story for the front and a spread inside. In those days, on the *Express*, you were encouraged to write. It wasn't all crash, bang, wallop. Mind you, when the paper went tabloid, nobody told me.

We, the press, were much closer to things then. We knew the baggageman and the bus driver. There were a lot more Aussie journos there, all very supportive and close to their players, so there were few secrets.

Pat Gibson, *The Times*

I was staying with my brother in Doncaster and we went on the third day. Even in those days Headingley was a gimcrack sort of ground. Quite a number of fat men were wearing 'I bowled Boycott' T-shirts. They gravitated to the Western Terrace. We took our seats at the Rugby Stand End, fine leg to the right-hander. The players were then using the small pavilion side-on.

Of the play scarcely an image remains. Lillee fielding at long leg being offered a banana from the Western Terrace and being cheered when he ate it. Boycott being bowled almost inexplicably by Lawson bowling from the Kirkstall Lane End. It wasn't till I saw the highlights in the evening that I realised that he'd moved across to off stump and the ball had jagged back a long way and bowled him behind his legs.

I remember cushions being thrown on the outfield [when play was abandoned] and one man saying in a thick Leeds accent, 'I'm not coming here again.' He must have missed the Monday and Tuesday. Anger was in the air, partly fuelled by England's poor performance on a substandard pitch. One other thing I remember was the electronic scoreboard. I clearly recall seeing those 500–1 odds flashed up on the Saturday either at the end of their first innings or at the close of play when they had lost one wicket for very few.

On Monday I travelled back to London and caught the last hour or so of

Botham. Tuesday I returned to work and was phoned by a friend with news of England's victory. I even had a note of the book I was reading at the time: *Cricket Delightful* by Mushtaq Ali, a pioneer of India's early Test days. An apposite title.

Stephen Eley

As a boy growing up in Cumbria, cricket meant the horse's field with its allotment hut pavilion and birch tree-thicket sightscreens. And the Headingley Test match.

Dad took me every year. Leeds was a remote place, further than Glasgow, and its distance lent the day the flavour of an expedition. The fact that that year the likes of Botham, Willis, Gower, Marsh and Lillee lay at the other end, made it more of a pilgrimage. Not for my father. He hated the Stainmore Pass, which hacks its way through the Pennines like a blunt knife; he dreaded the maze of wrong turnings waiting to deceive us in that impossibly huge metropolis of Leeds.

It was a burden to him, I know. But perhaps it is the gifts that are difficult to give, that are truly blest. For that Saturday will stay with me until the end. And the fact that it wasn't even *the* day doesn't matter in the least.

In the memory that day burns with the intensity of Van Gogh's palette; the long-gone evergreens of Headingley still tower above everything like that artist's famous cypresses of the south. I see, portrait-close, the face of Dennis Lillee turned to catch the light as he signed autograph books whilst fielding at long leg. And I am dazzled by the lights of the electronic scoreboard, shining as brightly as 500 vases of sunflowers.

On the scoreboard the odds read 500–1. But there were no takers. Perhaps there were one or two in the drunken crowd surrounding us who were senseless enough to throw their money away. I hope they did.

The drunk hold a fascination for 12-year-old boys which is not shared by the population at large. And there was one person I studied with as much interest as if I had been an artist myself. He was not a trumpet player, although he played one incessantly. Propped up between two fellow drinkers, he blew his way through the day. There was precious little music, but his face achieved a redness that was positively symphonic.

But these were all sideshows. Inevitably it was the figure of Botham that persists most strongly. Not rampant as he was to be two days later, and no longer entirely snared in the uncharacteristic doubt of his pair at Lord's with the attendant sneers of MCC members. And it is for these very reasons that the portrait painted of him by that day is special.

180

For on that day we had The Hero caught in a time of never-to-be-repeated vulnerability, trying on the mantle of greatness but unsure if his shoulders were wide enough. On that day we had the breaking of silence, moments before destiny dawns. On that day we had the last few uncertain sketches, before the first strokes on the masterpiece are applied.

Thanks, Ian. Thanks, Dad.

Jonathan Tulloch

I went on the Saturday, and remember pondering on whether or not to have a bet on England at 500–1. Unlike Lillee and Marsh, I decided against it.

Geoff Lawson was fielding on the boundary just in front of us at one time, and engaged in some rather smug banter with the crowd. I often wonder if he was inclined to do the same during Botham's innings on Monday. I can also recall the controversy surrounding the decision to bring the players off for bad light during the extra hour, and leave them off when the sun broke out only a few minutes later. The Yorkshire public don't take kindly to being cheated of an hour's cricket. I wasn't too bothered though, as I felt such delays represented England's best chance of getting out of the game with anything other than a hammering.

I filled in the scorecard with the utmost care after the game, framed it, and it hangs today on my office wall (my wife wouldn't let me put it up at home).

David Thornley

In the spring of 1981, Irving Rosenwater, who was the usual BBC-TV scorer, announced that he would not, after all, be returning from his winter work for Channel Nine to work on the Ashes series.

As his number two (used on days when two matches were televised), I was invited by the producer of cricket, Nick Hunter, to score three Tests, with Michael Fordham doing the other three. It was decided that at the end of the season a decision would be made as to which of us would then get the regular position from 1982 onwards. (In the event, Michael died on holiday in America in the autumn of 1981.)

As it turned out, I had recently left Lord's, where I had been secretary to the secretary of the National Cricket Association, running their film lending library during the winter. Ted Dexter had kindly offered me a job where my cricket expertise could be put to better full-time use and I had worked with him for about two weeks when the BBC letter arrived. He very kindly let me take up Hunter's offer because, at the time, he was writing for a Sunday newspaper and we should be at the Tests in any case.

My three designated Tests were Lord's, Old Trafford and The Oval, so Ted and I were at Headingley, although I was not scoring; he was doing TV commentary. On the Monday morning we met up and he decided I should get the train back to London and get cracking on the pile of work we had in the office. 'I shall soon be following you down the motorway,' he said.

So you can imagine my surprise on arriving at Ealing to be met by Ted's wife, Susan, beaming and saying, 'Come in quickly! Botham's saving England!' I did not see any of that great innings and even after all these years I have only just about forgiven Ted.

The summer had a happy ending, for it started seven years of scoring Tests for the BBC and, at Lord's, I was advised by Bobby Simpson to apply for the same job in Australia with ABC. This led to 11 happy Australian summers, two trips to New Zealand and the Caribbean. But, for all that, I often wish I had seen the 1981 Headingley Test in its entirety.

Wendy Wimbush

I have only attended one day's Test cricket in the last quarter of a century but it does happen to have been Monday 20 July 1981. I live in Aberdeen and the nearest Test ground is some seven hours' drive away. However, I have made every attempt to bring up my two boys in the proper manner, complete with twice-weekly coaching classes at Aberdeenshire Cricket Club and educative sessions in front of the TV set. I decided it was time to induct Jonathan, my eldest, then 10, into the real-live drama of the Test match. We would book a summer holiday in Yorkshire; I selected the fourth day of the third Test as my opportunity.

My memories are structured by an acute sense of tension which, while it certainly changed in nature during the day, never entirely departed. The fact that I was trying to adjust my role of wise and experienced tutor to a stream of events which refused to be ordered simply added to my agitation. Neither of us was particularly intense about an English success – we saved that kind of emotion for Fergie's Dons – but for the sake of the day it was important that Brearley's team performed strongly enough to make a decent match of it. On the Saturday, driving down and listening to the radio, we had heard of nothing but English batting failures. By the close, my fears of an interminable six hours of hapless one-sidedness were replaced by concern that there wouldn't be a real day to go to at all.

The scruffy tiers of the Western Terrace, half-empty, looked bleak. It was difficult to maintain the conviction that we were attending a major sporting event. The Aussies strutted about, laughing and shouting. At the fall of each wicket they would rush together to embrace and to form their own little band of cacophonous self-sufficiency, indifferent to the silent despair that was seeping into every other part of the ground.

The odds of 500–1 appeared on the scoreboard; Jonathan asked me for an explanation. Naïvely, he suggested a pound on for each of us; I informed him that betting was a mug's game and that bookies always knew what they were doing. We were seated alongside a couple of backpackers from South Africa who had little detailed knowledge of English cricket. When they enquired about the prospect of England's number seven, I assured them that he was 'talented but unreliable – won't last'.

After the bails had been lifted, as my son was roaring his applause, I recall a quick moment of astonishment. The man with the marvellous 145 not out was, after all, not Jessop, not Hammond, or Hobbs but an individual whom the TV had made intimately familiar to us all. A very contemporary hero who advertised Shredded Wheat, someone who, between overs, habitually emitted little gobs of spit and who, when he had been congratulated on beating Hugh Trumble's record for the fastest 100 wickets in Tests, had shortly replied that he'd 'never heard of the guy'. It was my last and greatest surprise of the day; the thought that 'Good God, it's him who's done that ...'

Framed on the wall of my sitting room is a copy of the scorecard, purchased for 15p at 10.30am and on which I encouraged my son to fill in all of the batsmen's runs, stroke by stroke, as a way of maintaining interest through what was bound to be a turgid six hours or less. Beneath the glass, you can still make out the firmly-entered succession of fours and twos with which Botham opened his account, each separated by a suspiciously neat dot. And then, as you attempt to follow the line, you notice how the orderliness begins to fray and finally to collapse beneath a turbulent flow of entries, as the novice begins to search out the necessary space in which to cram it all. There is the result on the wall, the torrent of fours and the one golden six spilling over the columns, crowding out the rows of other batsmen, until they finally pour over into the space reserved for the bowling analyses.

The next day, Jonathan was all for going back. But England were still only 124 runs ahead and the Aussies were certain to move to an eight- or seven-wicket win by about 3 o'clock. I knew that what we had experienced the previous day had been an extraordinary gift. What, somehow, Jonathan had encountered on his very first attempt was something which I had spent 25 years pursuing. Time to resume the education. 'No,' I said, 'it won't be worth it.' We went shopping in Bradford instead.

David Northcroft

I'd just finished my A-levels and with time to kill before going to college, I persuaded a couple of schoolfriends to come along to the match with me in shifts. I was there on Thursday and Friday, but Saturday was spent at home in York listening on the radio.

Off we set on Monday and by close of play knew that the writing was on the wall. However, we were on such a high that we caught the train from Headingley to Leeds and phoned home from the station to ask our parents' permission to go back for the last day. Realistically, we knew that Australia still had the upper hand but were so exhilarated by Botham's batting we felt a real need to be there.

In the meantime, it was a time of great celebration – my sister had just got married and I took some of her wedding cake up to the *Test Match Special* box as a variation from their usual chocolate cake. Everywhere you went there were Union Jacks for sale and Sue and I had decided to take a couple with us to Headingley in a show of patriotism. For some reason I don't remember now, we'd taken a disliking to Trevor Chappell and as Botham sent one shot hurtling towards the boundary in our direction, Chappell set off in pursuit.

We'd secured good seats right on the boundary edge (mind you, we had to set off at the crack of dawn to do so) and were delighted to see the ball coming our way. We so wanted the entertainment and possible escape act to continue so we waved the Union Jack for all we were worth in an attempt to distract Chappell. As the ball clattered into the advertising hoardings we were on our feet, cheering and waving that flag like there was no tomorrow. Chappell pulled up right in front of us, giving us a look of such disdain and muttering at us under his breath. He obviously thought we'd been unsporting in trying to put him off.

When we watched the highlights, we were surprised to see our actions captured for posterity and we even made it on to the *Botham's Ashes* video. Loads of people claim to have been there, but we've got the proof on film. We also feel that we did our bit in helping Botham to score just a few of those precious runs!

Kate Hempsall

Owing to an accident at the close of 1980, I was unable to follow my profession as a freelance professional musician for the majority of the year. There were several possible uses of my weekly Sickness Benefit, none of which, sadly, included my attendance at first-class cricket matches. On the Monday I devised a devious method of entry to the ground which, if it came off, would enable myself, my wife and our nine-month-old daughter to see some of the match without the need to trouble my wallet. It seemed possible that around teatime the Headingley gates would be thrown open to all, sundry, my family and myself, assuming there was any cricket left to watch.

As we drove to Headingley shortly after lunch, the *Test Match Special* commentators were gloomily discussing how long it might be before Australia wrapped up the game (and probably whether or not the 'Cut'n'Come Again' cake would last the day). With great fortune, we managed to park the car on Kirkstall Lane. We could listen to the car radio and observe the reactions of the spectators perched on the indoor cricket school roof.

It was exciting enough sitting in the car, watching the paying customers going wild with disbelief, but when at tea, or shortly after, the gates were indeed thrown wide open, in we trooped to watch first-hand what we had so enjoyed second-hand. What superb entertainment. All free!

Prompted by my vast cricketing knowledge, I chose to watch the Bob Willis Show on television instead of somehow scraping together the entrance fee in order that I might legitimately watch 'what was left of the match'. I doubt I'll ever forgive myself.

Eddie Peacock

I was a teacher at Wolgarston High School in Penkridge, Staffordshire, and for two years we had run an 'activity week' during the last week of the school year (prompted by the cricket-loving members of staff who spotted the opportunity to whisk groups of youngsters off to different cricket grounds).

Usually, the fourth day of a Test fell on the first day of activity week and this was the case in July 1981. On the Monday morning 40 pupils and four staff gathered and piled on the coach. We made slow progress on the M1 and it was clear that we would be late for the start. As we came off the motorway Brearley was out, Gower went as we parked the coach and by the time we sat down on the Western Terrace, Gatting was out – 41 for 4. It is hard to describe the feeling at that stage – what do we do when the game is over at lunchtime? Is there anywhere else to go in Leeds?

There were very few on the Western Terrace – old wooden slatted benches then – and the atmosphere was low-key, certainly until Botham came in. Rather pompously and foolishly, I was dressed in a blue blazer and an MCC egg-and-bacon tie, having been elected a few months earlier. Sitting close to us was a group of Australians, one of whom had perfected the art of simultaneously balancing a pint of lager on his belly and verbally abusing a member of the MCC.

Three of the teachers, including myself, stood outside the betting tent at lunchtime and actually got as far as getting £5 together to put on England at

500–1, but of course we didn't. Everyone relished Botham, particularly when he batted with Dilley, as much for the instant entertainment as the likelihood of putting England into a winning position.

Everyone in the school party wanted to come back for the final day but we had already arranged to go to Lord's for the third day of Middlesex v Worcestershire – Wilf Slack, bless him, 248 not out – and a tour of the Museum and Long Room. Stephen Green showed us round but there were so many earphones plugged into transistors that, as the wickets fell at Headingley, the cheers rang round Lord's.

David Jenkins

I was driving to the Young Chelsea Bridge Club (in Earl's Court, naturally) from Forest Gate in the East End, where I lived. My car, a Fiat 126, was not fitted with a radio but I had a portable one in the car. Not surprisingly, reception (Medium Wave in those days) was erratic. I switched on for the first time to hear Bob Taylor's wicket go down. Depressed, I switched off; clearly, we were about to lose by an innings. On my arrival, about half an hour later, I switched on again and Botham and Dilley had taken the game to the Australians – the commentators were actually talking in terms of making them bat again! Of course, it was a lost cause ...

Richard Fleet

On the day of Botham and Dilley's partnership, having thought everything was lost, I went into town. Through a Radio Rentals window in Maidstone High Street, I watched in amazement as the innings unfolded. I must have stayed there for nearly an hour, pretending to be waiting for a bus. I then went home and forgot to purchase what I had gone into town for. But it was worth it.

John Edwards

Nothing sticks in my mind more than the Monday afternoon. At the time I was in the sixth form at school, studying for my A-Levels. I wasn't particularly 'sporty'; I had played a bit of rugby and cricket but that was about it. I would watch the occasional cricket match on TV (mostly John Player League) but had never gone to a live match or played club cricket. That day changed all that.

I remember watching the afternoon session in the sixth-form common room, waiting, I suppose, for the last rites to be served. Lesson times came and went

– with Botham and Dilley at the crease we were not going anywhere. Teachers complained and the head of sixth form (Mr Otterwell, I think) was called. He took one look at the TV and promptly sat down and joined us! It was a pivotal moment. Within weeks I was going to Sunday League matches and had started to play club cricket.

I'm still a keen cricket fan, a member of Surrey CCC and follower of Scotland and England. I've played regularly for the past 18 years (although a bad back has stopped me for the last two seasons). You could say that Messrs Botham, Brearley, Willis and Dilley et al have a lot to answer for!

David Flintham

I was in the BBC Club (now the Langham Hilton) in London at the time. In those days the place, like any watering hole in London at lunchtime, was usually extremely noisy and smoky. This day also. Except – once Beefy started really laying into the Aussie attack, slowly the hubbub started to settle. Being the BBC Club there were TVs hanging from brackets. Before you knew it, word got round that something special was happening. Botham was performing the hero act. We had no idea how it would end but it was astonishing – a usually vibrant bar all stood back and gawped at the telly suspended over our heads. I can't say absolute silence descended but I can say that, for a while, time stood still. We all stood in a huddle around the screen and marvelled.

Martin Booth

I was in the Press Club in Ludgate Circus, sharing a pint or two with some other journos, when Botham was progressing towards his century. When he reached it we all said how nice it was for him, how, even though the match was beyond recall, at least he had bounced back after relinquishing the captaincy. We liked him, liked the way he played, wanted him to succeed. Not until he was 130-odd did it occur that the result might yet be in doubt. At the close we were getting quite optimistic, but then we expected him to add a good few more the next morning ...

Bob Willis rose to a higher level in our estimation when he was bowling the Aussies out. I always thought he had a really silly action, and a silly hairstyle, but somehow, with the crowd roaring him on, it all looked so different. Even via TV, there was a sense of crowd and bowler coming together to make the Aussies' lives even harder.

Peter Chapman, *Financial Times*

After setting up on Wednesday 13 July at our usual caravan site just off Pool Bank, my son Colin and I savoured the pleasures of eating outdoors in the fresh air of a summer evening while lazily admiring the splendid panoramic view way over to the northeast in the direction of Harrogate. Colin had been chosen to open the batting for Scotland in the Under-16 match against Wales. It was due to be played on the following Sunday and Monday at Neath, so we were resigned to missing out on four sessions of play at Headingley.

We left in a miserable state of mind at the start of the tea interval on Saturday to drive down to Neath. Out of range of *Test Match Special,* we switched off and began talking more optimistically about the match against Wales, whose XI included one Robert Jones, later to make a name for himself on the rugby field. We all spent Monday afternoon with an ear to the car radio and an eye on the field. Colin put together a fine second innings, playing a major part in a Scotland win.

Having left our caravan behind, we drove back up to Leeds as quickly as conditions would allow through a night of filthy, depressing, unremitting rain. At around eight o'clock next morning, under unpromising skies, we came to and decided to take ourselves to the ground for the last rites. I missed out by a very short time on having my fiver accepted in the betting tent — events on the field kept me rooted to my seat and delayed a speculative visit to Ladbrokes at the foot of the Western Terrace until the lunch interval.

Peter West was giving his summary of the morning's play when I returned to my seat. An over-the-shoulder glance at a monitor in one of the commentary boxes made me suddenly aware that I was clearly in shot behind him, a few places along the front row of the upper tier of the main stand. Somewhere, tucked away in the BBC's archives, that record of my attendance remains as proof for posterity; and my voice may still be heard too. Rodney Marsh's hook flew straight towards us, before being caught just inside the boundary beside what Richie Benaud referred to as 'the confectionery stall'. Normally passive, I was up there on my hind legs, yelling out, 'Catch 'im, Dilley boy!' A nearby effects mike picked up that wild outburst; it remains for all to hear on the soundtrack of the video.

Without doubt it was the greatest cricket match I have ever seen. On the way out of the ground, a fellow spectator said something to us about Ian Botham's fantastic innings the previous day, and we explained why we had missed it. Colin was asked if he had 'done anything' in the match against Wales. With modest satisfaction, he was able to say he had. It's the sort of moment that sticks indelibly in the memory. As Shelley wrote: 'Rarely, rarely comest thou, Spirit of Delight'.

Alexander Scott

I have met many, many people who claim to have attended the match on all days – most are liars; there were only about 1500 on the last morning. My mum, my sister and I, however, have a good alibi. Mike Gatting, a family friend, provided us all with tickets for every day. Apart from the odd comfort break we didn't miss a ball.

It's funny but even at 15 (as I was then), I knew that I'd probably experienced the most exceptional day/days of my life. Since then I've acquired a degree, a wife, and three beautiful daughters, and they've all provided special moments – but nothing quite compares ...!

Particular moments? Well, two mates and I sat in Gatt's seats in the Grandstand every day. When Gower was out 'slashing at a wide one' on the Monday morning, we spared the southern Nancy Boy nothing. We may have done had we known his mother was sitting two seats away!

On the Monday morning we'd watched the nets (as I did every morning) and enjoyed some good banter with a very confident Terry Alderman. On the Tuesday morning we shouted 'Morning Terry' – but he wouldn't acknowledge us. The Aussies' mood had changed and I thought England had a chance.

The last three hours of Monday's play were remarkable. Tuesday's events have been repeated, but Monday's never will. As Botham walked out, I famously said to my mate: 'Well, he's not going to come off twice.'

One myth. Richie said of his six: 'That's gone into the confectionery stall and out again.' It didn't. It almost decapitated me, and I was sitting miles from the sweet stall. My dad (who was a GP) gave me ointment when I got home to ease hands made sore by clapping (honestly). That says it all.

My mum had never bet before, and has not done so since, but she had 50p on England at 200–1 (very few actually got the much-touted 500).

Richard Levin

A photo recently used in *Wisden Cricket Monthly* shows me in the background, directly behind Botham, half-hidden, grinning loopily and slightly out of focus. I was 17, so I now have a lot less hair and a lot less to grin about.

It was the first time I'd ever attended a first-class match. I went with a mate called Andy Mellor. I can clearly remember the thrill of seeing all those great players in the flesh for the first time and we nearly fainted with excitement when we shouted a matey greeting to Geoff Boycott and he replied, 'Awright lads'.

I'd love to be able to say our motivation for attending was premonitions of glory for England or some vague sixth sense that the game was not finished as a contest. But then I'd be lying. We had nothing better to do and the entrance fee had been reduced to half-price. We were bored and knew a bargain when we saw one. How very Tykish of us.

When Mike Gatting defied his legendary bulk and hurled himself forward to catch Lillee, I did a dance more mental than when they'd played a Sex Pistols song at the school disco. The roar that greeted the demolition of Bright's stumps was out of all proportion to the size of the crowd. Andy and I leapt out of our seats, hurdled the barrier and ran on to the pitch, along with just about everyone else. I slapped Botham heartily on the back as he hared for the pavilion. Clearly the aforementioned photo was taken just after this life-affirming experience. I enjoyed it as well. And I have washed the hand since.

If the Test had occurred a year earlier I'd have been blissfully unaware, as I wasn't really interested in cricket until that summer. Maybe I just started paying attention. There's no doubt that being at Headingley played a significant part in cementing my now unequivocal love of the game.

Russell Clarke

I saw and scored the whole game from the old bowling green stand (opposite the Western Terrace), together with my wife and group of friends from all parts of the country. If you were to ask about that game in Leeds today, you would think the ground on that last day had been packed to capacity, in view of the number of people claiming to have been present. In fact, there were probably no more than 6000 in total at the end.

One of the group I was with on that fifth day commented that, if Australia lost their fifth wicket by the time the score reached 65, England would win. The fifth wicket fell at 65 and he was proved correct. This same person also dissuaded another of our group from putting a £1 bet on England when the scoreboard showed the odds of 500–1 against. I don't know if they are yet on speaking terms.

Stan Dawson

I was 13 and it was the first live Test I had seen. My dad had promised to take me along for the final day, but midway through the fourth day it wasn't looking good. We'd missed out also in 1979, when we arrived outside the ground for the Test against India just as it started to rain. In 1981 I watched the fourth day on TV. My mood started to lift as Dilley and Botham had their fun, but it still seemed unlikely to get me my day out at Headingley. Finally, Botham, Old and Willis had teased out enough runs to make it worth the trip and when Dad came home he agreed we could go.

I was young enough to think that anything was possible – Dad's main hope was that Botham and Willis would score a few more runs. We sat on the Western Terrace; not the best view, but good for atmosphere. Dad told me to watch Dennis Lillee, since we might not see him again.

Those two days made a huge impression on me. It brought home to me how no cause is ever lost while there is a possibility of a recovery, and has given rise to many disappointments since, when England have failed to live up to the spirit of that match (how could they?). It was the first time I had been part of such a major event, such excitement, such exhilaration. When I had to write a sonnet at school later that year, I used this match as my subject.

Though Ian Botham hit a final four
Alderman got Willis out soon after
England were looking at defeat – no more
I thought I heard Australian laughter

Dyson and Wood came out to end the match
Botham was hit for consecutive fours
But Wood was soon out thanks to Taylor's catch
And just before lunch there were three more roars

After lunch Willis was bowling supreme
Soon the score was 75 for 8
Then Lillee and Bright tried to end the dream
Until Gatting's catch seemed to seal their fate

And Bright was bowled – the Aussies' last wicket
A good end to a great game of cricket

Richard Smith

It was thanks to Hermann Goering that I watched the events of Headingley 1981 in the splendour of King's College, Cambridge.

I was actually at London University at the time; at Queen Mary College in the East End to be precise. However, in the war years, the college's students had been moved to the calmer pastures of Cambridge rather than catching the full force of the Luftwaffe's attempts to flatten London. Since then, King's has invited students from Queen Mary back to Cambridge for the Long Vacation Term – to enjoy the distinct contrast in surroundings and to do a bit of relaxed work before their final year.

The college television room smelled of vomit. I never found out why and wasn't certain I wanted to know. Whatever the reasons, it was also short of cricket lovers as there were only two others there. I had met neither and never did really, but they were there every day. One was short, smoked constantly and looked like a 1970s' fashion casualty. The other was furtive-looking, red-haired, needed a shave and never seemed to wear any socks.

I popped in for a few hours each day as England dug themselves into a hole. By the Monday afternoon I was in my room in the building at the back of the College where, so I was told (by everyone), E.M. Forster had lived. I was trying to read *Heart of Darkness* but the contrast between Conrad's thick gloom and Brian Johnston's commentary was a little hard to take.

When Bob Taylor was out I decided to forsake Conrad for Peter West. I thought Dilley might go down fighting. Botham was still there too. My two silent companions were already in the vomit-scented atmosphere. The three of us made chortling noises but never really spoke. At the end of the day's play I staggered off in elated disbelief and met some friends for dinner in the college refectory. I jabbered about how I had just seen the most incredible session of cricket in my life ... and they treated me like a more than normally dim child.

The following morning I was back in the television room. The cricket groupies were – like the smell – firmly in place. When Willis beat Yallop for nerve, Mike Gatting and I flung ourselves into the air (he had the ball), and my lunch partner came in. He knew little of cricket and looked rather oddly at me.

It was over lunch that word spread. While most of the students were away on holiday, the choir was still in residence and now moved en masse into the television room. The room grew ever more packed as people heard what was happening and it became a magnet for anybody with a vestige of interest in the game. Every wicket was met with shouts and jumps, while the air was punched senseless. I can remember the expressions of people who I have never seen since that summer. The supremely dapper head chorister with a heavily cultivated air of calm felt moved to comment that, 'This is getting really rather exciting, isn't it?' Another had clamped to his ear a radio which fell apart as Lawson jabbed and Taylor caught. There were agonised gasps in the room (now quite literally packed to the rafters) as the ball flew high to Dilley and then so nearly short of Gatting. Lunacy took hold as Bright swung and the stumps flew. No one left the room during the interviews with the mystifying Willis and delighted Brearley.

Eventually we all dispersed. It was still quite early on a beautiful summer's afternoon and Cambridge looked especially lovely. In a bit of a daze, I walked to the Porter's lodge and picked up a letter from a friend.

The next day a NatWest game was televised and I went down to the scene of the previous day's hysteria. The diehards, smoke, bristles and all were there, but not the hordes of the Tuesday afternoon. It took something very special to get them watching.

Colin Mayes

'You know, the trouble with you Poms is you're always so bloody cheerful when you've got no hope.'

Craig had dropped round to my room for a late coffee to discover me glued to the radio. It was Tuesday evening, Australia were 50 for one, and Henry Blofeld (I think) had just said that if England could only take a couple of quick wickets things could get interesting. Like Blofeld, I was clinging on optimistically despite all the odds, because the previous day Ian Botham had turned my world upside down.

I was working in Botany Bay as part of my gap year and, until Botham's innings, had been feeling increasingly gloomy. A lone Englishman living in a student hostel with Aussies, I had had to put up with constant sniping about the inadequacies of my country, as represented by my cricket team.

This had become so bad that on the Monday, when Boycott was out in the second innings with England still about 100 behind, I could no longer bear to watch the TV in the common room. I had retired to my bedroom and switched on the radio. England's exhilarating recovery that Monday night meant that I was able to hold my head up at breakfast the next day, but nobody seriously thought that England had done anything more than delay the inevitable. And so on the Tuesday evening I decided that my best policy would be to stick with the radio commentary on my own rather than watch the final defeat in front of the communal TV.

When my neighbour Craig popped in for coffee, the game was slipping away from England. Then, shortly after Blofeld's optimistic comment, Willis struck. In no time, Australia had lost four wickets and it was game on. Muttering something about needing to get some sleep, Craig gulped down the rest of his coffee and left me to my radio.

With such a small target to defend, every boundary came as a hammer blow, and I feared Rodney Marsh would produce one of those match-turning innings with which Ian Healy has tormented England fans in more recent times. 'And Marsh hooks it,' (my heart sank). 'Dilley's under it, HE'S CAUGHT IT!' (I leapt off the bed, punching the air, shouting in whispers for fear of waking the neighbours).

When Bright fell, I could contain my excitement no longer. It must have been some time around midnight when I ran down the corridor and let off a single

'YEESSS!' I was surrounded by silence.

Not many people wanted to talk at breakfast. Craig said nothing at all. I went out and bought all of the papers, unable to get enough of the headlines and the descriptions of England's heroics. Not surprisingly, the reports tended to talk of Australian failings as much as England's strengths.

Rob Eastaway

I was 15 and bunked off a lesson with my cousin to go to a friend's house as he lived just over the road from school. We watched the climax of the match there, jumped up and down a bit and sneaked back to school. No one seemed to miss us. Teddy Sheringham, who was in our class, stayed in school – the swot. Apparently he wasn't that bothered about the cricket.

Paul Newman, *Daily Mail*

It is the only match when I have ever seen crowds gathered outside TV shops to watch what was going on. I can remember listening to the climax at lunchtime with my radio plugged in in the next-door office, and time after time being unable to bear the tension, going next door and turning it off, then being unable to bear the silence and going back in and turning it on again.

My story concerns the works council of the Duport Steelworks in Llanelli, formerly Llanelly Steel, nicknamed 'The Klondike'. Employment of a cricket pro on The Klondike works ground prior to the First World War produced the coaching that led to a host of good cricketers, including Dai and Emrys Davies and three other Glamorgan players, being produced from two streets opposite.

In 1981 it was announced that the works was about to close, despite the recent opening of the most modern arc furnaces in the world. On the last day of the Test, the works council, the unions and Llanelli Borough Council were meeting with Duport Ltd in Llanelli Town Hall in a last effort to save the works. They were unsuccessful and, after I had interviewed the union reps about what had happened in the meeting, I remarked, 'I've got some good news for you – England won.'

'We know,' they said. 'We smuggled a radio in with us so we could keep up to date with the score.'

Bob Harragan

July 1981. I was deputy head at a comprehensive school in Derbyshire and it was the last week of term.

On the Monday we had a Parents' evening. Having no appointments myself, I was able to keep an eye on the progress of the cricket. Every 20 minutes or so, I was going to those colleagues who were seeing parents and keeping them informed of the unbelievable development of the Botham/Dilley partnership.

The progress of the Test was at the forefront of my mind the following day – I watched it on TV in the school library with two or three other friends and colleagues during our lunch break. The bell went for afternoon school – it was all far too tense and exciting for us to move. We exchanged glances and stayed. After a few minutes the head looked in, gave a resigned smile and left us to it. When Willis took the final wicket we leapt from our perches, arms aloft, and celebrated – then we went to teach our classes (some 15–20 minutes late!).

John M. Brown
Scorer, Derbyshire CCC

I was 14 years old and attending High School in Barkingside, Essex. On the final day five of us were due to help a teacher redecorate one of the prefabricated classrooms, so I viewed this as a good opportunity to listen to the game on the radio. We all spent the afternoon session listening without any work being carried out.

Simon Lewis

I saw James Bolam, the actor, in King's Cross Station the day after the last day of the Test and the only thing I had that he could sign was that month's copy of *Wisden Cricket Monthly*. He said he'd been watching it and was 'glued to the screen'. Incidentally, the third part of the Beiderbecke trilogy has come out this week and I'm sure I remember two of the characters going to Headingley!

Scott McKie

Meanwhile, at South Kensington in London, Botham's deeds had interrupted cricket at that annual festival of music, the Proms at the Royal Albert Hall.

Before going into the hall to stand, sit or lie down, a more than usually energetic bunch of promenaders would while away the queuing hours with a game of cricket. The pitch was a flat paved area in the queuing area, the outfield a long flight of steps. The only boundary, Prince Consort Road, was a hefty swipe with an improvised willow, with the supreme hit a straight drive which bounced across Prince Consort Road and hit the Royal College of Music. Passing buses meant that few succeeded in threading the traffic. The umpire was Little Albert – a statue of the prince consort that stood immediately behind the batsman.

But when word got round of Beefy's bashings, play was abandoned to listen to radios of cars parked around the hall. Games of scrabble, backgammon and *vingt et un* in the various prom queues were disturbed by raucous cheers from the cars. As the innings grew, parking meters were fed (illegally). A normally Hitler-like traffic warden not only stopped to listen but also helped out with change for the meter.

Bob Benjafield

Unbelievable, preposterous, implausible ... not that I saw one ball bowled. And nor did I find out the result until more than a week after the Test had finished.

Uncle Richie described it as, 'The summer of summers for England', and it wasn't too bad for me either. Having just completed my first year at London University, I took off around Europe with fellow freshman Jon Davies, each of us armed with rucksack and InterRail card. And it was on reading a copy of the *Sunday Telegraph* as we trundled out of Vienna station on the evening of Monday 20 July that I pretty much knew the Ashes were Aussie-bound. England, following on, six for one in the second innings and Gooch gone for a duck. Two down, three to play. Gotta be.

There weren't too many British journals down Budapest way and it wasn't until we reached the Greek island of Ios over a week later that I was able to track down another newspaper. And there we were – sitting on a terraced bar under the scorching sun, cold beer and Marlboro to hand, *Daily Telegraph* about to be devoured. Forget the forthcoming Charlie and Di nuptials, it was straight to the sport.

The next two minutes were just extraordinary as my eyes began to dart with increasing haste between county reports. Tantalising snippets like 'England's fighting performance at Headingley'. OK, so we made a game of it. And then 'Willis's heroics'. And 'Botham's historic innings'. What on Earth had happened? Put me out of my misery, please. And there it was, lurking in one of the reports – a reference to an England victory.

'I don't believe it, Jon. We beat the Aussies.' And we ordered another beer. And another.

Chris Lyles, *Daily Telegraph*

Since I was only two at the time I can't remember Headingley '81 at all. However, it's interesting to consider how it still had a significant impact on myself and everyone else in my generation of English cricket-lovers. Growing up in the Eighties and Nineties, there were countless times on rainy summer afternoons during washed-out Test matches when I would sit on the couch, watching dumbfounded as the BBC replayed highlights of the game. And, such is the influence of TV on cricket-obsessed youngsters, I and my friends would inevitably re-enact some of Botham's more outrageous shots from his astonishing innings, and Bob Willis's wonderful leap of delight when he took the final Australian wicket.

I can also remember a school match when I was 14, which we won despite seeming well beaten at an early stage. We batted first and were in deep trouble at something like 30 for 6. It was one of those innings where the run-rate is so slow that you wonder where the next run will come from. Then suddenly a lad who had a great natural eye, but not the technique to score consistently at a high level, came in and scored a rapid, unbeaten 30-odd which ultimately turned the match on its head. We bowled them out cheaply in what was an exceptionally low-scoring match, and eventually won by 28 runs. Afterwards one couldn't help but compare it all to Headingley '81, and I think this shows again the uniqueness of this great match, since, as our history teacher no doubt noticed, it is pretty rare for schoolboys to compare current events to those of the past, especially when they can't remember them.

Headingley '81 has also had an influence on me as a hugely passionate England fan. So often since this miraculous game, during Test matches in which England are facing an uphill task, have TV and radio commentators said things like 'England need a Headingley '81 if they're going to win this match.' Through this continuous process, perversely, I find myself harking back to days which I can't recall at all, and in effect feeling nostalgia towards an event during which I was wearing nappies.

Jonathan Dyson

The Keith Boyce Story

'If this bugger goes up and down, I'm dead'

For one Englishman, Headingley 1981 was a nightmare. English cricket's greatest victory was not only a daily torment for groundsman Keith Boyce, it also destroyed plans three years in the making; plans which took five more years to revive and 14 to fulfil – and then still ended in tragedy.

Boyce arrived at Headingley from Yorkshire's Middlesbrough ground in 1979. He had a reputation for producing good, fast pitches and a fierce determination to tame the capricious nature of the Headingley track.

Nineteen years on, the wiry Boyce is still full of nervous energy, his skin browned and weathered by the elements. He stares out at the Headingley square – where England had just beaten the West Indies in the first two-day Test for 54 years – like Captain Ahab catching sight of the Great White Whale.

'If somebody said to me, "Do you want England to win?", I'd say I'm not really bothered,' says Boyce on preparing a Test pitch. 'I'd be more concerned to make sure there's good cricket on the fourth day, with a result on the fifth.'

Pitch preparation for the Headingley Tests of 1979 and 1980 had been badly affected by rain. In 1981 Boyce felt he had not yet been given the chance to demonstrate the talents which had won him the transfer to a Test venue. He also had growing doubts about the square and whether it could ever perform as he wanted. However, the weather in the run-up to the 1981 Test had been much better than in the previous two years. 'Finally, I thought I had the opportunity to prepare a good Test match pitch.'

On the Tuesday before the match, the Australians arrived to net and to inspect Boyce's work. 'The pitch was dry, with a few little cracks in it. It looked a very good surface. The Australians – Hughes, Lillee and Marsh, the manager Fred Bennett, even the commentator Alan McGilvray – all came to look at the pitch. They were very happy with it and so was I.'

The Australians asked Boyce few questions, but on the Wednesday Mike Brearley turned up and began gently pumping the groundsman for information.

'Brearley was a tremendous communicator and a very crafty man as well. He got more out of groundsmen than most. He would always be looking for as much detail on the preparation of the pitch as possible.

'He was suspicious because the pitch was so hard. You could see him thinking, "Is this going to hold together?" He immediately wanted to know how much water the pitch had been given.' Boyce had to admit that, in an effort to produce a good, dry pitch, he had not watered it for 16 days.

Boyce says that such a dry pitch would either eventually break up into blocks or that the surface layer would crumble. Pace bowlers would be more dangerous if the pitch broke up into blocks, the batsmen not knowing how high the ball would bounce. If the pitch 'dusted', the ball would grip the surface more easily, assisting the spinners. Brearley, by selecting four seamers, clearly thought he knew what would happen.

Hughes, who made a second inspection of the pitch with Lillee and Marsh 10 minutes before the start of play, was obviously less sure. Marsh and Lillee would have remembered the 1972 match at Headingley, which Derek Underwood won in three days on a raging turner. Maybe this influenced the Australian selection, but in his book, *Phoenix from the Ashes*, Brearley expresses his surprise at Hughes' decision to pick Ray Bright ahead of Rodney Hogg.

As play got underway Boyce waited to see how his pitch would perform. 'As a groundsman, you don't watch the cricket, you just watch the ball. You watch it hit the deck, you watch the bounce, you watch the wicketkeeper's hands, how high or low he takes the ball.'

Straight away Boyce realised he was in trouble, lulled into a false sense of security by his experience at Middlesbrough. 'The pitch had too much pace in it. Yes, it had uneven bounce, but that was only a problem because it was magnified by the pace of the pitch.'

The ghost of a troubled memory flashes across Boyce's face as he remembers the first morning, hand rubbing forehead in an effort to soothe the pain. 'We grade the pace of Test pitches from one to five. The truer the bounce, the more you can push the pace. With a Test pitch that was a bit untrustworthy you'd want to keep it around pace three. On day one, the 1981 Headingley pitch was pace four. My stomach was in a bloody knot. I thought: "If this bugger goes up and down, I'm dead."'

At the end of the first day's play – and throughout the match – Boyce watched the TV highlights while talking on the phone to fellow Test groundsmen or soil scientists at Aberystwyth University. The question he kept asking was: 'What will the pitch do next?'

As Brearley had appeared to predict, the pitch began to crack into a series of blocks and again, says Boyce, Hughes missed a trick. 'You can make the blocks loose and the pitch more uneven by using the heavy roller. The Australians didn't seem to understand this. If they had, they would never have declared at the end of the second day. If they'd batted on they could have used the heavy roller on the third morning. I was bloody relieved that the Australians didn't ask me about the pitch before declaring. Mind you, if it had been Yorkshire, I would have told them anyway.'

But if Boyce thought life could not get any more difficult, any complacency was soon shattered. 'Something started happening to the pitch that I'd never seen before and it was very alarming. When the pitch broke up, the blocks started curling up at the edges like pieces of dry bread. We had a series of mini-saucers on the pitch. If the ball hit an up slope it would fly and if it hit a down slope it would stay low. Batting became totally hazardous.' Then it got worse.

'Every day I did bounce tests on the pitch – literally dropping a ball onto the pitch to see how high it would bounce. I used to do it when everyone had gone home or early in the morning. You're not supposed to do it, see, when a game's underway, but groundsmen are curious people.'

And nervous ones, too. Something else had happened to this cracking, uneven, hazardous third-day pitch – it had got faster. 'It was now pace five,' shudders Boyce, still shivering at the shock of his discovery. 'It was then I realised that I'd got the pitch ready two days early. I could have slowed the drying down, watered it more. But I was so used to working with a square where you could prepare a pitch two or three days before the start of a match and still get a week's cricket on it.'

Brow furrowed, he continues: 'I quickly learnt that to produce a Test pitch at Headingley you had to leave a touch of moisture in it on the first morning. Not a lot. Good batsmen – the Boycotts and the Gooches – should be able to see out the first session and get the benefit of a dry pitch in the afternoon.'

This approach, of course, had its own dangers. 'If I got it wrong, and left too much moisture in, you could be four down by lunchtime.' However, when Boyce did get it right, he says that Headingley would offer a good batting strip on the second day of a Test; run-getting would become more difficult on the third as the bounce became a little unreliable. By the fourth, the bounce would be very erratic and on the fifth the pitch would be, in Boyce's words, 'totally dodgy'.

By preparing the pitch two days early, Boyce had produced a strip that had reached the 'totally dodgy' stage by Saturday. From then on, he says, it was simply 'unfit'.

The last thing Boyce needed now was a rest day – another 24 hours for the pitch to continue to dry and crack. He had to take drastic – and unauthorised – action.

'We're supposed to leave Test pitches open, but the Sunday was a lovely sunny day and I kept the covers on to stop the drying. I didn't want it to crack open any more. I needed to try to contain the steep bounce that was developing. It was against the rules. But I knew the pitch was unfit for Test match cricket and we still had two days to go. I was fearing something terrible taking place. I had visions of all sorts happening – I didn't want anybody to get hit.'

With a day to brood on how the pitch would perform, Boyce arrived at Headingley on the Monday morning feeling like a death-row prisoner heading for the chair. 'I didn't sleep at all. I was feeling bloody sick. I just wanted the match over. I couldn't stand another day. I was creeping around. I'd tried hard, but I knew I'd failed.'

Boyce still forced himself to watch how the pitch played. As Botham sailed into the bowling, Boyce observed how the pace of the pitch was helping to send even thick edges flying one bounce to the boundary. It was, he says, 'a relief to see people enjoying themselves', but he couldn't shake his depression or the fear of what was to come on the fifth day.

However, once Willis switched ends and found his length, Boyce's torture didn't last long – and no one, to his immense relief, was hurt. Ironically, Boyce reveals that the Kirkstall Lane End of the pitch – being higher on the sloping ground and therefore quicker to drain of any moisture than the Rugby Stand End – dried and cracked more alarmingly. Willis's success came while bowling to the less dangerous end.

With the Test over Boyce was awarded his match medal while the crowd cheered and shouted, 'Boycie, give us a wave'. But the groundsman was lost in a fog of despair.

'I got very stressed. It's one of the worst experiences I've had. My wife and I went to have a quiet pint up the road. But we just kept bumping into people who all wanted to talk about the bloody match.'

At least Boyce got off lightly in the post-match press conferences, Brearley even praising his courage. He told the assembled hacks: 'Boyce came from Middlesbrough where he produced good, fast pitches and he wanted to do the same at Headingley. But he hasn't succeeded. The wicket in the one-day international was a bit of a lottery and this is a worse pitch than in 1977 for the Australian Test. But you have got to give it to the groundsman for not playing safe.'

Boyce knew what he had to do to win plaudits for his pitches as well as his pluck. 'I realised that the pitch at Headingley hadn't got the ability to withstand five days of Test cricket. It needed digging out. My mind was made up – solid! I had soil samples taken and analysed – we would never get a good pitch from that square. The pitch was made up of bloody bad soil. It would crack. Moisture would hold it together for a while, but then it would go.'

Then, as if doused with ice-cold water, Boyce realised he had no chance of getting Yorkshire to agree to his plan. 'Bloody Botham and Willis knackered me up totally. When I requested that the pitch be dug up, people would just turn round and say, "Stop moaning Boycie, you're always going on about the Test match pitch, there's nothing wrong with the bloody pitch. We've just had the most exciting Test match ever, what do you want to dig the bloody thing out for?"'

So has Boyce ever told Botham of the trouble he caused him? 'Never. I wasn't brave enough.'

Straight after the end of the Headingley '81 match, Boyce found himself being trailed by a BBC film crew making a documentary about his preparation of the 1982 Test strip. That Test was against Pakistan and the English captain was one R.G.D. Willis.

'I remember Willis couldn't believe he was looking at the same pitch. This time I'd left moisture in it; there was no way I was going to repeat my mistakes of a year earlier. The ball was only rebounding knee-high and it wasn't a good pitch – but I had to play safe.'

The 1985 Australians also got a shock when they pitched up in Leeds expecting another terror track. 'They were bloody nervous,' remembers Boyce, 'and so was I.' In fact, Boyce was so on edge that when he was asked about the pitch, he told the press: 'There's a bastard in my family and it's sitting out there.'

Both the Australians and Boyce were in for a surprise. The Aussies racked up totals of 331 and 324, while England made 533 in their first innings and won by five wickets. But the Headingley track was soon up to its old tricks. In 1986 England were bowled out for 102 and 128 by India and lost by 297 runs. That most sedate of Indian medium-pacers, Roger Binny, took 7–58. England captain Mike Gatting offered to help Boyce with the spadework and the order to dig up the pitch was finally given.

However, even the new square still produced tracks that cracked too quickly or were sluggish seamers with extravagant seam movement. Boyce began to develop plans to lay a clay-based pitch and to replace the ash layer which was used to draw moisture from the square with a modern drainage system. But first he carried out some exploratory work. He remembers his first spade thrust with horrified clarity. 'I went into the ash and found it saturated. The ash had dipped in the centre of the square, which meant the water running down the hill from the Kirkstall Lane End was collecting beneath the square.'

Any moisture on the surface of the pitch would not be drawn down into the square. Instead it would stay within the pitch, cracking the surface as it evaporated. A proper drainage system was ordered and work on the clay-based pitch began in 1990, 12 years after Boyce had arrived at Leeds. Only then was the full horror of the Headingley strip revealed. 'We went through a farmer's sandstone wall 32 inches underneath the square. We found bottles, boots, cans – you name it. The ground had obviously been an agricultural field with all sorts of tip fill dumped on top of it.'

With the pitch he had always wanted finally under his command, Boyce began to work towards his original goal of a fast, true Test strip. This he finally achieved in 1995 with the pitch he prepared for the England v West Indies Test. The strip received the top possible marks. 'It was like getting a knighthood,' says Boyce.

But even in his hour of triumph the fates conspired against him. He had been able to battle so long with the pernicious nature of the Headingley pitch largely because of the support of his wife and family. They had recognised his dedication to excellence, accepted the inevitable black moods and kept him going. The '95 strip, he promised, would be their reward – proof that the struggle had been worth it.

Then – just before the Test – Boyce's devoted wife died. He 'simply couldn't go on'. In the same year he produced his perfect strip, he resigned.

Five years later, Boyce is back with Yorkshire cricket, enjoying his work on the county's academy ground. But his memories of Headingley are not warm. 'It is a graveyard for groundsmen,' he says bluntly, 'and as for '81 – that game's still an embarrassment to me.'

The Graham Dilley Story

'I was hoping they wouldn't pick me'

'Two weeks after Headingley I was bowling so badly I was playing for the Kent Second XI against the Army at Woolwich.'

Graham Dilley rarely tires of talking about the greatest Test match he ever played in, but he is honest enough to admit that he never should have been there.

Dilley is reminiscing on the boundary of the Oundle School ground in Northamptonshire during the summer of 2000. He is watching the England Under-19 women's team, which he coaches on and off, play Holland as part of the Dutch side's World Cup warm-up. However, mention Headingley '81 and he's a million miles away ... and not always in a happy place.

'I'd lost it totally. I was running up to bowl thinking, "I'm not too sure where this is going." Some people are relatively fortunate because once they lose it, it goes from being all right to not all right relatively quickly; with me it took three months. Eventually it got worse and worse, until I had no idea where the ball was going.'

Dilley had played in the first two Tests of the '81 Ashes series. 'I was having an absolutely dreadful time. I managed to pick up wickets, but I didn't bowl well. In the first Test at Trent Bridge Rodney Hogg chipped a half-volley to Boycs at midwicket. That's not how you get wickets if you're a Test fast bowler.'

Dilley's state of mind was not helped by his relationship with skipper Ian Botham, a man he respected and liked, but whose captaincy style was a mystery to him. 'There was an occasion in the West Indies during the 1980–81 tour when Ian sent Brian Rose up to me after I had bowled six overs. Rosie said: "Both wants to know if you've had enough or not?" So I said, "Yeah, I think six overs is enough," and went down to third man.

'At the end of the next over I wandered up to mid-off and Both turned round to me and said: "What's the matter with you then?" "I thought I'd finished," I replied. And he said: "Don't you want to f**king bowl? Well, f**k off down to third man." So, there I was, the opening bowler, doing third man to third man in the Caribbean heat.'

Nor could Dilley find much help off the field to sort out his bowling problems. 'It didn't happen in those days. You were left to your own devices. Some people might have the odd word with you – but there was no "come on, let's get into the nets and talk this through, see what's going on". It was more a case of: "Here's the ball, run up and bowl. What do you mean, you can't get it straight? Get it straight!" – and that was it.

'My problems might have started off technical, but they very quickly became mental. I was frightened to let go of the ball. Rather than just being relaxed and free-flowing, I was tense and stiff. It became a mental thing which turned back into a physical thing because everything was so stressful.'

One bright spot for Dilley in the run-up to the third Test was the return of Brearley. 'I was really pleased. He was the captain on my first overseas tour [to Australia in 1979–80] when I was only 20 years old and had played just one season of county cricket.

'We had to sign a whole lot of bats before we went away to Australia. I signed my name as far down on the bat as I possibly could, almost on the bottom. I was thinking, "What the hell am I doing here?" There were all these guys who I'd been watching on the telly until now – my heroes some of them – and I was going away on tour with them.

'If there had been a sports psychologist around he'd have picked up on it straight away. I felt like that for a while until we had a muck-about game of hand football. There was a 50–50 ball between me and Both and I didn't back down. A little while later Brears came up and put his arm around me and said: "You'll be all right." Suddenly I felt at home. I thought, "If he thinks that then it must be right."'

But despite Brearley's return, Dilley could not shake the feeling that he was not worth his place in the Test team. 'I was hoping – although I would never have admitted it to anybody – that they wouldn't pick me for Headingley. I'd got so worn down by going out in front of 10–14,000 people and not being able to do my best.'

No such luck: 'First it was, "Oh God, they've picked me in the 12." Then, "Oh God, they've picked me in the 11."'

Dilley's performance in the Australian first innings was a nightmare. While showering after Friday's play, he complained to his captain about being persuaded to bowl closer to the stumps. Brearley challenged this orthodoxy, citing the success of Croft, Procter, Daniel, Willis and Garner and suggested he consider going back to bowling from wide of the crease. Despite the respect Dilley had for Brearley he was in too negative a frame of mind to take up the suggestion and told his captain that changing his tactics would only make matters worse.

However, Dilley's swashbuckling stand with Botham on the fourth day led to Brearley handing him the new ball when Australia went in to chase 130.

'Brearley, Both and some of the others had been saying, "We can win this", and for Brearley to turn round to me and say, "Go on, go and do what you can do" – that made me feel good, made me feel that somebody believed in me.

'It didn't take away the fear of actually going out there knowing it hadn't been going well for three months. It was not suddenly going to change now just because I'd got a 50 and probably one of the best captains England has ever had had come up to me and said: "Tight situation, here's the new ball."'

Dilley was right. In a game packed with miracles he was not about to receive a second helping. 'From the first ball I knew nothing had changed. I felt exactly the same way running up to bowl as I had for the last few months.'

After two overs for 11 runs he was removed from the attack.

'I had a little bit of a thigh strain, went off, got it strapped up and went back on again. I knew I wasn't going to be asked to bowl again unless the situation was hopeless. Then Brearley might chuck me the ball and say, "See what you can do". But until then I wasn't going to get anywhere near the ball. Quite honestly, I was relieved that the torture had gone again.'

Dilley went back to Kent and straight into the second team, where he stayed until selected, much to his surprise, for England's 1981–82 tour of India. 'I knew I wouldn't play in the Edgbaston Test. I got into the squad, but only because they wanted to keep the same 12 together. With the mental state I was in when I had a ball in my hand, it was neither a shock nor a surprise to be left out. I was quite happy not to play.'

But did he change his mind after what occurred in the fourth and fifth Tests?

'Of course I wanted to be part of it, but without having the responsibility of having to run up and bowl. I was relieved to get rid of that responsibility, because I couldn't do my job.'

Part 6

What happened next (quite a lot actually)

The bet

'I don't bet on cricket. Is somebody having a go just because we lost?'

The statement was clear enough. Dennis Lillee was letting it be known in typically forthright fashion that no way would he have a plunge on the game. Only trouble was, he had and a lot of people knew it.

Two days after England's win at Headingley, the *Sun* splashed the story on its front page: 'Mystery of Aussie Bets Coup'. Next to photographs of Kim Hughes and Lillee, the story ran: 'Two Australian cricket stars allegedly netted £7500 between them yesterday by backing England to win the Headingley Test. The two players made their bets on Saturday when Ladbrokes offered 500–1 odds against an England victory. One put £10 on an Australian defeat and another put on £5.'

Australian manager Fred Bennett was quoted saying: 'I spoke to the entire team about it. It was emphatically denied by all the players. There is no law about betting in cricket. But I would certainly be concerned if this had been done because of the damage it could do to the image of the game.'

Unfortunately, a few column inches above he was contradicted by a Hughes quote which ran: 'Two of the lads gambled — not because they want to bet against their team, but because the odds were too good to miss.'

Lillee's angry denial followed. The Aussie fast bowler was to keep schtum about the bet until his retirement a few years later. His admission in a book that he had taken up the 500–1 odds greatly upset the other punter — his long-time mate Rod Marsh, who had hoped the allegations would be quietly forgotten. Twenty years later, he's still having to talk about it.

That a £15 bet would still be discussed in the next Millennium would have seemed ridiculous to Marsh, Lillee and their team-mates back in 1981. But when they arrived at Headingley on the Tuesday before the match, Australian eyes would have been eagerly scanning the ground for the Ladbrokes marquee.

With betting unknown on Australian cricket grounds, many of the touring press and players were drawn to the red candy-striped tent like bees to a honeypot. Most money went on the horses of course, but a favourite bet with the press was on Marsh to be highest scorer with some attractive odds set by former Kent and England wicketkeeper Godfrey Evans and Ladbrokes director Ron Pollard. Marsh told the newspaper boys they would get lucky soon, but was never able to deliver.

'It's part of the tradition of the Headingley game to have a Ladbrokes tent between the Western Terrace and the main stand,' says Yorkshire CCC secretary David Ryder. 'It's principally to take betting on the racing, the cricket's just an extra.'

It was late on the Saturday of the Headingley Test, after play had been halted for bad light, that the 500–1 odds were first posted – and not during the Monday lunch or tea break as is often claimed. 'We were absolutely certain we could not lose after England had to follow on. After all, no team has won from that situation since 1894,' Pollard told the *Sun*. Ladbrokes eventually paid out winnings of £40,000 on bets totalling just £25,000.

The odds set, they were chalked up on the blackboard outside the Ladbrokes tent. 'Somebody told the electronic scoreboard operator,' remembers Ryder, 'and he decided to put it up – to give everyone a laugh I suppose, a bit of black humour.'

Australian squad member Dirk Wellham saw the odds flash up. 'I can remember the whizzbang electronic scoreboard's tongue-in-cheek offering of 500–1 against England. I can even recall the crowd's spontaneous murmur of amusement at the sight of the board's message on that murky afternoon.

'As the light continued to fade and it was more certain that play would be over for the day, we relaxed in the first-floor dressing room, hearing the crowd meandering about below, muttering unhappily about the plight of English cricket.

'The black scoreboard stared at us from the opposite side of the field. In the brand new bright yellow dots, the Ladbrokes odds on the result of the Test were dramatically revealed for all who cared to revel in the plight of the English.'

Wellham claims that the cricketers from Western Australia, particularly Lillee, Marsh and Hughes – who were 'not so enthused by the conservative approach of those from the hypocritically corrupt eastern states' – found the 500–1 odds very interesting indeed. 'The odds were openly discussed in a light-hearted tone, as cricketers do when they are in England, touring, waiting for the weather to clear. It was just a joke, some relief at the end of a satisfying conclusion to a good day's toil. No one took the comments seriously. It was just a joke at England's expense.'

The timing of what happened next is not clear. It is possible – as suggested by the report in the *Sun* – that the Lillee/Marsh bet was placed during the brief resumption of play at 5 o'clock on the Saturday evening with England 0–1 in their second innings. However, Lillee himself and some of his team-mates seem to remember it happening on the Monday lunchtime with England still 149 runs behind and only six wickets left. Others claim the punt took place at tea, with Botham warming up but England dead and buried at 176–7. Speaking in 2000, Lillee claims to have 'sat down and thought about it' before placing the bet.

Many recall, as you have read, seeing the 500–1 being displayed on the scoreboard during Monday and believe that bets were still being taken by Ladbrokes at those odds. However, on Test Match Special Henry Blofeld began that morning's commentary by suggesting the odds against an England victory had been revised down to 200–1. What is clear is that Lillee concluded that he could not pass up 'the chance of a lifetime', even one supplied by 'such stupid odds'. Lillee declared that he was going to bet £50 of the team fund on England to win at 500–1. Marsh snatched the money away. The other players laughed, told Lillee he was mad and suggested he put the money behind the bar during the inevitable Aussie victory celebrations.

According to Allan Border that was the final straw for Lillee. He said that he was going to bet £10 of his own money and the rest could do as they liked. 'It was an instinctive and impulsive reaction – he couldn't resist it,' claims ex-*Daily Star* writer and close friend Ted Corbett. 'Dennis thrills at all forms of sport and loves a bet. Probably his best friend in England is Charles Benson, the Daily Express horse racing tipster.'

As it became obvious that Lillee was serious there was some half-hearted fumbling in pockets. 'Lots of guys threw in their small change,' remembers Peter Philpott. 'I think I threw in a couple of bob myself. Everyone was killing themselves laughing.'

'I actually looked in the pockets of my trousers hanging on the peg behind me in the search of money,' recalls Geoff Lawson, 'but I came up empty and my wallet was locked away in the valuables bag. As a poor uni student I could have paid my fees and rent for the rest of year had I found some loose change.'

Ray Bright too resisted the urge to chip in. 'Initially I was going to bet £2,' he says, 'but I thought about the lager I could buy instead and left it.'

John Dyson was more adamant. 'Dennis said, "Have a quid on it." I said I didn't want to waste the money and didn't think any more about it.'

Lillee was keenest of all that his mate Marsh should join him in the bet. 'Have a fiver on it, Bacchus, just to be with me,' he pleaded, but Marsh was having none of it.

Then came the question of who should place the bet. Lillee handed over his tenner – he did not bother with the loose change – to the Australian coach driver Peter Tribe. Tribe, or 'Geezer', as most of the Aussies called him, was a streetwise guy. He soon became an integral part of the squad and the person they turned to when they needed a favour.

Play then restarted and the Aussies returned to the field. Just as they were walking out to the middle, Marsh spotted Tribe walking round the boundary towards the Ladbrokes tent and changed his mind. 'Geezer,' he shouted and raised five fingers to indicate his stake. Tribe shook his head, as if to tell Marsh not to waste his money, and continued on. 'Geezer,' shouted Marsh again and then, as Tribe turned around, he waved his five fingers a second time before clenching his hand into a fist in mock anger to suggest what would happen if the bet was not placed.

Tribe nodded and set off, but again he thought how ridiculous the whole idea was and headed back to the dressing room, planning to return Lillee's money. Nearly there, he changed his mind for the last time. 'I've heard of these things happening, so I'd better not take the risk,' he thought, and turned around for the final time.

A man who knows both Australian punters well on and off the field, David Gower, is not surprised that Marsh eventually caved in to temptation:

'Marsh and Lillee would have a punt on the Martians landing if they had got [those] odds. They've had a few bets on horses that barely answered to the description.'

In fact, Ladbrokes had just offered an American woman 500–1 against aliens landing on Earth.

When they got back to the dressing room, the two Australians received confirmation that their bet had been placed. 'Lillee was standing at the top of the stairs,' remembers Headingley groundsman Keith Boyce. 'He was grinning and holding up both hands, fingers outstretched. Marsh was at the bottom, nodding and holding up one hand.'

But while Lillee and Marsh had got their money down, one England player had failed in his attempt. Bob Taylor was the unlucky man. 'During the Monday lunch break I was in the players' dining room with Mike Gatting and physio Bernard Thomas. Gatting, who was just out, was sulking [he was less than happy with his lbw decision]. Most of the Aussies were there as well. I was sat with my back to the ground, facing the Aussies' table. All of a sudden, the Aussies started laughing and pointing towards the ground. I turned round to see the scoreboard showing the 500–1 odds against us. I got my head down again but they kept pointing – I thought they'd mistakenly added a nought.

'I turned to Gatt and said: "See that? Good odds for a two-horse race, eh?" I asked him if he wanted a bet but he was too fed up. I nipped upstairs to the dressing room to get some cash. I offered the information about the odds to the other England lads, but they were too disappointed with their efforts to bother. That didn't put me off and I rushed downstairs to get the bet placed. As I walked out of the door, I ran into a swarm of children. There always seems to be more autograph-hunters at Headingley than at any other ground and I was besieged right away. I signed a few and yet the swarm began to increase. By this time the resumption of play was just ten minutes away and I still had to get to the other side of the ground. Yet I couldn't get away and was conscious that, if I walked away, I would get the usual subtle Yorkshire reaction of, "Hey, bighead, David Bairstow always signs, you know!" I was next but one man in and had to be padded up as the players walked out, so I had to give up and sign the rest of the autographs. I thought no more of it until the following afternoon when Australia's last pair were at the wicket. Then I turned around and, for the first time that day, my concentration was broken by the sight of the Ladbrokes marquee. I thought, "I could've won £1000". The irony was that those kids probably had my autograph many times over.'

Again, although Taylor remembers the events happening on Monday, they could have taken place on Saturday. Gatting was out in controversial circumstance on that day as well, with not everyone agreeing with the umpire that the ball hit his bat after colliding with his pad. Taylor was also the team's designated nightwatchman and therefore would have to be padded up as Brearley and Boycott returned to the crease.

Two other equally distinguished cricketers also believe they lost out on making a killing. 'Ted Dexter and I were in the habit of checking the racehorse fields each morning,' remembers Richie Benaud, 'and then leaving a note for Godfrey Evans when he came upstairs to the commentary box, as he did every day of a match, with a couple of Ladbrokes' pink slips. Ted and I decided that whichever of us was not on TV first would take the 500–1 on the fourth morning for a tenner each, just for the sake of not allowing something to run unbacked at that price in a two-horse race.' Unfortunately for Dexter and Benaud, Evans and Pollard had already left Headingley, thinking the match would finish that day. 'It was a good lesson for me never to bet on anything than can talk,' Benaud concludes.

News of the Lillee/Marsh bet began to leak out almost straight away. 'I was talking to Denis Compton,' says Frank Crook, then reporting for the Australian *Sun*, 'and he said he had heard a whisper that a couple of players had taken the 500–1 odds.'

Word reached the England dressing room, though Graham Dilley for one was not impressed: 'I remember thinking, "what a waste of money that is".' Gower, however, reckons that such experienced, if compulsive, punters knew, or thought they knew, that they were throwing their money away. 'As the England team at the time bore more resemblance to a donkey than a racehorse, they could scarcely have imagined that they would collect.'

The story reached the press the day after the match. 'I was driving home from Leeds when the sports editor called to say they'd had a tip-off that two Aussie cricketers had taken the 500–1 odds,' remembers Steve Whiting, then the cricket correspondent for the London *Sun*. 'Some guy in the Ladbrokes tent had heard Tribe laying the bet for Lillee. I spoke to Hughes and he confirmed the story.' Whiting then told Crook that he had the bet story and that it was going to run the next day. Crook had until 10 p.m. on the Wednesday to file a story of his own. As often happens on cricket tours when a big story breaks, the touring press gathered in a hotel room to talk it over. But to Crook's surprise, some of his colleagues thought there was nothing to talk about. 'I was astonished,' remembers Crook. 'I said: "If I file this story it'll be page one." And one bloke said: "Page One!? It won't even get a run at all." Then a guy from one of the Melbourne papers got a call from his sports editor asking him about the story and he said: "There's nothing in it, I'll give you a few paragraphs." By this time it's about 9.40. I excuse myself and go and write the story. Of course it's page one the next day.'

Brian Mossop, who was working for the *Sydney Morning Herald*, explains why most of the Aussie press corps did not share Crook's enthusiasm for the story. 'We thought it was a bit of a joke. Even after the story had appeared in the London Sun, we found it hard to take seriously. You just didn't think about bookies and betting then. Even the tour books didn't make much of it. We were pretty dismissive of the whole affair.'

So what happened to the Australian winnings? Lillee had won £5000 and Marsh £2500, which was a lot of money in 1981. If they'd wished, their cash could have bought Marsh a new Fiesta Popular, while Lillee could have had the latest Ford Capri shipped back to Perth. Back in the Antipodes, the money might even have bought a house.

Dirk Wellham remembers talk of Lillee giving some of his winnings to charity. Graham Yallop confirms that it did not go into the team fund, though the two West Australians were not allowed to be anything other than generous when it came to keeping their team-mates' throats well-lubricated. It was this expected largesse which Crook thinks might explain why the defeated Australians, once they got back to the hotel, 'were in high spirits, with everybody chortling and laughing'. Interviewed by the BBC for its *Clash of the Titans* programme, Terry Alderman recollects that, in the gloom of defeat, 'things perked up' once the Aussies remembered the bet.

The next day Crook gave Alderman and a 'chirpy' Kim Hughes a lift to

Edinburgh. 'What's the go on the betting?' asked Crook, only for Hughes to dismiss the story and claim that journalists had made up quotes from the Aussie players and management.

Lillee himself was treating the revelations very lightly. 'He revelled in the controversy, he didn't think he had done anything wrong,' remembers Corbett. 'His biggest concern was taking such a large sum of money out of the country.'

Geezer went to collect Lillee's and Marsh's winnings when the tourists played against Worcestershire just before the fourth Test – delivering it to the tourists' dressing room. The bus driver became one of the biggest beneficiaries of the bet. Marsh and Lillee used some of their winnings to buy Geezer a set of golf clubs. Later they flew him and his wife out to West Australia for a holiday.

So is there any possibility that the bet influenced Marsh and Lillee's efforts in the match? Few connected with the game think so. The SMH's Mossop has an unshakeable belief in the two Aussie legends: 'A lot of people say that Lillee and Marsh played some part in the defeat because of the bet. I'll never believe that because I know they loved nothing better than beating the Poms.' Graeme Wood is more succinct, but just as sure. 'It was a bit of a joke that backfired, but it certainly didn't affect their performance,' he insists.

Others had doubts. Dilley, who was hardly in the most positive frame of mind, admits: 'I can remember wondering about the result and being typically English in not totally believing we'd won entirely through our own efforts. The bet just put an element of doubt in my mind, even though I knew nothing dodgy had happened.'

Certainly, you would be wise not to suggest anything 'dodgy' to Dennis Lillee's face. A few years later he claimed: 'I'd flatten anyone who ever suggested I threw a game. I have a completely clear conscience over the betting incident. I believe my integrity as far as playing to win every game I've played is unquestioned. I didn't regard it as betting against my team or my country. At no stage did any of the other players think there was anything wrong with taking the odds and betting against Australia, just that it would be stupid to throw the money away. I just thought odds of 500–1 were ridiculous for a two-horse race. I was prepared to risk £50 on the off-chance that I might get £25,000. The thing that irks me is that it was by no means the first time players had bet on the other team. I certainly wasn't the first, although I was the first to be crucified for it. I'd planned to have £50 on England. That I got cold feet about virtually throwing big money away and only made it a £10 wager is still a matter of regret to me. At the time we realised we'd won the money we felt a bit bad about it, but what could you do?'

Fifteen years later his views had not changed. In 2000 he told the West

Australian newspaper: 'I have never lost a moment's sleep over it. You'd have to be very naïve to think anyone who knew what the result of a match was going to be would only bet £10 on it. If you knew the result you'd put your house on it.'

Marsh has always been much more tight-lipped about the bet. But, as head coach of Australia's ultra-successful Cricket Academy, he has had a hard time avoiding the subject. After lecturing his young charges on the dangers of match-fixing, he told the press: 'I have no conscience about that [the '81 bet], I have no problems about talking to anyone about that. That's something that happened, that's a fact of life. I had a five quid bet. I mean, big deal. Most Australians have done that.'

Few doubt Lillee's and Marsh's denials that the bet affected their performance, but Corbett believes the game's players, officials and fans were not, in any case, keen to think the unthinkable. 'So many people's perceptions of what's exciting, captivating and unpredictable about cricket stem from that game,' he says. 'That's why Lillee and Marsh got off lightly. It would be like finding that the Germans at Dunkirk didn't have any bullets. It would have destroyed the legend.'

It was almost exactly 16 years before Ladbrokes again offered 500–1 odds against an England victory. By a huge coincidence, their opponents were again Australia and the venue Headingley. England batted first and made 172, two fewer than in the '81 first innings. Australia again declared with nine wickets down, but this time added exactly 100 to their '81 score. England went in again, 329 runs behind and the 500–1 odds were posted. Nasser Hussain and John Crawley attempted a Botham/Dilley, adding 133 for the fifth wicket, but once their partnership was broken England crumbled to lose by an innings and 61 runs. Had any of the Australians fancied a punt they would have been taking a big risk. In the wake of the Lillee/Marsh bet a new clause was added to the contracts of all Australian players. It read: 'The player undertakes that he will not directly or indirectly bet on any match or series of matches in which he takes part.'

All bets, or so we thought, were off.

The match ball mystery

Mike Smith collects cricket memorabilia. Anything that moves (or, rather, doesn't) 'of a personal nature'. Among the most treasured acquisitions regaling his Tunbridge Wells home is a cigar box presented to Wally Hammond by the touring South Africans on the occasion of the Gloucestershire immortal's wedding in 1929. Then there's the coffee set Ranji gave to Mrs Murdoch, W.L.'s better half. And a silk menu from a dinner thrown for the Ashes protagonists in 1896 by the Earl of Sheffield. Pride of place, though, goes unerringly to the ball with which Bob Willis blitzed Australia at Headingley. Or so Mike thought until recently.

There were some juicy items up for grabs at Christie's on 20 October 1988. G.H. Phillips' engraving of The Cricket Match between Sussex and Kent at Brighton (1849), George Beldam's classic snapshot of Jessop jumping out to drive, a silk handkerchief commemorating the trailblazing 1861–62 England tour of Australia, even a cache of letters in W.G.'s own fair hand. Mike dived straight into the Willisana: Cornhill, Prudential, Gillette, NatWest and John Player medals, photos, touring blazers, sweaters, shirts, cap, ties, cufflinks, a cigarette box, a brooch from Pakistan, and the *pièce de résistance* – the ball with which Willis had demolished Australia at Headingley in 1981.

Mike recalls hoovering up all that for 'around £1600, which was still a lot of money at the time – and I had to push myself for that'. *Wisden Cricket Monthly*, to which Willis still contributed a column, reported that the entire collection of Willisana went for £3260. The estimated price for the ball had been £80–£120; so keen was the competition, Mike paid £1150 – £50 more than the 1979 World Cup final medal fetched.

'Those keen collectors would have been surprised by Bob Willis's matter-of-fact explanation for the sale,' wrote WCM's Steven Lynch. 'Laughing off suggestions that he was either hard up or disillusioned with cricket, he

216

explained: 'I've never been one to make my home into a shrine to myself. I always kept the trophies and things in a suitcase. Now I've moved from Birmingham to Clapham, and I've got less space.' What, though, of the ball – parting with that had presumably been something of a wrench. Willis, assuredly no sentimentalist, suggested Lynch had no need to worry on his account: 'I've never taken it out of its box.'

Scarcely able to believe his good fortune, Mike requested a note of authentication; Willis duly obliged. 'Then I had a look at the ball,' recounts Mike, 'and thought to myself, "It's well-marked for a ball that was only 36.1 overs old when the match finished." So I wrote to Willis seeking further authentication.'

Willis replied, reaffirming the ball's legitimacy and offering an 'amusing' tale by way of explanation. Amid the almighty kerfuffle at the end of the Test, it seems, the ball was retrieved by the good offices of Geoff Boycott, who returned it to Willis. Willis said he put it in his kitbag and headed back to Edgbaston for the following day's NatWest Trophy tie against Sussex. There, upon unpacking, he was 'horrified to discover that the ball had been borrowed by a Warwickshire colleague who'd been hitting it against one of the picket fences ... hence its lack of pristine condition'.

For Mike, Willis's missive represented far more than reassurance: 'That letter was better than anything I'd hoped for. The fact that he'd told me that story. I was as happy as a sandboy.' He gave the matter no further thought.

Then, while researching this book in the spring of 2000, a loose strand materialised. Ignorant – as yet – of the auction, we asked Bob Taylor whether he knew the whereabouts of the ball. As it happened, he did – 'It's sitting on my mantelpiece.' In an admirable show of selflessness, Willis, related Taylor, had given it to him as a memento; largely unnoticed as it went amid the breathless hubbub, the match had also seen the keeper break J.T. Murray's first-class record for catches. We would have left it there had we not subsequently run across the Christie's episode. When we informed him of this development, Taylor was as embarrassed as he was insistent; the last thing he wanted to do was create a fuss or be the cause of somebody else's disappointment.

'The first I heard about there being any doubt,' said Mike, 'was when Keith Hayhurst [Lancashire CCC committee member and secretary of the Cricket Memorabilia Society] rang me, shortly after the end of the [2000] season, if I recall right. "You've got the '81 match ball, haven't you?" asked Keith, so I said I did. "Well," he went on, "Bob Taylor says he has it."

'It was a bit of a shock. I've always considered it unique. If you look at it from the outside it's more likely to be Bob Taylor's, but I thought it was genuine. To me, that ball is a unique part of cricket history, of English folklore. I'd like to know if it's real.'

In the phantasmagorical world of sports memorabilia, £1150 for a ball, even for the ball used in the century's most memorable cricket match, is small beer. A Walter Johnson baseball card might set you back 30 times as much. The railway sleeper Ian Botham borrowed for his 149 not out raised £10,000. That, though, is hardly the point. Two men felt suspicious and dismayed. Only one should have had any need to be. Over to you, R.G.D. Willis.

'I have no recollection of giving the ball to Bob Taylor,' he stated in reply to our letter. 'Why would I keep a cricket ball for over seven years and send it to auction if I did not think it was the genuine article? If there is some doubt over the ball's authenticity I will quite happily give Mr Smith his money back.'

Hardening the myth

'He needs a father figure, and I need a younger brother.'
                                                    Brearley on Botham

'There's only one difference between the sides and that's Botham.'
                                                    Kim Hughes

Over the ensuing weeks, the rest of what the band Orbital refer to as 'snivilisation' seemed to have been suitably inspired. Within three days, the PLO and the Israelis were facing each other across a table in Lebanon and calling a ceasefire. On 5 August, Michael Heseltine announced a package of measures to regenerate depressed areas of Merseyside. Two days later, a million Solidarity members went on strike in protest over Poland's food and economic crises. On 24 August, Mark Chapman, John Lennon's murderer, was sentenced to life imprisonment. (As the new century dawned, he was being considered for parole.)

On the first Sunday of the month, meanwhile, Ian Botham chose one of the posher suburbs of Birmingham as the stage for his next trick. As a contest, truth be told, this Edgbaston humdinger proved vastly more enthralling than its predecessor, even though Australia, once again, held the whip hand until the last. During the entire shebang, for the first time in 668 Tests, not one batsman reached 50; the most compelling games of cricket are almost invariably those where bowlers rool OK.

England recalled Emburey for the deflated Dilley. Australia, who had replenished stocks and humours with a relaxing few days in Scotland ('Everybody up there was on our side,' recalls Peter Philpott), sought to stiffen their batting by swapping Martin Kent for Chappell while replacing the injured Lawson with Rod Hogg. The ball deviated off the seam from the outset, though not so vindictively that Michael Melford could resist reporting in the *Telegraph* that the batsmen 'found ways of getting out which are unlikely to figure prominently in their autobiographies'. Only one man survived 60 balls and that was Brearley, who knuckled down to make 48 – the highest score of the match, as it transpired – in two-and-three-quarter hours after demoting Gooch and backing himself to tackle the new ball.

Opting to bat, England were indebted to a last-wicket stand of 24 between Old and Willis in mustering as many as 189 as Alderman (5–42) resumed his stranglehold. Old sent back Dyson and Border before stumps but Australia refused to be daunted by the spectre of Headingley. Wood (38) resisted for nearly three hours before Kent (a relatively freewheeling 46 off 81 balls), Hughes (47) and Yallop (30) led the way towards a muscular lead. Emburey's four late strikes limited the damage to 69 but Lillee had trapped Brearley by the close, and despite Boycott's resolutely non-stentorian 29 in three hours, England were fewer than 30 to the good when Gooch, yorked by Bright, was fourth to go. Botham fell at 115–6, bottom-edging a cut off Lillee, his match haul to date 26, 3 and 1–64; the advantage, at 46, was still wafer thin.

Gatting and Old – elevated by Brearley under express orders to have a welly against Bright – thrashed 39 in 27 minutes before Alderman elicited an edged drive from the Yorkshireman; Bright then beat Gatting in the flight to nudge leg stump, gleaning his fifth wicket. Lo and behold, Emburey and Taylor now constructed England's first half-century stand of the match, diligent defence spiced with the off-spinner's inimitable rustications. Even so, 151 in two-and-a-bit days, for all that Old had pinned Wood on Saturday evening, seemed eminently gettable. There were wobbles aplenty on Sunday morning when Hughes' pluperfect hook off Willis flew straight to deep square leg, reducing Australia to 29–3, but Border and Yallop forged the highest stand of the game, 58, whittling the target down to 64. Headingley hangover? Pah.

If anyone was going to induce panic it was Emburey, and he duly plucked a pearler out of the hat to have Yallop edging into his boot and thence to Botham at silly point. Better yet, with 46 required, he unstapled Border with one that spat out of the footholds and reared, eschewing all consideration for the basic principles of fair play. 'I think we knew at that point we had won,' Botham would claim; few witnesses were so convinced. Marsh and Kent had trimmed the target to below 50 when Brearley persuaded an unusually reluctant Iron Bottom to bowl, contrary to Dickie Bird's recommendation.

'Brearley came up to me at square leg for a natter. We often had chats out there on the field, and he always had something significant to say, but on this occasion he did not seem to know quite what to do. "What do you think, Dickie?" he asked.

'"Captain," I replied, "I reckon you've had it."

'"Oh dear," he said. "Do you really think so?"

'"Just look at the scoreboard," I said.

'Brearley persisted, "Well, what would you do if you were in my shoes?"

'"What would I do? If I were you, Captain, I'd put myself on to bowl, chuck them up, let them get the runs as quickly as possible, and then we can all shoot off home."

'"Good thinking," he said, and strolled off. Then he stopped, turned, came back to me and said, "Dickie, thanks for your suggestion, but I've decided to try something different."

'"You need a miracle, man," I told him. "What can you possibly do?"

'Brearley replied, "I'm going to bring on the Gorilla at the City End."'

The plan was for the Gorilla to keep an end tight, leaving Emburey to do the attacking, a job Botham felt would be better served by Willey, reasoning that the pitch was more conducive to spin. Brearley, in fact, had already asked Willey to loosen up. Unaccustomed to such humdrummery, Botham yomped in, sun blazing, shirt billowing, crowd roaring. In his second over, Marsh was bowled swinging across a yorker; next ball, Bright fell leg-before to one that snuck back and squatted. Lillee stayed awhile before fishing at one in the realms of the wide blue yonder and edging to Taylor, who dived and pouched, albeit at the third time of asking. Kent continued to cut a composed figure, refusing singles, protecting Hogg. He had just turned down another when he drove across a fullish inswinger. Three balls later came the inevitable inswinging yorker to Alderman; cue a set of shivered timbers and victory by 29 runs. Now came pandemonium as Botham grabbed a stump and set off for the pavilion, waving it above his head, a Viking who had enjoyed a jolly decent spot of pillaging but was by no earthly means replete.

In all he had whisked out five men for one run in 28 deliveries, the most destructive spell to conclude a Test, hardening the myth. Emburey had unquestionably done ample with bat and ball to warrant the Man of the Match award, yet even a crusty adjudicator like Trevor Bailey was swayed by the astounding denouement and plumped for Botham. 'Sure, I had bowled fast and mainly straight – but enough to deserve the figures of 5 for 1? Surely not,' reflected Botham. 'The Aussies had lost their bottle, there was no other explanation. In fact, I can recall the look on the faces of the batsmen as I ran in. It was exactly the same shell-shocked expression as I had seen at Headingley.' Hughes, all the same, had every cause to echo the words of Bob Hoskins' bemused Harold Shand in *The Long Good Friday*: what a diabolical liberty indeed.

'He just brushed the batsmen aside by the force of his personality,' marvelled Taylor. 'The noise [of the crowd] was so loud that I was worried that any snicks to me might not be given out by the umpires … the whole carnival atmosphere was inspiring. I have never known such an excited, animated crowd in England.

It was almost as if cricket had suddenly become the most important thing for most of the country.'

Willis had accepted Uncle Rupert's shilling (24,000 of them to be precise) after Headingley, contributing a column to the following day's *Sun*. This was an action he would soon regret, as friends pointed out his crass error of judgement in getting into bed with the very paper that embodied everything he had purported to detest about the press (in fairness, he did agree to it in the immediate aftermath of victory). Not that this deterred the sports editor from publishing a photo of a palpably exhausted Willis, taken during the NatWest tie against Sussex that very day, beneath the headline 'One Over The Eight'. The implication, claimed Willis, was horribly unfair: 'By the time I got back to Birmingham [from Leeds] I was almost dead on my feet, and the "wild celebrations" consisted of staying in, having an early teetotal supper and going to bed.' He duly apologised for his Headingley outburst − sort of − in his *Wisden Cricket Monthly* column: 'I am sorry I could not instantly appreciate the emotion and atmosphere.'

Willis had arranged a benefit bash for the Sunday night of the Edgbaston Test: a ball at the Albany Hotel, where the tourists were staying. 'Kim Hughes danced on the table and Dennis Lillee led a chorus of singing,' recollected Gooch, 'not so much celebrating as trying to forget. Only two of the Australians lingered after the formal part − captain and star bowler − and if the departure of the rest was disappointing, it was also understandable. I know how I would have felt.'

Nor did the fifth Test at Old Trafford do much to reinvigorate spirits. Harried by Willis, Botham and Lancashire's Paul Allott − making his debut in place of the injured Old − Australia, having dismissed England for 231, were shot out for 130 in 30.2 overs, their briefest innings since 1902. In a Channel Nine studio, Ian Chappell and his fellow pundits donned black armbands. Leading by 101, England had lurched to 104–5 when Brearley, back down the order, glanced Alderman to Marsh. With the arrival of the bareheaded Botham, the Saturday afternoon gathering was yanked from its flat-beered torpor and dunked into a vat of purest Perignon.

Wary and restrained at first − he had, after all, gone first ball on Thursday − Botham gradually began to tuck into Bright, prodding Hughes to bring back Alderman and Lillee ahead of schedule. The latter's first over went for 22, including two pristine examples of Botham's latest speciality − the duck-hooked six. In the space of 26 balls Botham made 47 as the total surged by 52; in eight overs before tea it rose by 76 − 65 of them bearing his imprimatur. Unlike at Headingley, the strokes were almost entirely authentic, the ball met squarely and staying mainly on the plain; both chances he offered, if they can be so termed, were fiendish.

Having taken 59 balls and 65 minutes to get to 28, he expended a further 27 balls and 37 minutes romping to 100. By scaling three figures off 86 balls he had registered the second swiftest century in Ashes annals, and the fastest for England full stop since Jessop 79 summers earlier. Half-a-dozen sixes constituted a fresh Ashes peak. 'I was completely ready for the new ball,' he would remember. 'I didn't deliberately set out to take the Australian attack apart. At the same time I was determined they were not going to dominate me. It was not until I saw a television re-run that I realised I twice hooked [Lillee] off my eyebrows for six. Perhaps that was the reason I connected so well – out of sheer self-preservation.'

On a technical level, most are agreed. This was Botham's most resplendent innings, even if the context meant it lacked the air of heroic defiance that underpinned his Headingley sally. It made him the first – and to date the only – player to win the Man of the Match gong in three successive Tests. John Woodcock advanced the question in *The Times*: 'Was this the greatest Test innings ever?' Even without the benefit of hindsight, this seems an unusually exaggerated reaction from such a judicious writer. Unlike Jessop, who entered with England on 48–5, needing a further 215 on a pitch that had hitherto prohibited any specialist batsman from making 50, both conditions and situation favoured Botham. And what of Stan McCabe's 187 against the full might of bodyline at Sydney in 1932? Or that same worthy's 232 at a run-a-minute in the opening instalment of the 1938 Ashes rubber, the innings that prompted Bradman to advise his players to 'come and watch this – you may never see its like again'? Or, to draw from Woodcock's own extensive experience, Len Hutton's 205 to set up a series-squaring win at Sabina Park in 1954? The only thing that can be said with any certitude is that Botham's Mancunian masterclass, which sealed the retention of the urn, was up there. Way up there.

By the time he had had his fill, caught behind for 118 out of a stand of 149, his last 90 had come out of 103 in 55 minutes and inside 14 overs – a cracking rate for a Sunday League match. In going from 5 to 118 in 70 balls, moreover, the roistering had been even speedier than that of Roy Fredericks at Perth in 1975 (his pal Viv Richards, mind, would in due course eclipse both, with Botham on the receiving end). At the other end, Chris Tavaré, brought in alongside his Kent elder Alan Knott at the expense of Willey and Taylor as England again searched for a less compliant order, had reached his 50 in 318 minutes, the slowest in a Test on an English field. Not that the tourists went down without a growl or two, Border and Yallop running up hundreds as Australia, 'chasing' 506, reached 296–6 and 373–8 before Botham and Willis restored order. Yet without Tavaré's tally of 147 runs in a dash under 12 hours, England would have lost. It takes all sorts.

A week later, Botham slugged his way to 106 in a John Player League match against Hampshire, piling on 179 in 67 minutes with Viv Richards. His second 50 came amid a fusillade of blows that yielded a run every 10.8 seconds. At one juncture he hurtled from the forties to 100 while the world's best and most consistently explosive batsman remained 'mired' in the eighties. 'I can count better than he can,' he reasoned, 'and knew when the sixth ball was coming up so that I could sneak the single to make sure I kept the strike.'

The Oval was Brearley's *adieu*. He had only ever intended it as a fling with an old flame, strictly for old times' sake. Midway through the match, the selectors announced that Keith Fletcher would lead the tour to India. The series won, they had decided it was both safe and pertinent to experiment. With the off-colour Gower and Gooch making way for Wayne Larkins and Paul Parker, Mike Hendrick's recall for the still-injured Old meant that only five of the Headingley XI survived. Australia, still shorn of Hogg and Lawson, retained Mike Whitney, the left-arm ringer plucked from Gloucestershire Twos to play at Old Trafford. Ditching Dyson, they also capped Dirk Wellham, who responded with a second-innings century, the first Australian to reach such heights on debut in England in 88 years.

In clean-bowling Lillee on the second day, Willis surpassed Wilfred Rhodes' English record of 109 Australian victims, but Border (106 not out) had already extended the score past 350. Then Lillee (7–89) and Boycott (who passed 1000 runs in a season for the 19th consecutive summer en route to 137) wrestled for bragging rights until Australia led by 38. Set 383 on the final day after Botham had taken his match haul to 10–253, England stuttered to 18–2 and 144–6 as Lillee topped Botham, improving his figures to 11–159, but Gatting (56), Knott (70 not out) and Brearley himself (51) secured the draw. 'I knew I was having problems with my technique,' Lillee would relate, 'but I was so perpetually exhausted that I simply couldn't do anything about it. It was a matter of survival and nothing more every time I went near a cricket ground. If I'd been fit [throughout the series], I could have got 50 wickets.' In Bedford, a painting of W.G. Grace on the exterior of The Cricketer's Arms was replaced by a passable likeness of G. Boycott Esq.

In December, BBC viewers voted Botham their Sports Personality of the Year – to date, the last cricketer to be so honoured. The competition was anything but negligible. Two days after the Old Trafford Test, in Zurich, Seb Coe broke the world mile record, triggering a nine-day private duel in which he ceded the palm to Steve Ovett then regained it. The world's foremost middle-distance runners, soccer team (Liverpool), snooker player (Steve Davis), speedway rider (Michael Lee), ice dancers (Torvill and Dean) and cricketer were all English. Even James Bond was now being played by Roger Moore, a pukka old fruit from south of Hadrian's Wall. All of a sudden, it was a heady time to be a Pom.

Rod Marsh declared that the omission of Doug Walters 'may well have cost us the Ashes'. Colleagues chose a more obvious tack. Hughes, unsurprisingly, traced the rot back to Headingley. 'If we had won that match,' he would chuckle through gritted teeth many years later, 'there was going to be no more Botham, no more Gower, for the rest of the series. Brearley's comeback would have meant nothing.'

Peter Philpott was of a similar mind: 'A lot of psychological damage was done by Headingley. It wasn't a great Aussie side and it put a real dent in our morale. Test cricketers are proud people and that sort of loss can be very damaging – it will hurt.'

Come the end of the Old Trafford Test, his 40th, Botham was 42 runs and eight wickets shy of the 2000 runs–200 wickets double previously achieved by only two men, Benaud and Sobers. Surprisingly, typically, the trickier part of the equation came first, via those 10 scalps at Kennington; the requisite runs followed in his next outing, in Bombay three months later, as he outpaced both colossi by an avenue or two. His wickets had cost 21 apiece, the runs coming at a steady 33. The finer print read eight centuries, 17 five-wicket bags, four of 10-plus. In that 1981 series he had collected 399 runs and 34 wickets; only that prodigious South Australian George Giffen had amassed more runs (475) in a rubber while claiming as many victims – and that was back in 1894–95, scene of that century's 'follow-on' victory. Sobers' 722 runs and 20 wickets in 1966 provided the only other comparable instance of English audiences seeing a single man exert such inordinate influence over the destination of a series. Gary *Who*?

Quite rightly, Brearley shared the plaudits. 'He was a marvellous captain to me,' said Botham. 'He encouraged me when I needed it and restrained me if he thought I was in danger of over-stepping the mark. Most important, though, he listened to me.' Brearley, on the other hand, was honest enough to suggest they fulfilled a mutual need: he was the father substitute, Botham the kid brother he never had.

Having served his Leicestershire apprenticeship under Ray Illingworth, Gower is ideally placed to compare the two outstanding England captains of the past half-century. 'Brearley made the right bowling changes, field placings, squeezed the runs. As a captain, in those circumstances, you can't afford to make a wrong call. Every decision is crucial. I'd have agonised, questioned every decision 10 times, but he was very decisive. He knew what he was doing. We didn't question him.

'The essence of both men is the same. Strip away the appearances, the Cambridge University versus University of Life debate, they're two people with a great understanding of the game and how people operate. They acquired that understanding by being good observers and by compiling a mental library. They both had the confidence to decide and lead, to sell their decisions to the team. The difference is simply one of style. Ray talked to me in a bluffer, more dogmatic fashion; Brears would sell things to me. The steel was there but he had a gentler approach.'

'Both were authoritarians, completely confident in their ability to control a situation,' amplifies Bob Taylor, who toured Australia with Illingworth in 1970–71. 'Ray was the professional captain, defending the players and fighting their corner. Mike was more of an amateur captain, although he did say to us that when Lillee came in to bat that on no account were we to talk to him because that got his adrenaline going, giving him an excuse to have a go at the Poms.'

So far as Chris Old is concerned, Brearley had the edge: 'Because he used his training, his psychology. I enjoyed playing under him. I had a great respect for him and he had respect for what I could do. He knew when to put an arm round you, to kick you, how to make you feel good, how to get the best out of you, which is a captain's job.'

In *Wisden Cricket Monthly* (under the heading 'Brearley – has there been a better captain?'), John Arlott, having acknowledged that, 'I really did retire one series too early,' sounded an ominous but timely warning: 'Unhappily, his captaincy – happy in itself – is not of a type that can be taught, nor, except in the rarest – apart from this case unknown – circumstances, is it natural in cricketers.'

Some years later, a less reverent overview came from the pages of the fanzine *George Davis Is Innocent*:

Third Test 1981: Day Five – Headingley. Post-match interview.
Mike Brearley: Of course I let them force us to follow on. I knew Headingley would be a devilish pitch on the last day. It's like chess, Richie, you've got to be two steps ahead of the opposition.
Third Test 1981: Day Four – Headingley.
Mike Brearley: Five men out and we're still behind their first-innings total. Basically we're buggered, Ian. So, heads you poke around, tails you hit the bejesus out of it.

Two decades on, when his patients are getting him down, does Brearley find his dreams being saved from unexpurgated gloom by the fortifying glow of 1981 and all that? 'Not as much as I [dream about] getting myself run out [for five] in India, in my first overseas Test, or as much as I think about batting badly for England. But I do quite often think we could have lost the series 4-0, 5-0. Very lucky. Not all luck, but we were lucky.'

Conspiracy – a theory

'No matter what his [Willis's] physical condition he could at least have raised a glass or two to the most knowledgeable and patriotic cricket supporters in the country.' Thus wrote Noor Abdullah in a letter published in *Wisden Cricket Monthly* shortly after the magazine's star columnist had electrified Headingley and elected to badmouth the press. 'Kim Hughes could certainly teach some of our cricketers the art of sportsmanlike diplomacy.' Had he been privy to what went on behind closed doors, Mr Abdullah may have tempered his enthusiasm.

On returning home, Hughes was still in diplomatic mode. He had related well to the players, he said, and enjoyed the captaincy. 'You don't become an overnight sensation in a very hard and competitive field,' he asserted. 'It took Mike Brearley 10 to 12 years and he still makes blues.' Relations with the media, he told friends, could have been better. During the tour, indeed, he was reported as saying that, if anyone in the street spoke to him the way he was being addressed by the fourth estate, he would have 'decked' them. Here, deduced Alan McGilvray, was *prima facie* evidence of the naked aggression that blighted Hughes as leader and batsman. To the wizened but still perceptive broadcaster, he was the quintessential angry young man, forever wavering between joy and despair.

Greg Chappell had stayed up and winced through ABC's coverage of the final day of the Headingley Test. 'In a situation where you couldn't lose, they lost it,' he assured his biographer, Adrian McGregor. It hardened his resolve to carry on, to reclaim the accursed urn before summoning pipe and slippers. Sounding out Lillee, Marsh and sundry other members of the touring party, he was universally encouraged, wrote McGregor: 'For God's sake take it. If you'd seen what happened in England. Don't bail out on us.' He returned to the helm that winter, as he was always going to so long as that was his desire, even if the vote was not unanimous. For Hughes, who was never granted the luxury of picking and choosing when or if he toured, whose commitment could never be questioned, it must have felt like a slap in the face from an extremely wet and unreasonably cold flannel.

By comparison with his feted opposite number, rather inevitably, the consensus on Hughes' leadership acumen was positively fetid. 'He has several endearing qualities [but] I thought him a poor captain and I was no orphan on that score,' opined Dennis Lillee. 'The thing that irked me the most was that the bloke wouldn't listen. For some reason or other he thought he knew better and this led to some bitter conflicts.' For which Lillee himself, felt Geoff Lawson, was at least partly to blame. He had scarcely stinted, reasoned Lawson, in his efforts to undermine Hughes' authority.

After contradicting Fred Bennett over the betting shenanigans – honestly, if unshrewdly – Hughes' friendship with the tour manager had dissolved. 'Peter Philpott and Hughes worked together as though they were from rival countries,' noted Dirk Wellham, a chapter in whose autobiography went under the title of *Dr Kim and Mr Hughes*. 'Perhaps as a New South Welshman and a West Australian, respectively, they were from different cultures.'

As an interested onlooker, David Gower cannot claim to have noticed the fissures, at least not before Headingley: 'It was a bit early to say there were ructions. They were winning the series. But if the respect isn't there and the pressure is on, that's when you get potential for divisiveness.'

Graham Yallop, for one, had a fair-sized bone to pick. During their first-innings stand at Headingley, Hughes, recalling the problems Bob Willis had caused the ex-skipper at Lord's, sought quite conspicuously to protect his partner when the Warwickshire man was in the attack, even to the extent of declining a single to fine leg. Not unnaturally, Yallop felt humiliated. His manhood had been publicly demeaned. While it is highly improbable that this was Hughes' intention, its impact could not be gainsaid. When the players came off for lunch, team-mates saw a Yallop far removed from the mild man they knew. He was speechless; the eyes raged. Stoked by Lillee and Marsh, the mood was mutinous. 'The sentiment was evident,' decided Wellham, 'but the method of execution ... left a lot to be desired. Hughes certainly didn't find a warm reception in his dressing room when he followed a livid Yallop through the door. I found the situation slightly confusing. I had always felt that the Australian team was 'one for all and all for one'. The latter part of that phrase seemed to be more appropriate than the first.'

Is it that big a stretch of the imagination, then, to interpret Australia's collapse at Headingley, not as an attempt to lose the unloseable Test and hence win the unwinnable bet, but as the subconscious by-product of the antipathy engendered by their captain? Sigmund Freud might well have nodded his assent. The anti-Hughes brigade, he would surely have contended, would have been, if not happy, then certainly not overly depressed at a defeat that would prick his bubble, deflate that lofty air. Such a reversal would not cost them the Ashes, they might have rationalised, merely delay eventual victory.

Is it conceivable, on that last day, that any disaffected New South Welshman or West Australian tried less than his utmost, however unwittingly? 'Absolutely not,' avows Lawson, piqued at such an outlandish insinuation, and understandably so. Look at how Lillee and Bright almost saved the day. Look at the dedication shown by Chappell and Dyson for most of the morning. Think how hard men have to struggle to be considered worthy of that baggy green cap, and how much pride they invest in representing their country. 'It was a freak game on a pitch that seamed and bounced for five days and contained a number of remarkable individual performances. There was a huge shovelful of depression in our dressing room after it was over. It was very quiet. No one even spoke in the showers.'

Chris Old, too, scoffs at the idea that Australia threw the match. 'There was never a hint of match-fixing – an Australian would rather die than lose to England, especially Lillee – and no matter how anti-Hughes they were, they wouldn't have done it to spite him.'

From those involved, it scarcely needs adding, one can hardly expect unalloyed objectivity. Might it possibly be, though, that heads made promises that hearts were unable to keep?

Just a theory, folks, pure conjecture ...

What became of the boys of '81?

Saturday, 1 July 2000. Nineteen years to the month since Headingley 1981. England are playing the West Indies at Lord's.

The match has entered its third day and a remarkable finish is on the cards. After bowling the West Indies out for 54, England have to make 188 to win. They lose Ramprakash early, but then Atherton and Vaughan begin to build a stand. The day is close and muggy – Ambrose and Walsh have the ball on a string.

At the Nursery End, the Media Centre hovers over the ground like the spaceship from *Close Encounters*. Inside are no fewer than seven of England's Headingley XI, six of them ex-England captains.

David Gower is sitting in the bar with comedian and *They Think It's All Over* co-star Nick Hancock, watching the game on television. Geoff Boycott, wearing a tank top, talks to no one. He comes down from the commentary boxes on the top level, asks for a cup of tea and retreats to his sanctuary. Sitting on the other side of the bar is his old opening partner, Mike Brearley. Whiter of hair and even frailer than in his playing days.

Ian Botham, hotfoot from the Sky commentary box, doesn't once glance at the cricket. He is buzzing around, arranging the evening's entertainment and, no doubt, planning a round or two of golf now that Sunday looks like being a free day.

Bob Taylor, now employed by match sponsors Cornhill, is also busy, shepherding guests including TV's Bob Holness, singer Suggs and Sports Minister Kate Hoey to the executive boxes.

Bob Willis, also taking a break from the microphone, stands at the back of the viewing area as Ambrose surges to the wicket, the Antiguan fast bowler's duel with Atherton every bit as mesmeric as his own victory charge in 1981.

And then there's Graham Gooch, down from the radio box. He's nervous — really nervous. With Cork and Gough at the wicket and still 28 to get, he freezes in the corridor, unable to see the game, but afraid to move in case it disturbs some cosmic balance that may be helping England towards the winning runs.

Then it's all over. Cork runs from the pitch, punching the air. The boys of '81 slip away, all except for Brearley, who has his *Observer* column to write. He sits there, gazing out over the ground, thinking, no doubt, of other narrow escapes and famous victories.

Key:
* National record (as of 1.1.2001)
**World record (as of 1.1.2001)
HS: Highest Score
BB: Best Bowling
5w/i Five wickets in an innings

ENGLAND

Graham Gooch
In 1981: Rich but unfulfilled promise.
In 2001: An Essex legend, more admired than loved elsewhere. Remembered, not always fondly, as much for his work ethic as for his sometimes imperious batting.

Clearly among the three most talented batsmen in the country, Gooch remained maddeningly inconsistent. Uncertain of his future, he decided to captain the first rebel tour side to South Africa. He was banned for three years.

The ban was lifted in time for the 1985 Ashes series and Gooch cruised back into the England team like *The Bismarck* on steroids. In a vintage year for English batsmen, Gooch scored 487 Test runs at 54.11. However, he struggled for most of the late Eighties and by the end of the 1989 Ashes series had played 76 Tests, scoring 4724 runs at 36.90. Between the start of the 1990 series against the West Indies and his retirement in 1995, he won 42 more caps, made 4176 runs at 51.56, hit 12 more centuries and was ranked as the best batsman in the world.

The making of him was the England captaincy. Determined to instil some discipline, he began to approach fitness and match preparation with an intensity previously unseen outside First Division football. England had lost all five Tests on the 1986 Caribbean tour; Gooch's side were defeated 2–1, but could have easily reversed the result had fortune smiled on them.

Against the 1990 Indians he scored 752, at an average of 125. Astonishingly, nearly half of those runs came at Lord's, where he made an instantly brandable 333. A year later came an undefeated 154, out of 252, against the West Indies at Headingley. The PricewaterhouseCoopers rankings suggest it was the greatest Test innings of modern times.

The 2–2 series draw against the West Indies was followed by victories against Sri Lanka and New Zealand. England won four consecutive Tests, something that they had not done since 1979 and (at the time of writing) have not done since.

A fractious and unsuccessful series against Pakistan was trumped by a 3–0 thrashing away to India and the first-ever defeat by Sri Lanka. Four matches into the 1993 Ashes series Gooch passed the captaincy on to Mike Atherton. Remaining in the side until the 1994–95 tour of Australia, he retired from international cricket at the end of the series but kept going for Essex until 1997, by which time he had led them to three Championships.

In retirement he has become a highly-valued batting coach and irregular broadcaster. His stint as a selector ended when he was scapegoated for the selection of Graeme Hick against New Zealand in 1999.

Test career stats (1975–95)
118 matches*, 8900 runs*, HS 333, average 42.58, 20 centuries

Geoff Boycott

In 1981: The most controversial figure in English cricket. A master technician with a flawed character.
In 2001: The most controversial figure in the cricket media. Respect for an acute mind and fearlessly unbiased opinions is set against further evidence of those character flaws.

Boycott ended the 1981 Ashes series just a few runs shy of Gary Sobers' Test aggregate record. He beat the record in Delhi that December and a few weeks later it emerged that he was joining Gooch on the rebel tour of South Africa. He played another five seasons for Yorkshire and his total of 151 first-class centuries and 48,426 runs is unlikely to be surpassed by a modern player.

Much to the surprise of those who believed him to be the taciturn Yorkshireman of popular myth, Boycott quickly set about carving out a second career as a highly opinionated, knowledgeable, resolutely unbiased, even colourful commentator.

His life then took a bizarre turn. A former lover accused him of assaulting her while on holiday in France. A French court tried and convicted Boycott and the broadcasters dropped him like a hot potato. He has now found a new home on Talk Sport Radio, and was recently recalled by Sky.

Test career stats (1964–82)

108 matches, 8114 runs, HS 246 not out, average 47.72, 22 centuries*

Mike Brearley

In 1981: The best Test captain, possibly ever.

In 2001: A private man. An intriguing and modest sage who keeps a low profile.

Brearley's short, but eventful, Test career came to an end with the close of the 1981 Test series. He led Middlesex for one more season, winning the County Championship as his swansong.

After that he disappeared from public view to build his career as a psychotherapist. He once told the authors that he could no longer afford to be a public figure as this might interfere with the analyst–patient relationship.

Since the mid-Nineties he has edged back into the limelight, writing for the *Observer*.

Test career stats (1976–81)

39 matches, 1442 runs, HS 91, average 22.88

David Gower

In 1981: Still English cricket's golden boy, despite recent travails.

In 2001: Universally loved for his graceful batting and his accident-prone captaincy. A high-profile media figure.

August 1982 saw Gower get his first taste of the England captaincy. Bob Willis was injured and he took charge for the second Test against Pakistan. England lost by 10 wickets; it was a taste of things to come.

By the time the West Indies arrived in 1984 he was first choice as skipper. Overwhelmed by a vastly superior team, England went down 5–0.

The next 12 months were the best of his career. First England won in India after going one down in the rubber. Then he led from the front against Australia, winning the man of the series award by creaming 732 runs at 81.33, a record for England in a home Ashes series, and regaining the urn.

Standing on the balcony at The Oval, Gower joked that the West Indies – England's next opponents – would be 'shaking in their boots'. Some shaking – the result was the same as in 1984. After defeat at the hands of India in the first home Test of 1986 he handed the captaincy – along with an 'I'm in charge

T-shirt' – to Mike Gatting.

He won it back in 1989 but it was another catastrophe, England losing 4–0 to Australia. He was dropped for the 1990 Windies tour, before being reinstated against India and selected for his fourth Ashes tour. Unfortunately, a run of dismissals which Gooch perceived as ill-disciplined, plus a jaunt in a Tiger Moth, put him firmly out of favour. He returned briefly against Pakistan in 1992, and overtook Boycott as England's leading run scorer. Yet much to his disgust – not to mention that of his many admirers – he was not selected for the tour of India and Sri Lanka, effectively ending his international career three years prematurely.

He is now suavely settled into the role of frontman for Sky's cricket coverage. On terrestrial TV he deals with the jibes directed his way on *They Think It's All Over* as easily as he once countered the swiftest of bowling.

Test career stats (1978–92)

117 matches, 8231 runs, HS 215, average 44.25, 18 centuries

Mike Gatting

In 1981: Not yet proving to be the new Patsy Hendren.

In 2001: A Middlesex legend, whose captaincy of England was first praised, then pilloried. Known for his waistline as well as his batting, which never consistently convinced at Test level.

Gatting's Test career continued in fits and starts until the 1984–85 tour of India. As England crashed to defeat in the first Test, he finally made his first Test century in his 31st game. In the fourth Test of the tour, he made 207. The Middlesex man then pulverised the Australian bowlers during the 1985 Ashes series. He was finally bracketed with Gooch and Gower as a Test-class batsman.

In 1986 Gatting found himself in the captain's hot seat. After a poor summer, England arrived in Australia and proceeded to win the opening Test, the series 2–1 and both one-day tournaments, defying suggestions that they could neither bat, bowl nor field.

However, the captain's nemesis was already looming in the far from insubstantial shape of Shakoor Rana. The now infamous altercation with the Pakistani umpire created the impression that Gatting was a loose cannon. He survived as captain until the first Test against the West Indies the following summer, whereupon a salacious story involving a barmaid and alleged sightings of Gatting's naked, heaving bottom hit the tabloids. The selectors finally decided he was too hot to handle and gave him the boot.

Halfway through the 1989 season he accepted an invitation to lead the second English rebel tour to South Africa. He spent four years out of international cricket before Ray Illingworth overruled his captain, Atherton, and insisted on his inclusion in the 1994–95 Ashes squad; his penultimate Test brought a century.

He captained Middlesex from 1983, during which time they won three Championships and four one-day cups. His stint as a national selector came to the same sticky end as Gooch's and, like the Essex stalwart, he retreated once more to the bosom of his county, only to be sacked as coach at the end of a disappointing 2000 season.

Test career stats (1978–95)
79 matches, 4409 runs, HS 207, average 35.55, 10 centuries

Peter Willey

In 1981: The hard man of English cricket, although that reputation was undermined by a stance which brought spontaneous laughter at first sight.
In 2001: An international umpire with a growing reputation.

After 20 Tests it seemed as if Willey's international career might be over. But in 1985 he was back at Headingley, facing the Aussies again and enjoying his third consecutive victory against the old enemy.

Selected for the infamous 1986 Caribbean tour, he played in four Tests but was mown down along with the rest of the English batting. He got one final game – against New Zealand at Lord's in 1986 – but the jury was in and he was found guilty of lacking Test 'class'.

Willey lives and breathes cricket and few were surprised when, a year after retiring, he rejoined the county circuit as an umpire in 1993. In 1996 he was promoted to international level and now wears the Happy Shopper logo with a mixture of wry incredulity and authority.

Test career stats (1976–1986)
26 matches, 1184 runs, HS 102 not out, average 26.90, two centuries, seven wickets, BB 2–73, average 65.14

Ian Botham

In 1981: The best-known English cricketer since W.G. Grace.
In 2001: Still the nation's most admired cricketer nine years after his final Test.

Botham's Test career never again quite reached the heights of 1981. Back problems, stiffer opposition, a lack of commitment and constant press harassment have all been put forward as reasons why his performances, particularly with the ball, declined. He toyed with public affection, constantly involved in scandal but also raising money for leukaemia research.

In retirement Botham continued his charity walks and joined Gower and Willis on the Sky team. He briefly held aspirations to become chairman of selectors, a campaign energetically backed by the tabloids but few others. Fit, tanned and apparently comfortable with his lot, there is little sign yet that he is going to go the way of most brilliant, instinctive cricketers and descend into bitter disparagement of future generations.

Test career stats (1977–92)

102 matches, 5200 runs, HS 208, average 33.54, 14 centuries, 383 wickets*, BB 8–34, 5w/i 27*, average 28.40

Bob Taylor

In 1981: In the eyes of many judges the best wicketkeeper in the world, kept in the shadows by Alan Knott's superior batting.

In 2001: Conducting his business for ball manufacturer Dukes, with the same neat, unshowy efficiency.

He may have turned 40 at Headingley but Taylor was only halfway through his Test career. With Knott joining the rebel tour to South Africa, he wore the national gloves for the next three years.

While never keeping less than immaculately, his batting was constantly disappointing for a man with a highest Test score of 97. In 1984 he was replaced by Middlesex's Paul Downton.

He played one more season for Derbyshire before retiring at 44. After that he again became a fixture at UK Tests, this time working for Cornhill.

Test career stats (1971–84)

57 matches, 1156 runs, HS 97, average 16.28, 167 catches, seven stumpings.

Graham Dilley

In 1981: The first genuinely quick English bowler since Bob Willis, although there were question marks over temperament.

In 2001: Despite two excellent years in the late Eighties, still best remembered for his stand with Botham.

Not until 1986 did Dilley become a Test regular again. Nineteen wickets in four Tests against India and New Zealand won him a place on the 1986–87 tour of Australia. The Brisbane Test produced his first five-wicket haul, seven years after his debut.

He remained in form for the next two years, capturing six 'five-fers' in the space of 15 Tests during which he took 59 wickets at 26.14. However, two games against the 1989 Aussies suggested the fire had died and he joined Gatting's ill-fated tour of South Africa. At the age of 30 he found himself on the international scrapheap.

In 1987 he left Kent, believing they were not paying what he was worth, and joined Worcestershire, whom he helped win two Championships. He retired in 1992 and now makes his living coaching at both international and county level.

Test career stats (1979–89)

41 matches, 521 runs, HS 56, average 13.35, 138 wickets, BB 6–38, 5w/i 6, average 29.76

Chris Old

In 1981: A classic English seamer, especially on home soil. Injury prone.

In 2001: A clever bowler, if not quite of the top rank; would have got into most England sides of the last two decades – if fit.

After playing in the 1981 Edgbaston Test, Old's international career came to an end with his decision to join Gooch's rebel tour. The same year was his 17th and last for Yorkshire, as he tired of the constant in-fighting and headed for the Midlands. Three seasons with Warwickshire followed before Chilly finally retired.

He then mixed hospitality and PR work with playing for Northumberland in the Minor Counties Championship. Later he managed a sports complex in Teeside, before ending up on the south coast, where he became Cornwall's Cricket Development Officer. Today he coaches in Falmouth and runs a restaurant, Chris Old's Clipper.

Test career stats (1972–81)

46 matches, 845 runs, HS 65, average 14.82, 143 wickets, BB 7–50, 5w/i 4, average 28.11

Bob Willis

In 1981: Once again England's spearhead. Perhaps the true phoenix from the Ashes.

In 2001: England's best fast bowler since John Snow, a commentator whose voice undersells his often thoughtful views.

Headingley was Willis's 60th Test; that he would play another 30 would have seemed madness on that rest day back in July 1981. The idea that he would also become captain less than a year later would have appeared just as dotty.

On the 1983–84 tour of New Zealand and Pakistan he passed Fred

Trueman's total of 307 Test wickets to become England's most successful bowler. Picked for the first three Tests of the 1984 Windies series, the edge had gone and he was savaged by Greenidge, Richards et al.

Typically, he did not hang around and retired the same year. He became involved in corporate hospitality and in August 1997 it was reported that he and his brother had paid £1 million for a business which hosts sports events at London's Cafe Royal. Another member of the Sky commentary team.

Test career stats (1971–84)

90 matches, 325 wickets, BB 8–43, 5w/i 16, average 25.20

AUSTRALIA

John Dyson

In 1981: The next Bill Lawry, possibly.

In 2001: One of the late Seventies generation given a chance by the Packer defections who would never otherwise have played at international level.

Ironically, the workmanlike Dyson is best remembered for two pieces of supreme athleticism. During the fifth Test of the 1981 series he took a brilliant diving catch at third man to dismiss Alan Knott. In the 1982 Sydney Test against the West Indies he outdid even that effort, sprinting 25 metres and flinging himself goalkeeper-style to take a more astonishing outfield catch.

He lost his Test place after the 1982–83 Ashes series, was briefly recalled in 1984–85 and then took the South African krugerrand, playing on two rebel tours.

A computer studies lecturer, he has also coached the New South Wales team. He now works in a PR role at the NSW School Sports Foundation.

Test career stats (1977–84)

30 matches, 1359 runs, HS 127 not out, average 26.64, two centuries

Graeme Wood

In 1981: Opener with all the strokes but a flawed defensive technique.

In 2001: Another Packer era stopgap, albeit one with flair who occasionally flowered.

Wood returned to England in 1985, scored just 260 runs in five Tests – 172 of them in one innings – and lost favour with the selectors. Guiding Western Australia to three Sheffield Shields, he was recalled to the national side in 1988. But despite a century against the rampaging West Indies he won just one further national cap.

As WA's chairman of selectors for three years, he oversaw two more Shield triumphs. He is now the general manager of brewer Carlton and United's Perth office.

Test career stats (1978–88)

59 matches, 3374 runs, HS 172, average 31.83, nine centuries

Trevor Chappell

In 1981: Greg and Ian's brother. A decent one-day cricketer.

In 2001: 'I didn't know there were three Chappell brothers. Oh, that's right, the underarm bowler.'

Chappell's only taste of Test cricket came on the 1981 tour. However, his energetic fielding, unfussy batting and medium-paced bowling kept him in the Australian one-day side until 1983. Retiring in 1986, he was recently appointed coach to Test cricket's latest entrant, Bangladesh.

Test career stats (1981)

Three matches, 79 runs, HS 27, average 15.8

Kim Hughes

In 1981: Australia's David Gower. A controversial choice as captain.

In 2001: Unable to withstand the pressure of captaining a poor side. A national scapegoat, although his batting still gets some misty-eyed.

Immediately after the 1981 Ashes tour, Hughes handed the captaincy back to Greg Chappell, and did not become first choice until the 1983–84 home series against Pakistan, at the end of which Lillee, Marsh and Chappell all announced their retirements – leaving Hughes to face ... the West Indies. After five consecutive defeats spanning two series, he resigned in tears, complaining of press harrassment and 'criticism and innuendo' from former players. That eminent Victorian Bill Lawry said he had been 'dragged down like a dingo', while Richie Benaud expressed 'complete astonishment' that he had quit.

Overlooked for the 1985 Ashes tour, he reacted by agreeing to captain a boycott-busting tour of South Africa. He was banned from international cricket and spent his last two seasons of first-class cricket captaining Natal before retiring in 1991.

Test career stats (1977–84)

70 matches, 4415 runs, HS 213, average 37.41, nine centuries

Graham Yallop

In 1981: A classy batsman better remembered for captaining Australia at their Packerised nadir.

In 2001: Unfairly consigned to Australia's forgotten generation.

Injury lost Yallop his place after the 1981 Ashes series. Not until 1983 did he become a regular again, and he responded by scoring 554 runs against Pakistan at 92.33. However, another run of injuries jeopardised his position and he joined Hughes on the rebel tours of South Africa. He spent his last few cricketing years playing in the Melbourne grades. Today he has branched out from running several sports centres into the tourism sector with an Internet booking firm.

Test career stats (1976–84)

39 matches, 2756 runs, HS 268, average 41.13, eight centuries

Allan Border

In 1981: Already establishing a reputation as one of cricket's toughest and most talented players.

In 2001: A national treasure.

Following Hughes' and Yallop's decision to go to South Africa and Chappell's retirement, Border was really the only decent, proven Test batsman Australia could boast about. That he also had guts became plain on the disastrous 1983–84 tour of the Caribbean. Over the course of the series he made over one fifth of the team's runs.

His reward for this heroism was the poisoned chalice of the captaincy. He failed to win his first seven series. Apart from Sri Lanka, Australia were the worst side in the world.

However, he then took a little-fancied side to the World Cup in India and Pakistan; Australia lost one game out of eight and defeated England in the final.

The one-day champions then set about climbing the Test ladder. When the 1989 Australians arrived in England, Border was fed up with being a loser. In what the *Oxford Companion to Australian Cricket* calls 'an unblinkingly hostile campaign', he jettisoned the nice-guy image nurtured on the previous Ashes tour and led his side to a 4–0 win. This gave the 34-year-old a new lease of life. Over the next four years Australia became the second-best side in the world.

He continued to play for Queensland and in 1994–95 helped them win the Sheffield Shield for the first time. He is now a national selector and broadcaster.

Test career stats (1978–94)

156 matches**, 11,174 runs**, HS 205, average 50.56, 27 centuries

Rod Marsh

In 1981: The archetypal Australian cricketer: brave, aggressive and matey. Liked a drink.

In 2001: One of the architects of Australia's renaissance.

Post-1981 there was nothing left for Marsh to do but increase his personal tally of runs and dismissals. In 1982 against the West Indies he became his country's most capped player. Against England in Brisbane later that year, he equalled Gil Langley's national record by pouching nine catches, finishing the series with a world-record 28 dismissals.

As head coach of the Australian Cricket Academy, he has sent Glenn McGrath, Ricky Ponting and Jason Gillespie, among others, on to Test honours.

Test career stats (1970–84)

96 matches, 3633 runs, highest 132, average 26.51, three centuries, 343 catches, 12 stumpings

Ray Bright

In 1981: A fringe player, whose selection for the Ashes series underlined how bare the Australian spinning cupboard was.

In 2001: The man whose cartwheeling middle stump is enjoyed over and over by England cricket fans to this day.

Bright's performance on the '81 tour failed to convince the selectors that he was a better spin-bowling all-rounder than Bruce Yardley and the WA off-spinner was preferred until his retirement in April 1983. After that Bright played the odd Test, but rarely made any impact.

He continued playing first-class cricket until 1988, captaining Victoria for four seasons and becoming his state's most capped player. Today he works for sporting supplements company Musashi and is a specialist spin coach.

Test career stats (1977–86)

25 matches, 445 runs, HS 33, average 14.35, 53 wickets, BB 7–87, 5w/i 4, average 41.13

Geoff Lawson

In 1981: Together with Alderman and Hogg, he inspired hope that the Australian tradition of incisive fast bowling would prosper.

In 2001: Remembered for one great Ashes series, injury prevented him from consistently fulfilling his potential.

It was not until the 1982–83 Ashes series that Lawson's Test career finally got going. Following injuries to Lillee and Alderman, he was asked to take the new ball and responded by taking 34 wickets at 20.20.

Lawson seemed the obvious candidate to succeed Lillee as the side's cutting edge, but he lacked consistency and missed a number of Tests between 1985 and 1987 through injury. By the time he returned to England in 1989 he was thought to be well past his prime, yet 29 wickets at 27.28 played a big part in regaining the Ashes.

Captaining New South Wales astutely for three seasons, Lawson led them to the Sheffield Shield final every time, winning one. He became NSW coach in 1995 and remains a thoughtful commentator on the game.

Test career stats (1980–89)
46 matches, 894 runs, HS 74, average 15.96, 180 wickets, BB 8–112, 5w/i 11, average 30.56

Dennis Lillee

In 1981: The paragon of pace bowling, still a sight to freeze the blood.
In 2001: A global ambassador for his craft.

During the first Test against the West Indies in December 1981, the Lillee legend was polished to a blinding sheen. In one of the most dramatic opening days in Test history, Australia were bowled out for 198 (Hughes 100) before Lillee ripped into the visitors to reduce them to 10–4. The last wicket, that of Viv Richards, drew him level with Lance Gibbs' world record of 309 Test scalps, and the job was duly completed as he finished the game with 10 wickets, taking his Test victims for the year to 85, a world record.

From then on, the injuries began to multiply and when Lillee did play he often bowled first change. However, his final Test was a triumph as he took 8–153 and together with Lawson (9–107) drove Pakistan to defeat.

Lillee is now the world's most in-demand pace bowling coach and runs his own cricket academy in Madras.

Test career stats (1971–84)
70 matches, 905 runs, HS 73 not out, average 13.71, 355 wickets, BB 7–83, 5w/i 23*, average 23.92

Terry Alderman

In 1981: The biggest find of the year.
In 2001: Probably more highly regarded in England.

The Australian public was keen to have a look at the new discovery. Initially, Alderman did not disappoint, taking 6–79 against Pakistan, but he only took two more wickets in the three-match series.

In the first Test at Perth during the 1982–83 Ashes series, he chased a pitch invader and successfully rugby-tackled him before he could escape. However, in making his citizen's arrest, he dislocated his shoulder, writing off his entire season.

He returned for the 1984 tour of the Caribbean but took just four wickets; in 13 Tests since the 1981 tour he had taken 28 wickets at 48.75. Thinking his international career was going down the pan he signed up for Hughes' South African rebel tour.

Part two of his international career got underway at Headingley on the 1989 Ashes tour. The 33-year-old finished the series with 41 wickets, one fewer than in 1981. All told, nearly 60 per cent of his Test victims were culled from the ranks of the oldest foe, against whom he collected almost six wickets per outing; among those taking 100-plus in Ashes contests, only Charlie Turner, marginally, has done so at a more prolific rate.

He was back to haunt the Englishmen in 1990–91, though half his 16 wickets came in the first Test. He toured the West Indies later that winter but only featured in the fifth Test. It was to be his last.

He continued to play for WA, for whom he took a record 433 wickets, and was player-coach in his final season, 1992–93. He now sells real estate and occasionally broadcasts on ABC.

Test career stats (1981–91)

41 matches, 170 wickets, BB 6–47, 5w/i 14, average 27.15

Blessing and curse

May 2001. The nigh-on invincible baggy-green 'uns touch down at Heathrow Airport. Fourteen years, 32 Tests, half-a-dozen tours and more than 2000 episodes of *Coronation Street* have passed since England last held the Ashes. Not even in the Bradman era were Australia so remorseless in their gum-mangling stranglehold. Will the urn go the way of the Wightman Cup and the non-Euro Ryder Cup, abandoned on the grounds of pointlessness? The bane of the competitive arts, after all, is one-sidedness. Maybe the Danes and Dutch could lend a hand?

For Australia, the ramifications of that 1981 series were both superficial and profound. Ray Bright still bears the scars: 'Yes, I suppose that shot of my middle stump disappearing does get a bit of airing. I don't need to see it again, that's for sure.'

As, for quite some time, did Allan Border: 'It took me many years to come to grips with what happened to the pride of Australian cricket in 1981. It was the lowest point I can remember in my career.' As was borne out by a subsequent exchange with Dean Jones, still a couple of years away from the onset of his own dynamic international career.

'It was hard to stand there in that crowd of cocky Yorkshiremen and watch that,' related Jones.

'How,' wondered Border, 'do you think it felt out there in the middle then, mate?'

The fourth-innings disasters of Headingley and Edgbaston became, if not the norm, then certainly a periodic irritant. At Sydney in 1994, chasing 117 against South Africa, Australia were dismissed for – you guessed it – 111. At The Oval in 1997, chasing 124, they fell for 104. Most recently, in the Melbourne Ashes Test of 1999, they were set 175, reached 130–3 and folded for 162.

Kim Hughes, meanwhile, was pigeonholed as a chap who never got going when the going got tough, and is mostly remembered as a loser – for all that his four wins and 13 losses as captain bettered the 5–18 and 2–5 records of David Gower and the well-thought-of Mike Gatting. Had Rod Marsh not made that bet at Headingley, it is not inconceivable that the selectors may yet have relented and asked him to be captain whenever Greg Chappell was otherwise engaged. After Hughes resigned, and subsequently took a batch of good men with him to South Africa, Border stepped up and, crucially, was afforded some breathing space to rebuild the side. One of the first infusions of fresh blood came from a sharp-nosed New South Welshman, Steve Waugh, who had, it was said, an equally-gifted twin brother.

Shame begat action begat Shane. A simplistic progression perhaps, but the chain of events did, broadly-speaking, take that very course. When the 1985 Ashes series was lost, plans for a national academy were hatched. It opened for business in Adelaide two years later, ostensibly as an arm of the newly founded Australian Institute of Sport. Deploying scientific training techniques, sophisticated monitoring programmes and technical experts, the goal was to hot-house and fast-track. Ian Chappell, Dennis Lillee, Marsh and Terry Jenner all lent their expertise. It was there that Jenner worked with Shane Warne, a tubby blond from Bondi with a Bothamesque swagger, not to mention a similar lust for life and disdain for authority. Expelled for failing to show sufficient rigour and dedication, he encountered rejection early but ploughed on regardless, stretching and straining every sinew to master the game's most taxing art.

In 1995, led by Mark Taylor, an earthier Brearley, Australia went to the Caribbean and became the first country to defeat the West Indies in a Test series for 15 years, the spoils sealed by a fourth-wicket stand of 231 in Jamaica between Mark and Steve Waugh. Of the XI that set a world record at Perth against the West Indies in 2000, recording Australia's 12th successive Test victory (a sequence ultimately extended to 16), all bar the Waughs and Matthew Hayden were Academy old boys. Absent through injury was Warne, the star graduate; the larrikin who revitalised leg-spin and gave the gnarled old game a long-awaited facelift. The coach was John Buchanan, an intent and ingenious Queenslander umbilically linked to clipboard and camcorder, whose methods had caused too great a culture shock at Middlesex CCC. At the time of writing, the English Cricket Academy, following in the wake of other Australian-inspired models in New Zealand, India, Zimbabwe and South Africa, is due to open in the autumn of 2002.

And then there's the bet. Had the Australian board punished Marsh and Lillee, it has been suggested, the current match-fixing crisis, the gravest dilemma cricket has ever confronted, might never have arisen. 'That set the standard of inaction and complacency on the part of cricket's administrators – that the whole thing didn't matter,' Matthew Engel, editor-in-chief of *Wisden*, told ABC Radio in the spring of 2000. 'I found it shameful then and I find it shameful now.'

Hard as it may be to credit amid the incessant scapegoat-herding, England won more Test matches and series in the 1990s – 26 and seven to 16 and five – than they did from September 1981 until the end of that decade. The most revealing auguries furnished by the summer of '81 came courtesy of the teenyboppers. Of the HMC Schools and English Schools Cricket Association XIs invited to the Eastbourne festival at The Saffrons, for instance, only Graham Cowdrey, James Whittaker, Huw Morris, Peter Moores and Graham Rose would win a county cap; their combined collection of Tests would be four. That season also saw an Indian Young Cricketers party tour Britain for the first time. Captain Ravi Shastri, Navjot Singh, Maninder Singh and Laxman Sivaramakrishnan would all do stirring deeds at a more exalted level (within three years Shastri and Sivarama were doing them to England). Of their counterparts only David Lawrence, Alan Wells and Neil Foster would meet them at the summit; only Foster made a lasting impression.

The winter of 1981–82 brought anti-climax on a depressingly grand scale. India won the first Test in Bombay whereafter the remaining five saw Sunil Gavaskar and Keith Fletcher take turns to slow proceedings down – at one juncture the rate sank to nine overs an hour, with the spinners on. Clement Freud and Henry the basset hound made a cheerier pair. The tedious purposeless of it all, Graham Gooch would claim with a modicum of credence, helped drive him into the arms of South Africa's propaganda-mongers. Five days after beating Sri Lanka in the latter's inaugural Test, Gooch led his 'rebels' out of Heathrow in strictest hugger-mugger – final destination the cradle and grave of apartheid.

Boycott, Emburey, John Lever and Underwood had all been on the subcontinent with Gooch; two more Headingley contributors, Old and Willey, were in tow, as were Woolmer, Hendrick, Larkins, Amiss, Humpage, Sidebottom, Les Taylor and Knott (the chap who'd given up touring ...). All 15 tourists were banned from Test cricket for three years. However, since only

Emburey and Gooch had greater things ahead of them, this does not explain the rapidity with which England's fortunes subsequently withered. This was because the decay was already well-entrenched.

The Class of '81 was almost certainly the last England side to strike fear into the breasts of the best. Between them, the top seven batsmen at Headingley wound up with 37,480 runs and 86 centuries in Tests, the bowlers – Botham included – 989 wickets. The corresponding figures for their counterparts come to 26,790 runs, 59 hundreds (all but half of them by Border) and 758 wickets (more than 40 per cent of them Lillee's). Some gulf. (By way of further comparison, those for the England XI that won the fifth Test at The Oval in 2000, thus prevailing in a series against the West Indies for the first time since 1969, were 24,388 runs, 49 hundreds and 455 wickets.) Boycott, Underwood, Knott, Old and Hendrick never played another home Test, and Willis was finally spent by 1984. An exceptional generation – particularly in the seam department – was passing (making it all the more regrettable, not to say unaccountable, points out Old, that the likes of Boycott, Gooch, Emburey and himself are currently deemed surplus to requirements as national coaches). Was the cupboard really that bare or had the world moved on? Did habits become vices? 'I don't think Headingley papered over the cracks,' contends Graham Dilley, 'because nobody was prepared to look at the cracks anyway. Back then we were still in the mentality of, "We invented the game, we've got to be doing it right."'

Let's be frank. Even to contemplate a reassessment of those breathless events 20 Julys ago would be to scale the topmost peaks of treachery. To even hint that there may have been certain, er, drawbacks, would be perceived as a gross insult to those who on that tumultuous Tuesday contributed, witnessed, experienced and sustained problems with heart, breathing or faith. A dash of perspective? A spoonful of proportion? Not if you value your credibility and/or neck. So, profuse and humble apologies in advance ...

'Botham made Brearley look like the messiah,' asserted Kim Hughes. Not that the victimisation of Australians stopped there. In 1985, having averaged 27 with the bat and 40 with the ball when the Ashes were lost in 1982–83, Botham terrorised them anew with bat, ball and hairdo. Bleaching his roots and letting his locks flow, as was the fashion, he added a good couple of yards in pace, grabbed 31 wickets, swashed 250 runs that were worth double in terms of their psychological impact, pulled off some stupendous catches, and generally contributed as much as Gower to the retrieval of the urn. In the opening Test of the next Ashes altercation, in Brisbane the following year, he settled the outcome with a savage 138.

'Australia always went on the defensive against Botham as soon as he came in,' recalls Trevor Chappell. 'It's like they were trying to keep him quiet rather than get him out.' When the urn was retained in Melbourne, He Who Must Be Obeyed claimed five first-innings scalps with a confidence trickster's aplomb. Even in 1992, then 36 and at least five years past his prime, Botham clobbered the Cobbers in Sydney, winning a World Cup match off his own bat, the spell undimmed.

Call it Bothobia. 'Up until 1981 the Aussies had underestimated Botham,' remembers Frank Crook. 'It was hard to find any Aussie who thought he was a great Test cricketer. After '81 they developed a real phobia about him.' Even when England recalled him in 1989 – 'and he was obviously over the hill' – the reaction of tourists and visiting press alike bore an uncanny resemblance to Colonel Hall's response whenever Sgt Bilko appeared to be on the level. 'We were all wondering, "What's going on, what have they got planned?"'

Had Australia been England's only opposition this would have been fine and dandy. Only once, in his first six Ashes series, did Botham taste failure. From the 1981–82 trip to India to the summer of 1988, unfortunately, India, Pakistan, Sri Lanka, New Zealand and the West Indies were also on the fixture list. Of the 15 Test rubbers with other adversaries during that period (as yet, Sri Lanka were deemed unworthy of such prolonged contests), England lost 10 and won four – and not one after 1985. Against the West Indies they lost 14 Tests out of 15, drawing the other. No shame in that, true, yet nor can there be any doubting that Australian weaknesses masked British flaws.

Comparisons between Sobers and Botham, by and large, have been pooh-poohed. So much so, few have bothered. The industrious Bob Bee is a noble exception. Botham played 102 Tests to Sobers' 93, so Bob, writing to *Wisden Cricket Monthly*, analysed their records by including only the Somerset man's first 93. The conclusions made eye-rubbing reading. Whereas Sobers made 1.62 times as many runs (8032 to 4972), Botham (370 to 235) harvested 1.57 times as many wickets. Against, arguably, stronger opposition. And while Sobers ran up nearly twice as many centuries (26 to 14), Botham had four and a half times as many five-wicket hauls (27 to 6). All that said, however, Headingley can be seen as the plateau.

In his remaining 62 Tests, Botham took 191 wickets at nigh-on 36 and stockpiled 3207 runs at much the same average as hitherto. He clocked up six further centuries and 11 more nap hands, but the rate was half as frequent. Granted, any chairman of selectors would probably give both arms to be able to call on somebody who could be relied on for 70 runs per outing as well as a wicket every 10 overs, yet the capacity to astonish, for the most part, had melted. At 30, a prime age for a cricketer, he was already spiralling down the greasy pole. Had he reached that pot at the end of the rainbow too soon?

Mozart, James Dean and Byron, Jimi Hendrix, Jim Morrison and Kurt Cobain – you name 'em, they burned out and/or died before they got old. Rusting and fading before our very eyes, the gods of sport degenerate for our delectation. Every creak and buckle is visible; X-rays by kind permission of the action replay. For excruciating voyeurism, what could possibly match Diego Maradona's descent into a bloated, coke-addled, gun-toting, wholly deluded thirtysomething? Endlessly recycling the same old riffs, Botham, who had almost as far to fall, merely descended from Led Zeppelin to Status Quo.

Not that this stopped him looming large and brash as ever in the popular prints, whether for allegedly breaking beds with Miss World, pulling on a joint in New Zealand or assaulting fellow passengers in mid-air. Provoked as he often was by the envious and those desperate for notoriety, some excesses could be attributed to onfield frustrations. Had Brearley and Barrington still been on the scene, he contended, 'it is possible that ... a lot of the problems I encountered in future years might not have arisen'.

After 1985, once back problems began to impair his bowling, the drop was not so much steep as sheer. Up to the start of the 1986 Caribbean 'blackwash' tour, he had played 79 Tests, scoring 4409 runs at 36.14 with 13 centuries, and taking 343 wickets at 26.37 with 25 five-wicket hauls. Thereafter he played 23 times, scoring 791 runs at 23.97 with one century, and taking 40 wickets at 45.8 with two five-fers. His last eight Tests spanned five years. Only his catching improved, remarkably so for a fellow of mounting bulk. Overtly reliant on psychological subjugation and that dazzling CV, he became all-too mortal. Not for him the single-minded drive of a Hadlee or Marshall. Boys just wanna have fun. And why ever not?

Because the team suffered. Because colleagues allowed themselves to be influenced by his approach. The superheroics of 1981 appeared to have persuaded Botham – and others – that he was capable of pulling off miraculous rescue missions, not via the conventional routes of preparation, planning, practice and training, but through sheer force of will. There was no need for a phone booth; the cape never came off. 'Botham's kamikaze approach would have been extraordinary in any other batsman,' wrote David Frith in *Wisden Cricket Monthly* after the third Test in Barbados in 1986. 'His aim in this hopeless crisis seemed to be to smash a rapid 149 not out and let [Greg] Thomas or somebody – his desperate self? – follow up with 8 for 43. We all continue to suppose this to be an impossibility. Ironically, Botham died feebly with an off-side waft after having thumped 21 off 14 balls.'

It is not beyond the bounds of possibility that responsibility would have helped him approach matters with greater gravity. The captaincy, however, had been out of the question since 1981. By 1989 – at 33, an age at which he may once have envisaged leading the side again – Botham was little more than a bit-part player dealing almost exclusively in boundaries, military-medium and extremely occasional tonics for the troops. Still, he was recalled to face Australia, in the not unreasonable hope that Bothobia still festered. A 4–0 series drubbing, celebrated with especial relish by Border, Alderman and Lawson, the veterans of '81, affirmed that it did not. The first Test, auspiciously enough, was at Headingley, and the media made the most of it. 'There were all the usual references in the build-up to Both's 149 not out and it gets up your nose a bit really,' admitted Border. 'After all, that was one brilliant knock and England's been living off that for a long time.'

And still the hacks and snappers snapped at his heels. In part, believes Peter Willey, the motivation was revenge. 'After 1981, because certain people had a go at the press, the press wanted to get back. Both was the first cricket superstar to get on the front page. He started to attract the paparazzi. And Both being Both, you've always got the chance of a story. They hounded him – it was stupid, it really was.'

At the same time, nevertheless, Botham's virtues continued to be extolled and exploited, his musings published regularly in the *Sun* and, later, the *Daily Mirror*. Did he begin to believe the hype? 'Yeah, yeah,' says Willey. 'When we went to the West Indies in 1986, Both thought he could blast people out. He wasn't anywhere near '81 form. He couldn't slog the fast bowlers but he still had this bravado. I think Both believed he was a hell of a lot better than he was. He couldn't accept that he became an ordinary cricketer who was playing on the memory of two or three Test matches. Unfortunately, perhaps we relied on him too much. I wonder if he covered up for the deficiencies of others?'

At bottom, Botham spoilt us. The resultant expectancy was cruel, debilitating, to his purported heirs as much as to the man himself. It massaged his ego but gnawed at his marrow. It convinced him (and others) that he could only truly enjoy – and hence fulfil – himself if he was constantly in the thick of things. How much more formidable a batsman could he have become had he acknowledged the decline of his outswinger and the alarm bells ringing in his spine, and jumped a couple of places in the order by way of compensation? He would doubtless take umbrage, as he has in the past, charging that the two skills were mutually dependent, that without being trusted at one he could not make the most of the other. But then he would, wouldn't he?

'In India in 1981–82 Botham played – and batted – as a batsman,' notes Scyld Berry, who covered the tour for the *Observer*. 'But then we ran out of bowlers against Pakistan the following summer and he regressed.' The salient, unavoidable point is that every time he gripped handle or seam, Botham was expected to play Merlin. Lancelot at the very least. He loved the burden, thrived on it, ignored it at will, wallowed in the clamour. The burden did not so much flatten as blind him.

Then again, how could it have been otherwise, for him or British cricket? Well, here's a theory. Had the 1981 Ashes series been regarded as it should have been, as a freak of nature, the defiant growl of a dinosaur, facts may have been faced far sooner, the rebuilding process begun that much swifter. As 'but ifs' go, admittedly, this is up there with JFK's assassination, the state of George III's marbles and God's whereabouts on the seventh day (if he/she/it hadn't been resting, he/she/it would surely have realised the need to think the whole thing through again, notably the bits about property, religion and animal extracts). There, though, lies the delight of hindsight. 'Can't buy a thrill,' Bob Willis's favourite songwriter once complained. Beg to differ, Mr Zimmerman: provided you're willing to pay the price, any form of orgasm is feasible.

No matter how bad things got – and a 5–0 hiding in the Caribbean followed by consecutive series defeats at home to India and New Zealand count as pretty dire by any standards – there was always the memory of '81 to soothe and comfort. If the miracle didn't happen today, there'd be another along soon enough (hence the players' tendency to save their best – a relative expression – for the second innings). Everything, the administrators and county chairmen banged on, was cyclical. It was a matter of personnel, not structure (hence those umpteen one-, two- and three-cap wonder-blunders). The attitude was reminiscent of Groucho Marx's stance in *Horse Feathers*: 'I don't know what they have to say/It makes no difference anyway/Whatever it is, I'm against it … /No matter how they've changed it or condensed it/I'm against it.'

Complacency reigned. The players' call for a four-day County Championship, bringing it into line with its international counterparts, went unheeded for years (introduced piecemeal in 1988, it finally took root in 1992). Nor did the ostrich tendency make the connection between those new-fangled video thingies and studying the opposition. Less forgivably, they failed to act when it became abundantly clear that the constant flitting between first-class and one-day formats might be doing irreparable harm to techniques, not to mention appetites. Accept that the rest of the world was developing faster than anticipated (the Packer Factor)? Not likely. Instead, the mandarins of British cricket blamed the ills on a surfeit of foreigners, cut quotas, handed out a few flags of convenience by way of sneaky recompense, then proceeded to struggle and fiddle and muddle. A struggle fuelled and perpetuated by post-Imperial arrogance and Munchausen self-delusion. Talk about a Faustian pact. 'Look here, Brears old man, you can have the Ashes if you must, but from here on in, you're on your tod …'

And so they waited patiently, with scant fear of disappointment, for Godot

Almighty, aka The New Botham. Derek Pringle, capped in 1982 while still at Cambridge, was the first poor sod. Well, he did wear an earring, had been an extra in *Chariots of Fire*, and once went shark-hunting. An intermittently useful bat and clever, occasionally Test-class, seamer – albeit well-nigh exclusively on the green, green grass of home – he served as a role model for subsequent pretenders, each of whom might well have accomplished more but for the ridiculous demands that dogged their every shadowed step, and the obligation many felt to try to live up to them. Then came Ian Greig, Phil DeFreitas, David Capel, Chris Lewis, Craig White, Dominic Cork, Mark Ealham, Adam and Ben Hollioake, Ronnie Irani and Andrew Flintoff. As the century drew to a close, few mentioned that Alec Stewart had long been the game's best wicketkeeper–batsman. Much less that genuine all-rounders – those capable of deciding games with bat and ball – don't grow on trees. Not since Alan Davidson retired in 1963 has an Australian Test XI featured one. Has it hurt them? Has it heck.

Of the New Bothams selected then anointed, drooled over and finally ridiculed by the media, the only aspirant worthy of licking the Gorilla's Doc Martens, in terms of consistency with bat and ball, has been White – and he took six years to recover from the initial overkill. DeFreitas and Cork are alone in taking 100 Test wickets, and while both turned Tests with their runs, their respective batting averages are 14 and 18. Lewis alone has managed a century, coming within seven wickets of being the first Briton since You Know Who to complete the 1000–100 double, yet averages of 23.02 (bat) and 37.52 (ball) made him Imran Khan in reverse. Flintoff and Ben Hollioake appear to have the makings of top-notch batsmen yet neither, perversely, has yet been urged/permitted to narrow his focus.

Again, the blindingly obvious was being glossed over in the quest to flog newsprint and airtime. The New Botham was/is every bit as misplaced and histrionic a concept as the New Dylan, or a Monroe Nouveau. This is not to say that British cricket cannot unearth a Bruce Springsteen, though White may turn out to be more of a Tom Waits. One can only hazard a guess, nonetheless, at what Lewis, the likeliest lad of the lot, felt about being labelled a 'black Botham'.

Belsize Park, North London, July 2000. The sun is showing no inclination to penetrate the Saturday morning grizzle. Mr and Mrs Brearley are about to take the short hop to a Lord's hospitality box for the Triangular Trophy one-day final between England and Zimbabwe. Home is a spartan-looking corner house surrounded by plush Victoriana. The black Jaguar XJS in the drive is the sole concession to ostentation. Garage, front door and window frames are all a pale shade of grey; just the ticket for a well-known psychotherapist who wants clients to feel unthreatened and has no wish whatsoever to draw attention to himself. Downstairs at least, primary colours are restricted primarily to the Joán Miró paintings that hog the walls.

As the last England captain bar one to bow out with a record worth telling his grandkids about (Willis, with seven wins and five defeats, is the only successor to have retired in profit), what did Brearley the psychotherapist regard as the source of the national cricket team's ills? Big sigh. 'I don't know what it is. Something to do with proper toughness, which comes from leadership, personality-types. Once you get the bit between your teeth, don't give up. The best Aussies have that but we don't seem to. It's parent v child; deposed authority figures can be ambivalent, often resentful.'

What, then, did he make of the contention that Headingley '81 was quite possibly the worst thing that could have happened to British cricket and Ian Botham? 'That theory is very hard to establish or disestablish. Perhaps the miracle success added to Botham's idea that he didn't have to work at his game, to practise. For the first three years of his Test career he was a wonderful cricketer. As a bowler he was quite fast, very aggressive, swung it both ways. Unlike Hadlee and Imran Khan he deteriorated rather than improved. When his back went I hoped he'd develop as a No. 5 and bowl a bit, but he didn't. He never quite learned not to play across his front pad to get off the mark, or hit inside out, so if people bowled very, very straight at him ... That series made him, but it might not have helped his long-term development.'

Others express similar views. 'It is possible that the Headingley victory worked to the detriment of England,' admits Bob Taylor.

'That summer probably did do us more harm than good,' affirms Pat Gibson. 'The selectors believed Botham could do anything, and he could at that time. But they spent 10 years looking for his replacement. He could never put together three performances like that again – who could? What he did in that series camouflaged our weaknesses. We were still looking for miracles a decade later.'

'I don't think what happened at Leeds and Edgbaston blinded English cricket to its faults, by deluding people that another miracle was always around the corner. I do believe, however, that the selectors went on too long with Botham,' says Christopher Martin-Jenkins.

'I was in awe of Botham, what he did to a crowd,' confesses John Emburey, 'but I think the expectations created by that match, and those at Edgbaston and Old Trafford, were bad for Botham, bad for English cricket.'

Geoff Lawson agrees: 'Those games certainly wallpapered over the widening cracks of the system. Individual performances often do that in team sports. But take out the results at Headingley and Edgbaston and England's performance was not too good against a team that was at the bottom of its learning curve and had the internal wrinkles.'

We hereby promise to head straight for Tyburn Gate and take our punishment like men ...

And yet, maybe this is all a touch ungracious. On 20 and 21 July 1981, for 24 hours more or less, a game of cricket held Britons in thrall: young and old, rich and poor, lefties and Tories, punks and New Romantics, the vast majority anything but leather-and-willow fetishists. That in itself is now unimaginable. And not just because soccer is now first, last and everything. British cricket followers have grown so accustomed to humiliation/failure/inefficiency that the act of outsparkling Zimbabwean *vin ordinaire* and Caribbean plonk is hailed as a renaissance (the subsequent triumphs in Pakistan and Sri Lanka are considerably more worthy of hype). The price for such comparatively rude health has, moreover, been high. For all their manifold qualities, Nasser Hussain and his team are found wanting when it comes to sex appeal. With one exception – Darren Gough – they are character actors not bill-toppers, men more obviously aware of their duties and limitations, ever cognisant that victory is something to be earned, not expected or conjured. Ah, humility at last.

Judged by the size of Test crowds, the Headingley Effect is debatable. The aggregate attendance for 1981 was 380,000 – 63,000 per Test. That the 1997 Ashes series drew more than 440,000, 73,000 per Test – on a par with those in the heyday of Boycott and Edrich, Illingworth, Knott and Underwood 25 years earlier – is not to be sniffed at, especially when the worldwide trend is downwards, let alone that the home team had not won a five- or six-Test series for more than a decade. Having convinced witnesses that drama (or at least horror) was always lurking around some unsuspected corner, the events of 1981 must be considered catalytic. Members of the self-mockingly-titled 'Barmy Army', those hardy loyalists who spend their winters cheering on Nasser's Army in distant if more clement climes, were certainly old enough to have drawn inspiration. Indeed, who can say what benefits were reaped by Test cricket as a whole?

Cricket-following in the late 20th century, though, was less about bums on seats than potatoes on couches and mugshots on back pages. At first glance, the tabloidisation of the game, instigated unwittingly by Botham, cannot be characterised as A Good Thing. By plastering the players' nocturnal activities – and even some of their daily ones – over the front pages, tours were disrupted, most notoriously during the 'sex'n'drugs'n'rock'n'roll' trek to New

Zealand in 1984 and, worse, the Caribbean trip under Gower two winters later. How could such unheard-of invasions of privacy – incited by circulation wars, justified or otherwise – *not* affect performance? The relationship between the two seemed symbiotic. The intrusions also led, indirectly, to Mike Gatting's sacking as captain in 1988, and in turn to him going off in a huff to captain another rebel tour to South Africa. On the other hand, this led to Gooch's appointment, which in turn brought, if not a major revival, then assuredly a renewal. Furthermore, without such unprecedented coverage, and the interest it revived – or, in many cases, stirred for the first time, *despite* the team's conspicuous lack of success – cricket in Britain may well have receded to minority status.

As it is, *Test Match Special*, despite a bumpy ride, is still with us, bless its chocolate socks. The Headingley Effect may also be seen as having revolutionised the way the game is broadcast, and hence financed. It was surely a factor in persuading TV executives and accountants at Sky and Channel 4 that it was worth raiding the coffers to prise live coverage away from the Beeb. An important social function was served, moreover, by all those comings and goings, rows and blow-ups, writs and counter-suits, grudges and gripes. Sometimes it felt like *Dallas* without the guns and padded shoulders. Sometimes it was *Crossroads* with knobs on.

In the Eighties and Nineties, England's cricketers were the Dukes of Displacement, the Earls of Transference. Long before the muddied oafs started getting it in the neck, they were the ones widely perceived as overpaid and inveterately useless. An easy target, granted, but a necessary outlet for all that, enabling the great, recession-hit unwashed to vent spleens and hone sarcastic witticisms. For many, the decline of the national team became a metaphor for the decline of a nation; in both cases, a wake-up call was imperative. Besides, *schadenfreude* is meant to be fun. What with all those yuppies and dinkies and Durannies, ethic-free brokers and conscience-deprived endowment salesmen, life would certainly have been a good deal less bearable but for the presence of such handy pin-cushions. In or out, swing or roundabout, up ladder or down snake, we wouldn't have missed it for the world. Besides – as those who were at Lord's, Headingley and The Oval to see the West Indies beaten in 2000 will readily testify, ditto those who tuned into the climaxes in Karachi and Colombo by kind permission of Uncle Rupert – delayed gratification is much the best sort.

Above all, though, Headingley '81 gave people a pleasure to treasure. It was an event that united them, not in woe and angst like the death of Princess Diana or the Aberfan disaster or the Dunblane massacre, but in wonder. In March 2001, India beat Australia in Calcutta to become the third side to win a Test after following on: so, once a century it is. England's victory, from a far more perilous position, still feels every whit as impossible, every iota as self-pinchingly, gobsmackingly implausible. To liken it to, say, Coventry City winning after being 4-0 down with 10 minutes to go, is to damn with faint praise. 500-1 against in a two-horse race! Small wonder the BBC's *Botham's Ashes* video remains among the market leaders nearly two decades after release.

As the years seep by, as the inquests and arguments rave on, a truth of sorts emerges. Headingley '81 was less a victory for Britishness or Englishness (whatever we mean by either) than for the captivating uncertainty of sport and the extraordinary resilience of the human spirit. To submit that British cricket and Ian Botham – let alone humankind in general – would have been better off had it never happened is the very height of ingratitude.

Around the turn of 2001, not long after Botham's publicity people had announced that he and his trusty mucker Allan Lamb would be staging another of their 'roadshows' this summer to mark the 20th anniversary of 1981 and all that, *Observer Sports Monthly* trumpeted the results of a readers' poll to discover Britain's 'Most Memorable Sporting Event'. Remarkably, Geoff Hurst's hat-trick, Manchester United's treble and Steve Redgrave's quintet all bowed the knee to the Both 'n' Goose Show. 'What sort of moment, then, have readers of the *Observer* chosen?' wondered Brearley. 'It is not an aesthetic moment, classical, unflawed. Nor is it in any sense predictable, or automatic. It is not to any degree tricky, subtle, or surreal. Its potency does not derive from an over-arching idea or vision. Rather the most telling achievements that turned this match were human, flawed, comical, and earthy.' As he embarked on his reminiscences for the umpteenth-and-first time, Botham encapsulated the enduring allure, precision personified: 'It was one of those crazy, glorious, one-off flukes.' The very quintessence, in other words, of what distinguishes sport from every other branch of civilised culture.

Hosannas, ladies and gentlemen, please, for Dr Feelgood and his mighty assistants.

ENGLAND V AUSTRALIA
Third Test at Headingley, Leeds
July 16-21, 1981

Australia	First Innings	R	B	M	4	6	Second Innings	R	B	M	4	6
J Dyson	b Dilley	102	234	294	14	-	(2) c Taylor b Willis	34	83	119	3	-
G M Wood	lbw b Botham	34	55	71	4	-	(1) c Taylor b Botham	10	10	9	2	-
T M Chappell	c Taylor b Willey	27	135	161	2	-	c Taylor b Willis	8	56	68	-	-
*K J Hughes	c & b Botham	89	208	270	8	-	c Botham b Willis	0	9	14	-	-
R J Bright	b Dilley	7	36	48	1	-	(8) b Willis	19	32	49	2	-
G N Yallop	c Taylor b Botham	58	167	208	5	-	(5) c Gatting b Willis	0	3	2	-	-
A R Border	lbw b Botham	8	20	35	1	-	(6) b Old	0	8	13	-	-
†R W Marsh	b Botham	28	50	65	5	-	(7) c Dilley b Willis	4	9	18	-	-
G F Lawson	c Taylor b Botham	13	35	45	2	-	c Taylor b Willis	1	2	4	-	-
D K Lillee	not out	3	6	8	-	-	c Gatting b Willis	17	15	22	-	-
T M Alderman	not out	0	-	-	-	-	not out	0	5	6	-	-
Extras	(b4, lb 13, w 3, nb 12)	32					(lb 3, w 1, nb 14)	18				
TOTAL	(155.2 overs, 609 mins)	401-9 declared					(36.1 overs, 169 mins)	111				

Fall of wkts:

1-55 2-149 3-196 4-220 5-332 6-354 7-357 8-396 9-401

1-13 2-56 3-58 4-58 5-65 6-68 7-74 8-75 9-110

England Bowling

First Innings	O	M	R	W	Second Innings	O	M	R	W
Willis	30	8	72	0	Botham	7	3	14	1
Old	43	14	91	0	Dilley	2	0	11	0
Dilley	27	4	78	2	Willis	15.1	3	43	8
Botham	39.2	11	95	6	Old	9	1	21	1
Willey	13	2	31	1	Willey	3	1	4	0
Boycott	3	2	2	0					

England	First Innings	R	B	M	4	6	Second Innings	R	B	M	4	6
G A Gooch	lbw b Alderman	2	7	17	-	-	c Alderman b Lillee	0	3	2	-	-
G Boycott	b Lawson	12	58	89	-	-	lbw b Alderman	46	141	215	1	-
*J M Brearley	c Marsh b Alderman	10	53	64	-	-	c Alderman b Lillee	14	29	33	3	-
D I Gower	c Marsh b Lawson	24	50	58	3	-	c Border b Alderman	9	22	36	1	-
M W Gatting	lbw b Lillee	15	29	58	2	-	lbw b Alderman	1	10	10	-	-
P Willey	b Lawson	8	22	29	-	-	c Dyson b Lillee	33	56	84	6	-
I T Botham	c Marsh b Lillee	50	54	80	8	-	not out	149	148	219	27	1
†R W Taylor	c Marsh b Lillee	5	23	36	1	-	c Bright b Alderman	1	9	9	-	-
G R Dilley	c & b Lillee	13	17	30	2	-	b Alderman	56	75	80	9	-
C M Old	c Border b Alderman	0	4	4	-	-	b Lawson	29	31	54	6	-
R G D Willis	not out	1	4	5	-	-	c Border b Alderman	2	9	31	-	-
Extras	(b 6, lb 11, w 6, nb 11)	34					(b 5, lb 3, w 3, nb 5)	16				
TOTAL	(off 50.5 overs, 245 mins)	174					(87.3 overs, 396 mins)	356				

Fall of wkts:

1-12 2-40 3-42 4-84 5-87 6-112 7-148 8-166 9-167

1-0 2-18 3-37 4-41 5-105 6-133 7-135 8-252 9-319

Australia Bowling

First Innings	O	M	R	W	Second Innings	O	M	R	W
Lillee	18.5	7	49	4	Lillee	25	6	94	3
Alderman	19	4	59	3	Alderman	35.3	6	135	6
Lawson	13	3	32	3	Lawson	23	4	96	1
					Bright	4	0	15	0

England won by 18 runs

Bibliography

Peter Ball & David Hopps *The Book of Cricket Quotations* (Stanley Paul 1990)

Richie Benaud *Benaud On Reflection* (Willow Books 1984)

Dickie Bird (with Keith Lodge) *My Autobiography* (Hodder & Stoughton 1997)

Peter Biskind *Easy Riders Raging Bulls* (Bloomsbury 1998)

Ian Botham (with Peter Smith) *The Incredible Tests* (Pelham 1981)

Ian Botham and Peter Roebuck *It Sort Of Clicks* (Collins Willow 1987)

Ian Botham (with Peter Hayter and Chris Dighton) *My Autobiography* (Harper Collins 1994)

Mike Brearley (with Dudley Doust) *Phoenix From The Ashes* (Unwin 1982)

Mike Brearley *The Art Of Captaincy* (Hodder & Stoughton 1985)

Richard Cashman, Warwick Franks, Jim Maxwell, Brian Stoddart, Amanda Weaver, Ray Webster (Eds) *The Oxford Companion to Australian Cricket* (Oxford University Press 1996)

Graham Dilley (with Graham Otway) *Swings and Roundabouts* (Pelham 1987)

John Emburey (with Pat Gibson) *Spinning In A Fast World* (Robson Books 1989)

Tony Francis *The Zen of Cricket* (Stanley Paul 1992)

Mike Gatting (with Angela Patmore) *Leading From The Front* (Queen Anne Press 1988)

Graham Gooch (with Alan Lee) *My Cricket Diary '81* (Stanley Paul 1982)

Gideon Haigh *The Cricket War* (Text Publishing 1993)

Gideon Haigh *The Summer Game* (Text Publishing 1997)

Dennis Lillee *My Life in Cricket* (Methuen 1982)

Dennis Lillee *Over and Out!* (Methuen 1984)

Christopher Martin-Jenkins *In Defence Of The Ashes* (Macdonald & Jane's 1979)

Christopher Martin-Jenkins (ed) *Seasons Past* (Stanley Paul 1986)

Alan McGilvray *Backpage Of Cricket* (Lester-Townsend 1989)

Adrian McGregor *Greg Chappell* (Collins 1985)

Alastair McLellan (ed) *Botham – Hero and Villain* (Two Heads 1997)

Michael Manley *A History of West Indies Cricket* (Andre Deutsch 1988)

Michael Melford *Botham Rekindles The Ashes* (Daily Telegraph 1981)

Rob Steen *This Sporting Life – Cricket* (David & Charles 1999)

Rob Steen *Poms and Cobbers* (Andre Deutsch 1997)

Rob Steen *David Gower – A Man Out Of Time* (Gollancz 1995)

E.W. Swanton (ed) *Barclays World of Cricket* (Collins 1980)

Bob Taylor (with Patrick Murphy) *Standing Up Standing Back* (Collins Willow 1985)

Dirk Wellham (with Howard Rich) *Solid Knocks and Second Thoughts* (Reed 1988)

Bernard Whimpress, Nigel Hart *Test Eleven – Great Ashes Battles* (Andre Deutsch 1995)

Marcus Williams (ed) *The Way To Lord's: Cricketing Letters to The Times* (Collins Willow 1983)

Bob Willis (with Alan Lee) *Lasting The Pace* (Collins Willow 1985)

Index

Subheadings appear in chronological order where entries refer to days in match

lack of stewards 142
scoreboard replacement 103-4
scorecards 167

S

T

U

V

W